DON'T TOY WITH ME, MISS NAGATORO

①

NANASHI

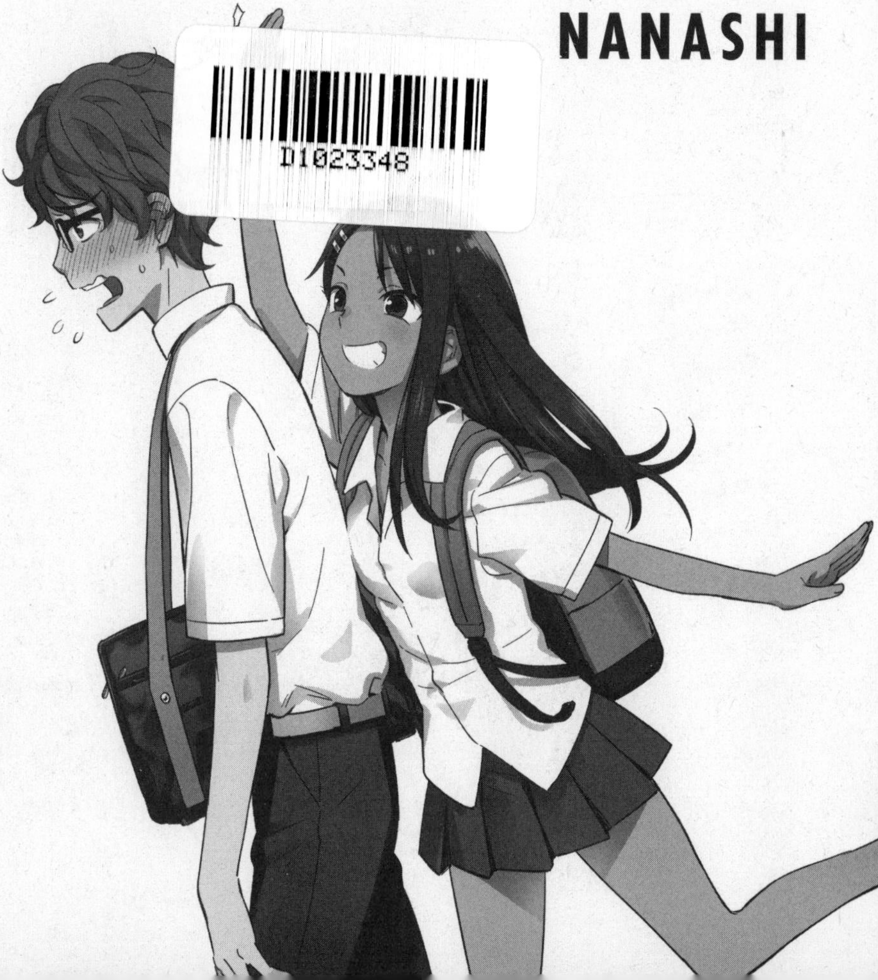

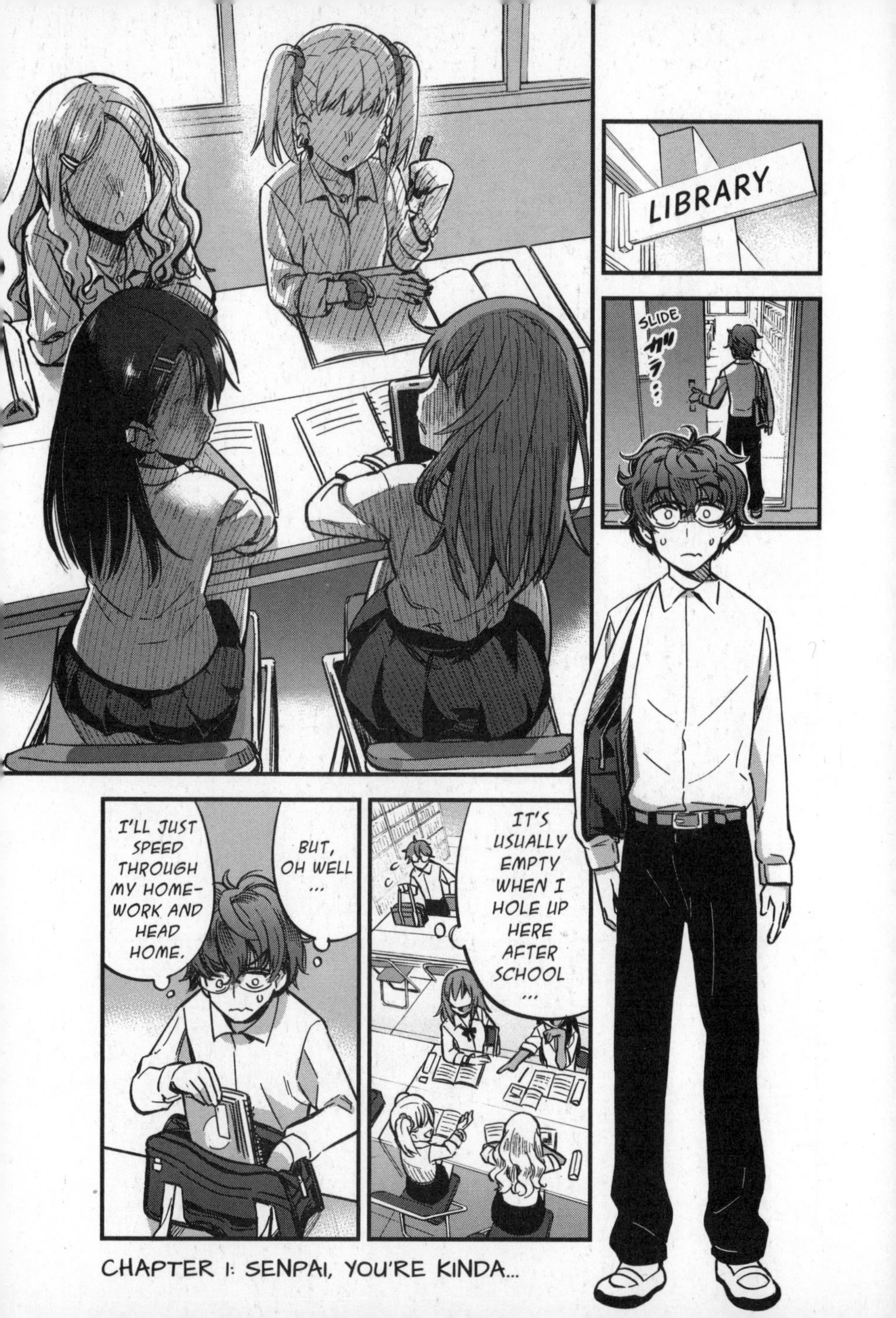
LIBRARY
SLIDE
ガラ…
IT'S USUALLY EMPTY WHEN I HOLE UP HERE AFTER SCHOOL ...
BUT, OH WELL ...
I'LL JUST SPEED THROUGH MY HOME-WORK AND HEAD HOME.

CHAPTER 1: SENPAI, YOU'RE KINDA...

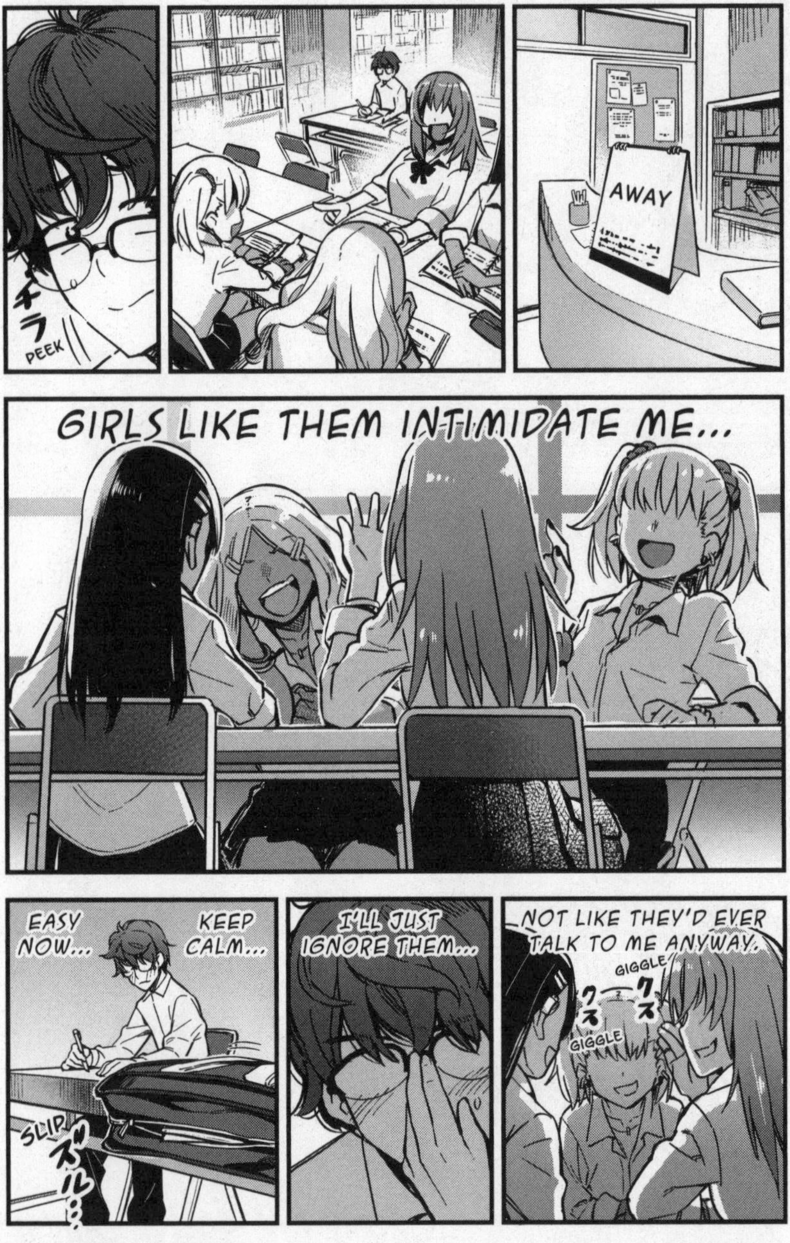
AWAY
チラ
PEEK
GIRLS LIKE THEM INTIMIDATE ME...
NOT LIKE THEY'D EVER TALK TO ME ANYWAY.
GIGGLE
クス
クス
GIGGLE
I'LL JUST IGNORE THEM...
KEEP CALM...
EASY NOW...
SLIP
ズル...

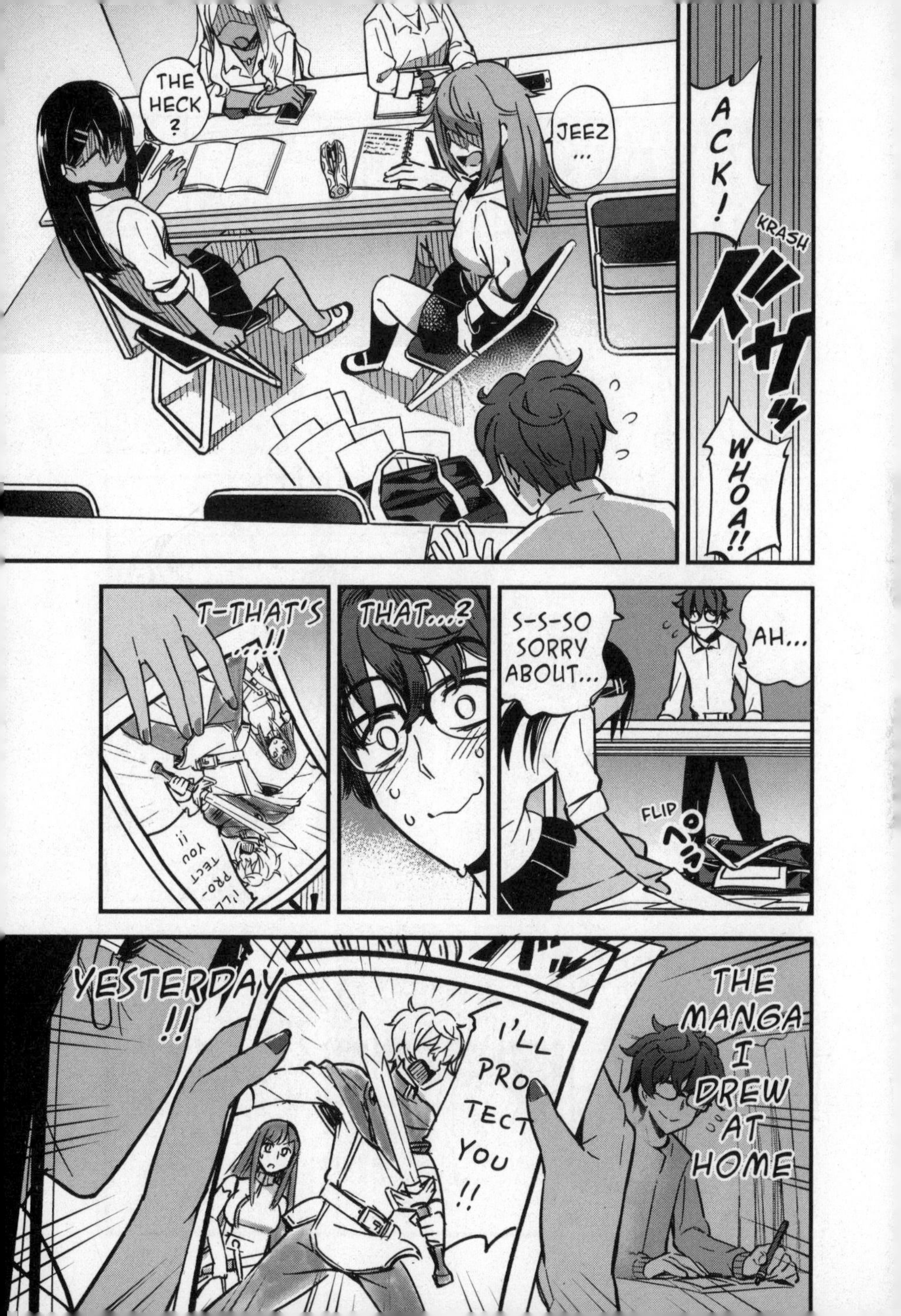
ACK!
KRASH
WHOA!!
JEEZ...
THE HECK?
AH...
S-S-SO SORRY ABOUT...
FLIP
THAT...?
T-THAT'S...!!
I'LL PRO-TECT YOU !!
THE MANGA I DREW AT HOME
YESTERDAY!!
I'LL PRO TECT YOU !!

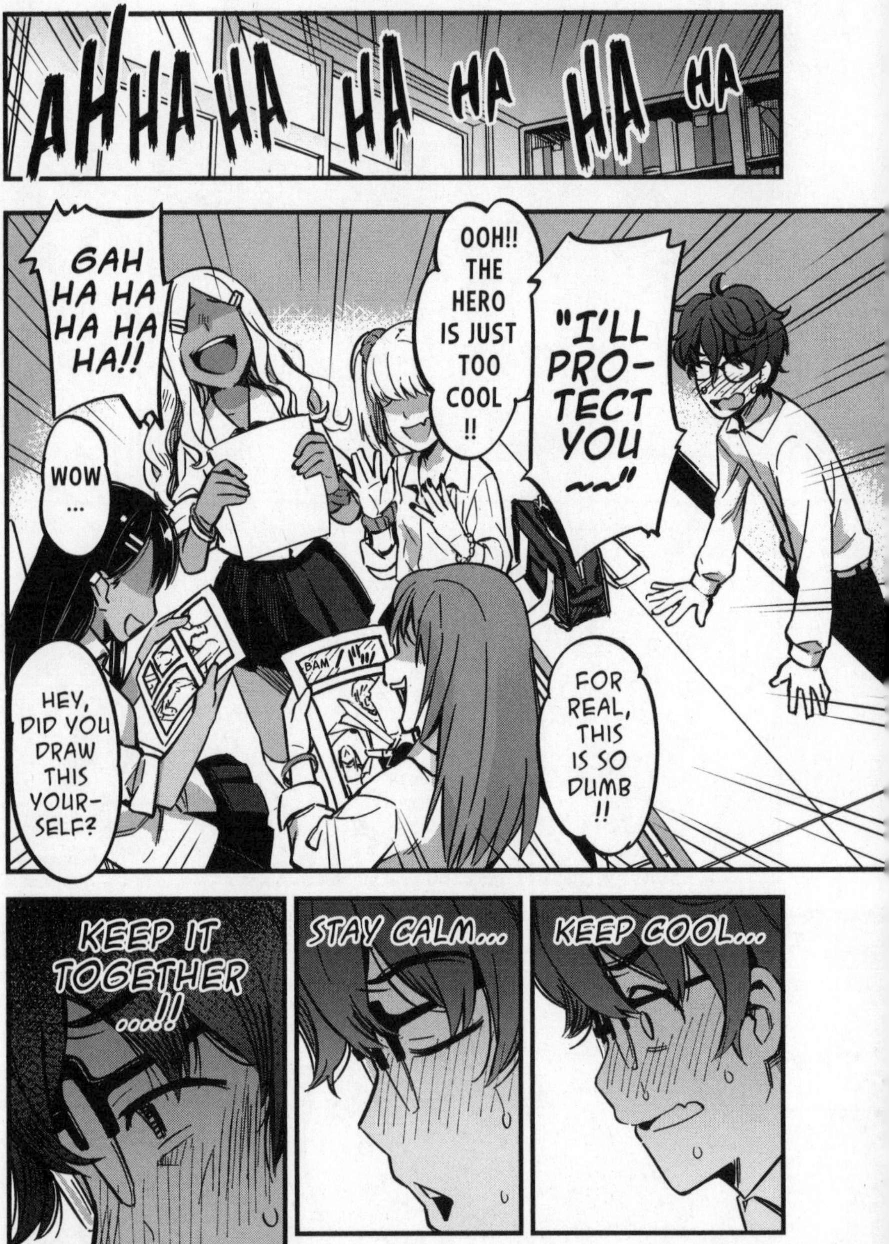
AHHAHA HA HA HA HA HA
"I'LL PRO-TECT YOU~~"
OOH!! THE HERO IS JUST TOO COOL !!
GAH HA HA HA HA HA!!
WOW ...
FOR REAL, THIS IS SO DUMB !!
HEY, DID YOU DRAW THIS YOUR-SELF?
KEEP COOL...
STAY CALM...
KEEP IT TOGETHER ...!!

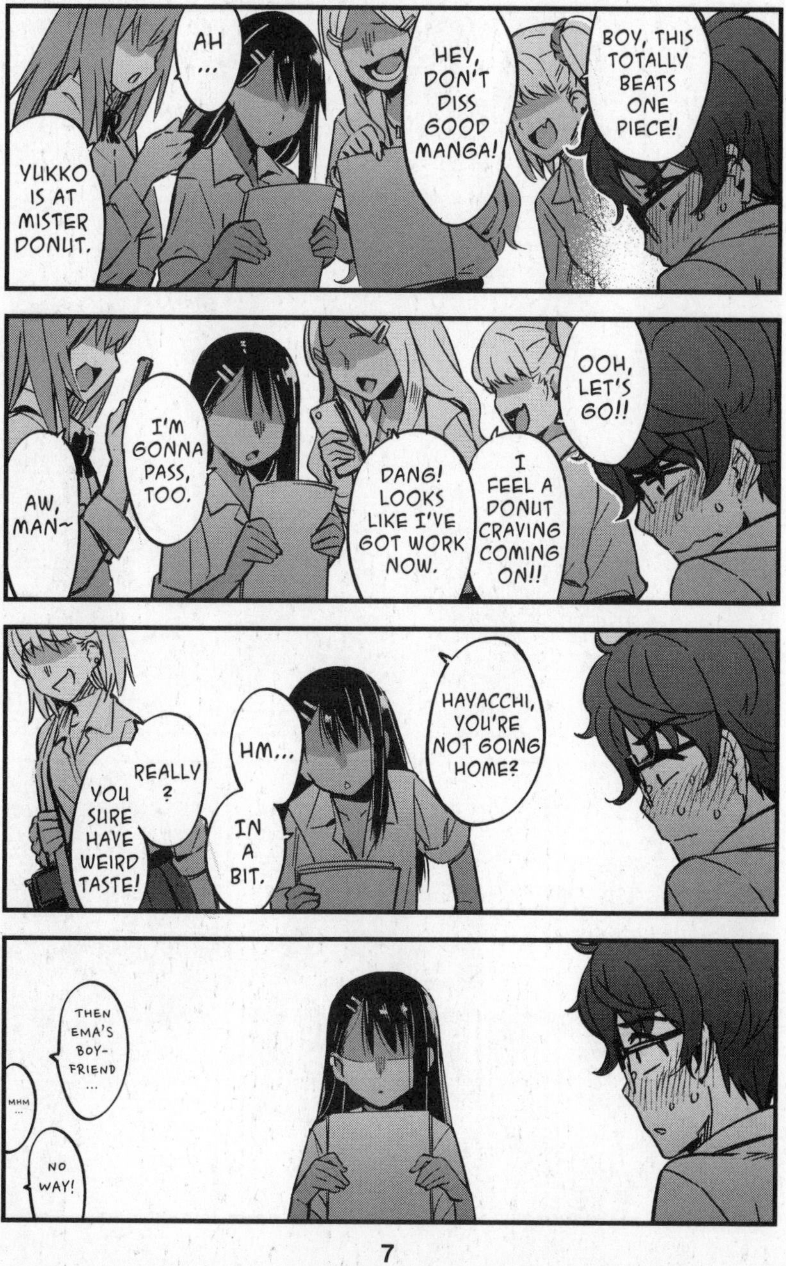
BOY, THIS TOTALLY BEATS ONE PIECE!
HEY, DON'T DISS GOOD MANGA!
AH ...
YUKKO IS AT MISTER DONUT.
OOH, LET'S GO!!
I FEEL A DONUT CRAVING COMING ON!!
DANG! LOOKS LIKE I'VE GOT WORK NOW.
I'M GONNA PASS, TOO.
AW, MAN~
HAYACCHI, YOU'RE NOT GOING HOME?
HM...
IN A BIT.
REALLY?
YOU SURE HAVE WEIRD TASTE!
THEN EMA'S BOY-FRIEND ...
MHM ...
NO WAY!

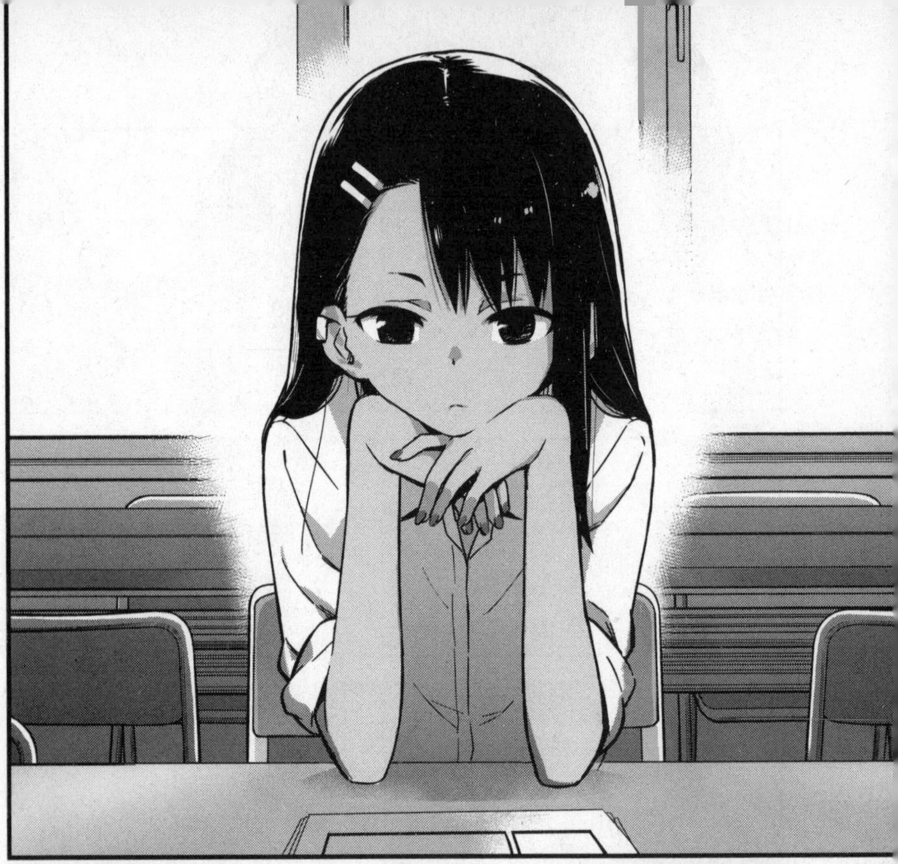

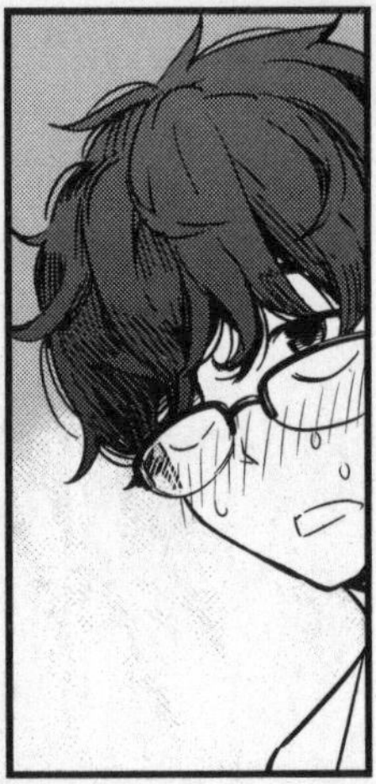

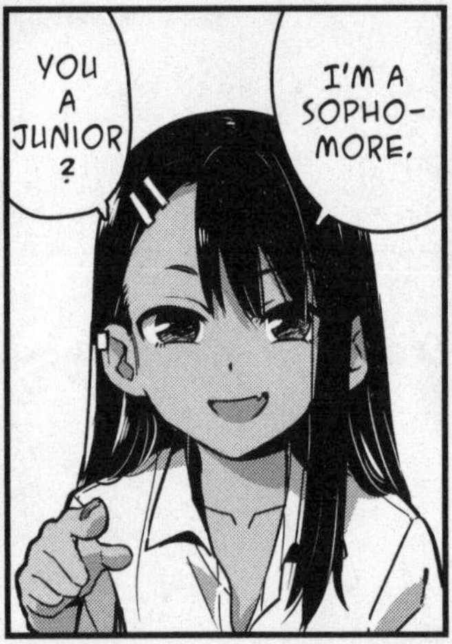
I'M A SOPHOMORE.
YOU A JUNIOR?

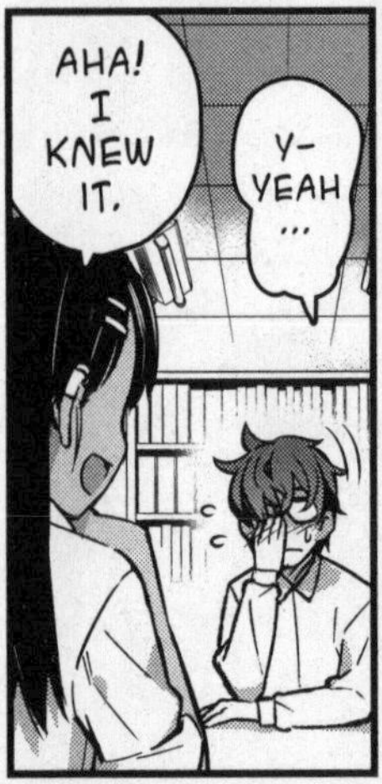
Y-YEAH...
AHA! I KNEW IT.

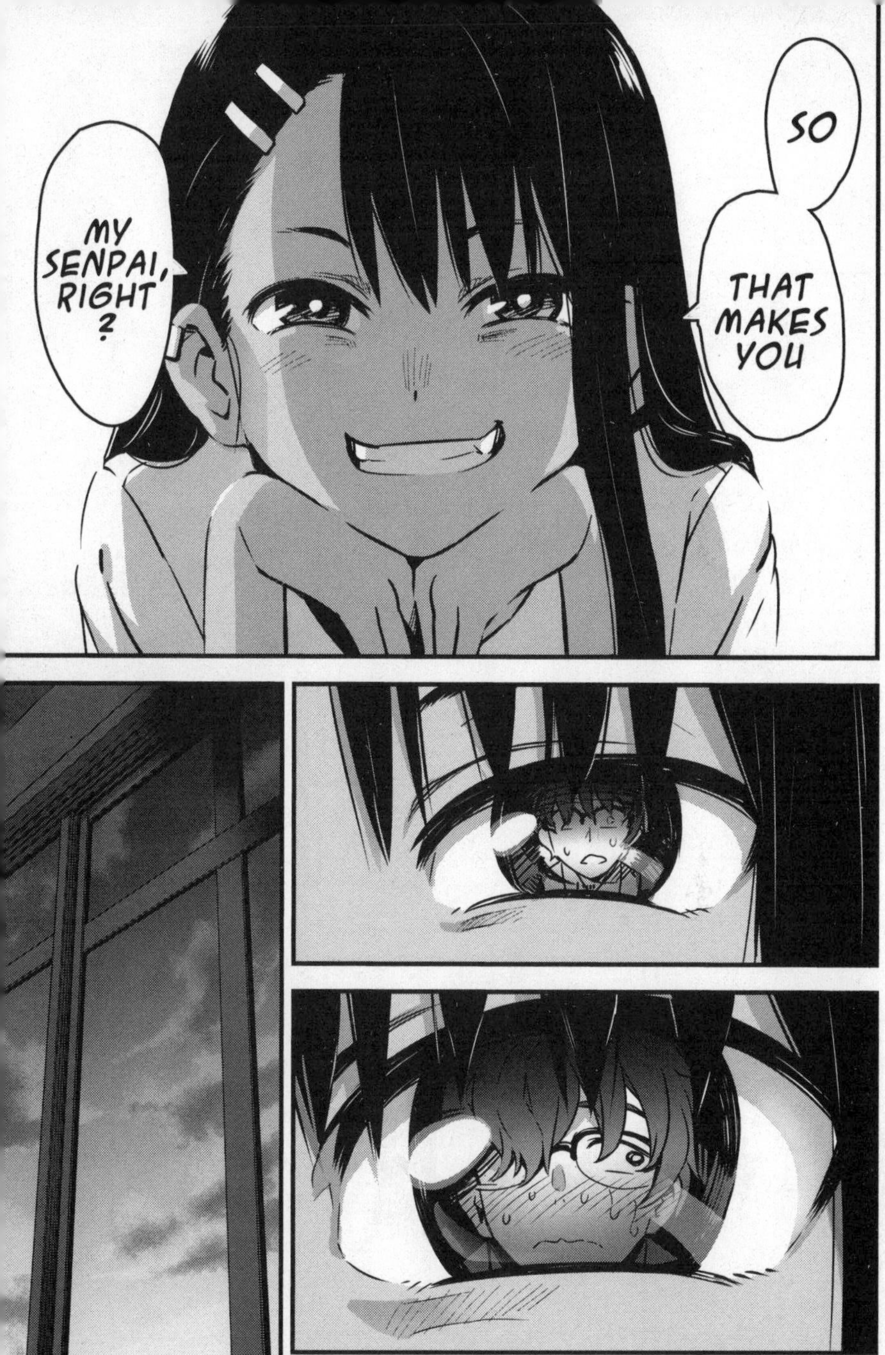
SO
THAT MAKES YOU
MY SENPAI, RIGHT?

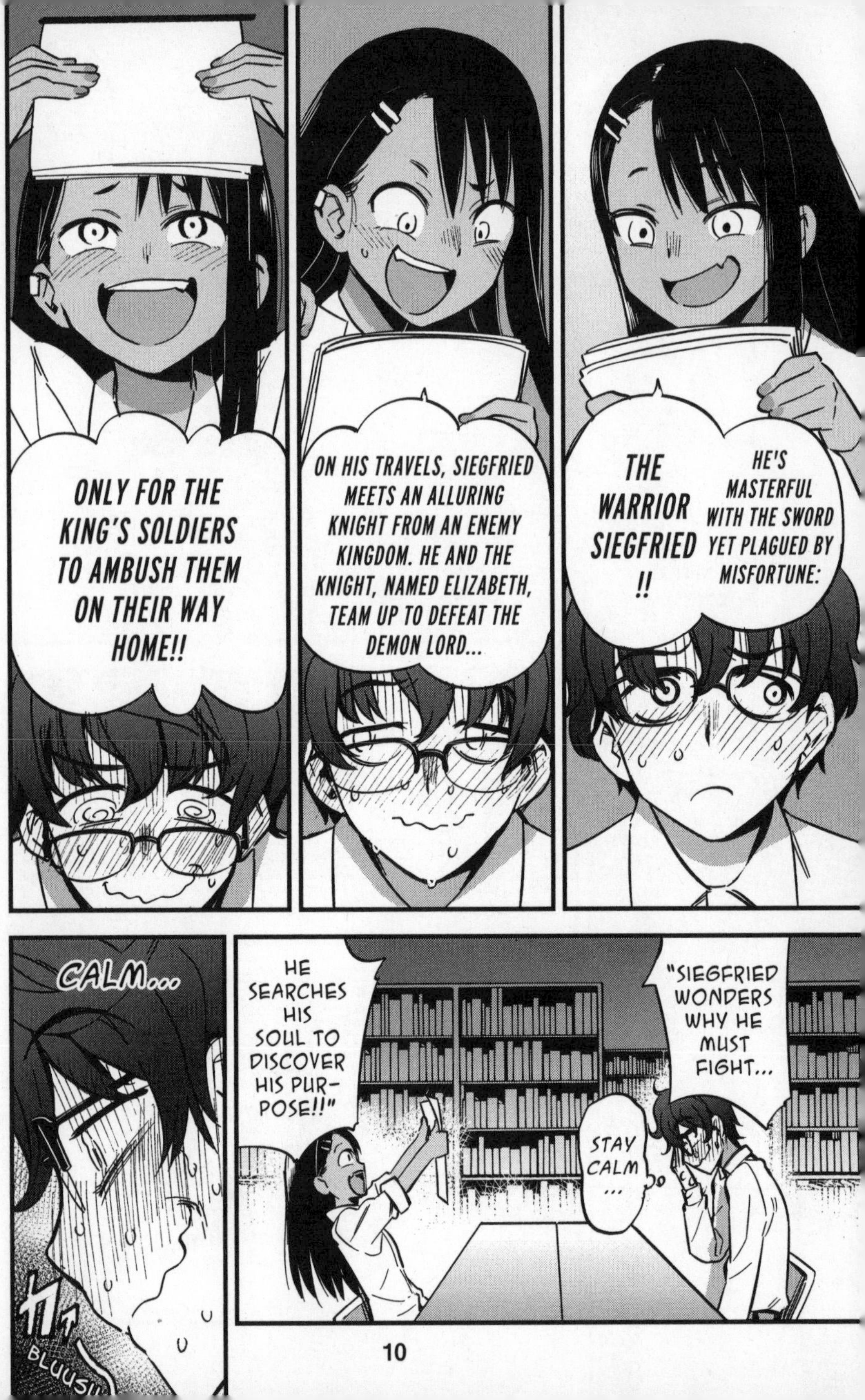
HE'S MASTERFUL WITH THE SWORD YET PLAGUED BY MISFORTUNE:
THE WARRIOR SIEGFRIED!!
ON HIS TRAVELS, SIEGFRIED MEETS AN ALLURING KNIGHT FROM AN ENEMY KINGDOM. HE AND THE KNIGHT, NAMED ELIZABETH, TEAM UP TO DEFEAT THE DEMON LORD...
ONLY FOR THE KING'S SOLDIERS TO AMBUSH THEM ON THEIR WAY HOME!!
"SIEGFRIED WONDERS WHY HE MUST FIGHT...
HE SEARCHES HIS SOUL TO DISCOVER HIS PUR-POSE!!"
STAY CALM...
CALM...
BLUUSH

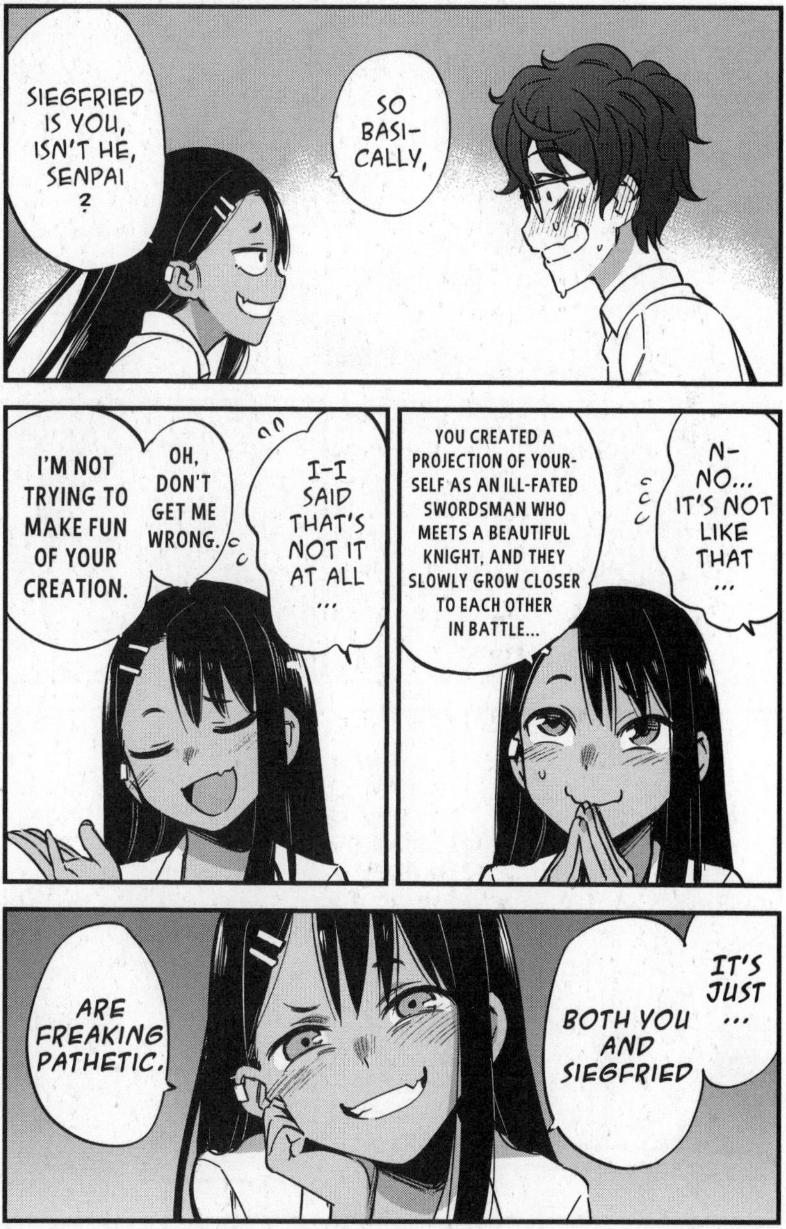
SO BASI-CALLY,
SIEGFRIED IS YOU, ISN'T HE, SENPAI?
N-NO... IT'S NOT LIKE THAT...
YOU CREATED A PROJECTION OF YOUR-SELF AS AN ILL-FATED SWORDSMAN WHO MEETS A BEAUTIFUL KNIGHT, AND THEY SLOWLY GROW CLOSER TO EACH OTHER IN BATTLE...
I-I SAID THAT'S NOT IT AT ALL...
OH, DON'T GET ME WRONG.
I'M NOT TRYING TO MAKE FUN OF YOUR CREATION.
IT'S JUST...
BOTH YOU AND SIEGFRIED
ARE FREAKING PATHETIC.

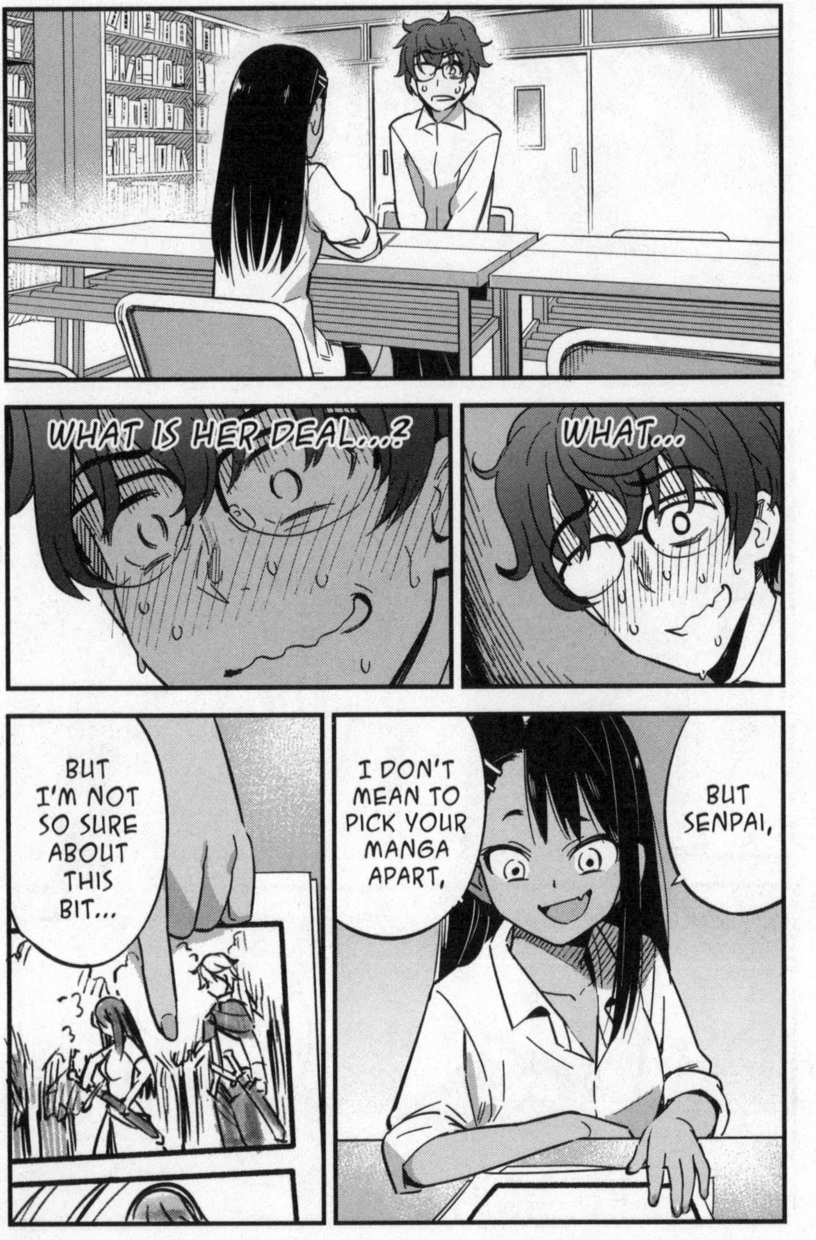
WHAT...
WHAT IS HER DEAL...?
BUT SENPAI,
I DON'T MEAN TO PICK YOUR MANGA APART,
BUT I'M NOT SO SURE ABOUT THIS BIT...

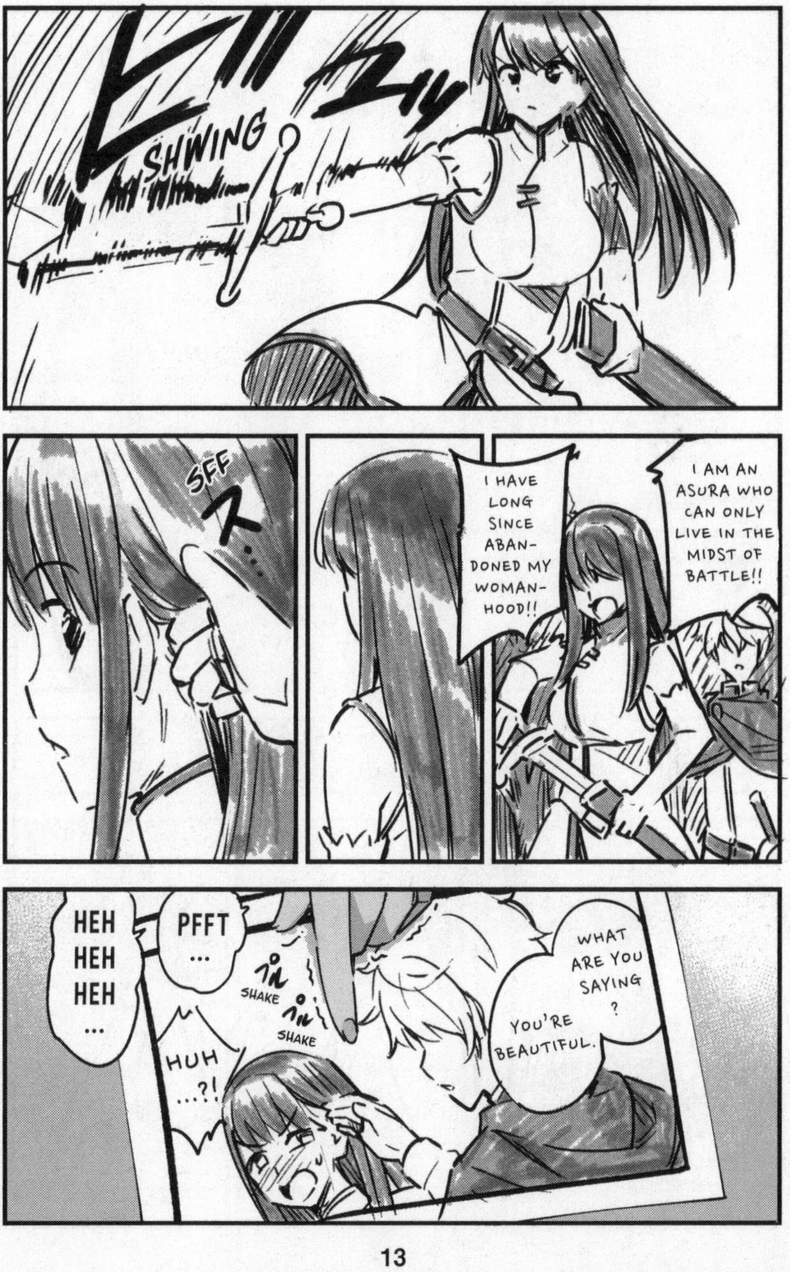
SHWING
I AM AN ASURA WHO CAN ONLY LIVE IN THE MIDST OF BATTLE!!
I HAVE LONG SINCE ABAN-DONED MY WOMAN-HOOD!!
SFF
WHAT ARE YOU SAYING?
YOU'RE BEAUTIFUL.
SHAKE
SHAKE
HUH ...?!
PFFT ...
HEH HEH HEH ...

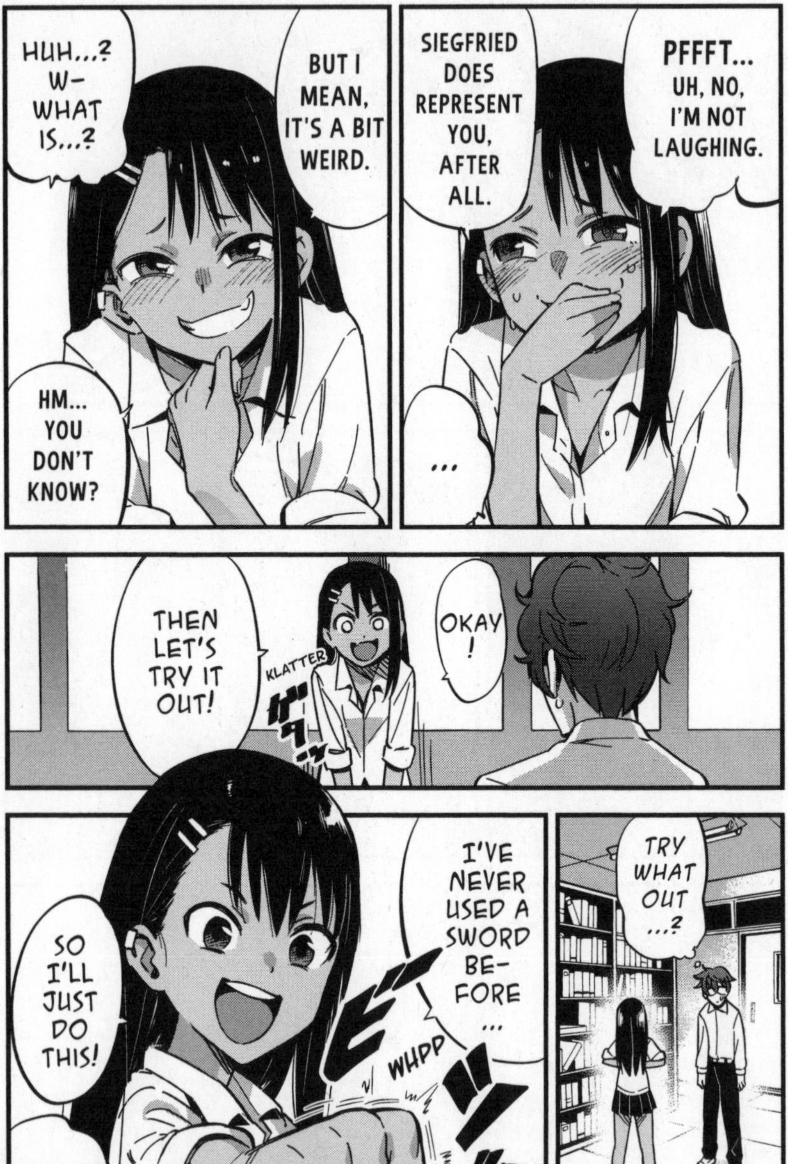
PFFFT... UH, NO, I'M NOT LAUGHING.
SIEGFRIED DOES REPRESENT YOU, AFTER ALL.
...
BUT I MEAN, IT'S A BIT WEIRD.
HUH...? W-WHAT IS...?
HM... YOU DON'T KNOW?
OKAY!
THEN LET'S TRY IT OUT!
KLATTER
TRY WHAT OUT...?
I'VE NEVER USED A SWORD BEFORE...
SO I'LL JUST DO THIS!
WHPP
"THIS?"

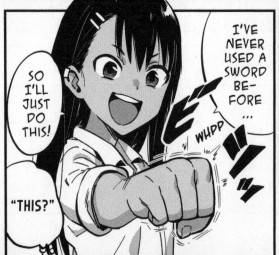

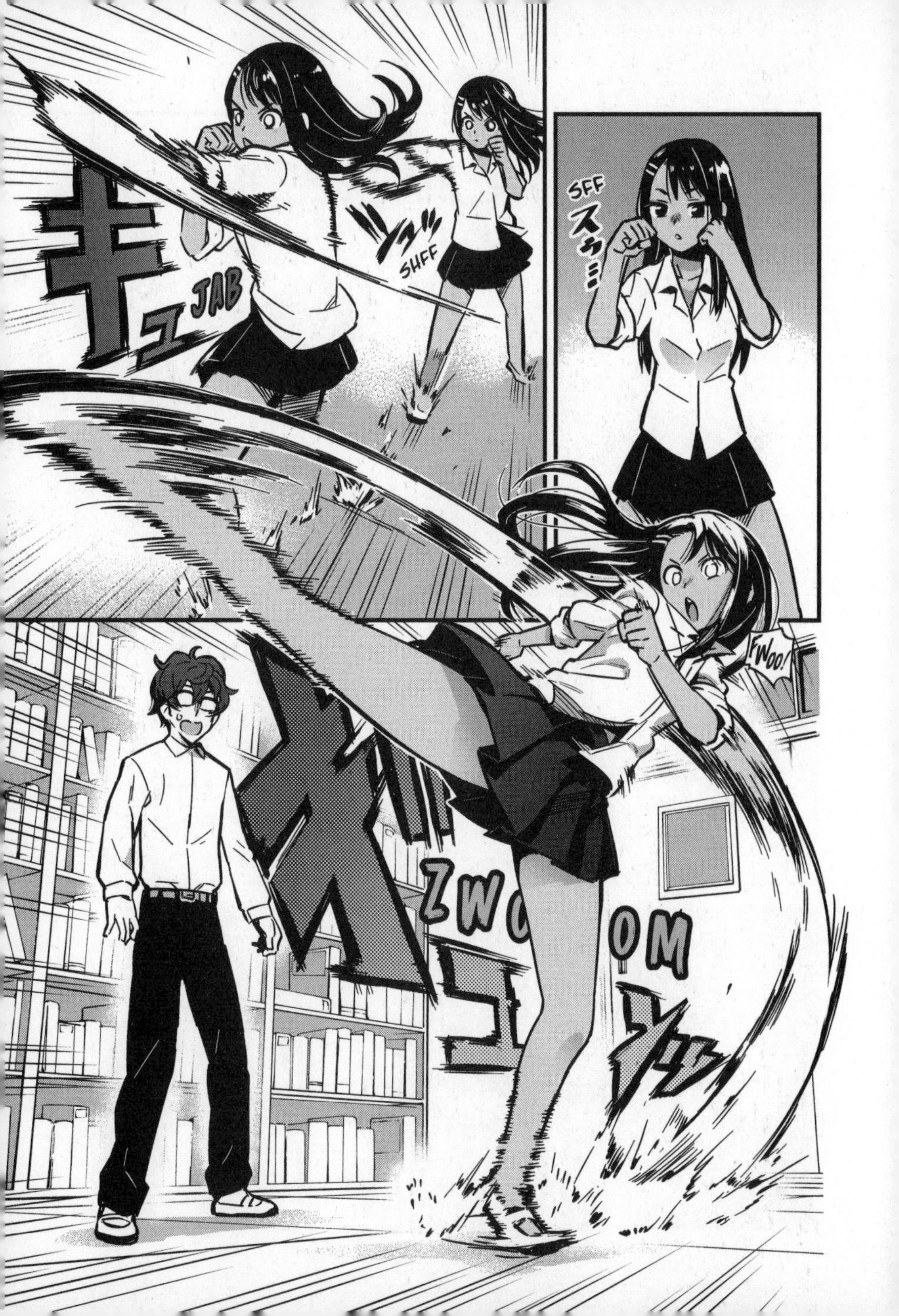
SFF
JAB
SHFF
FWOO!
ZWO OM

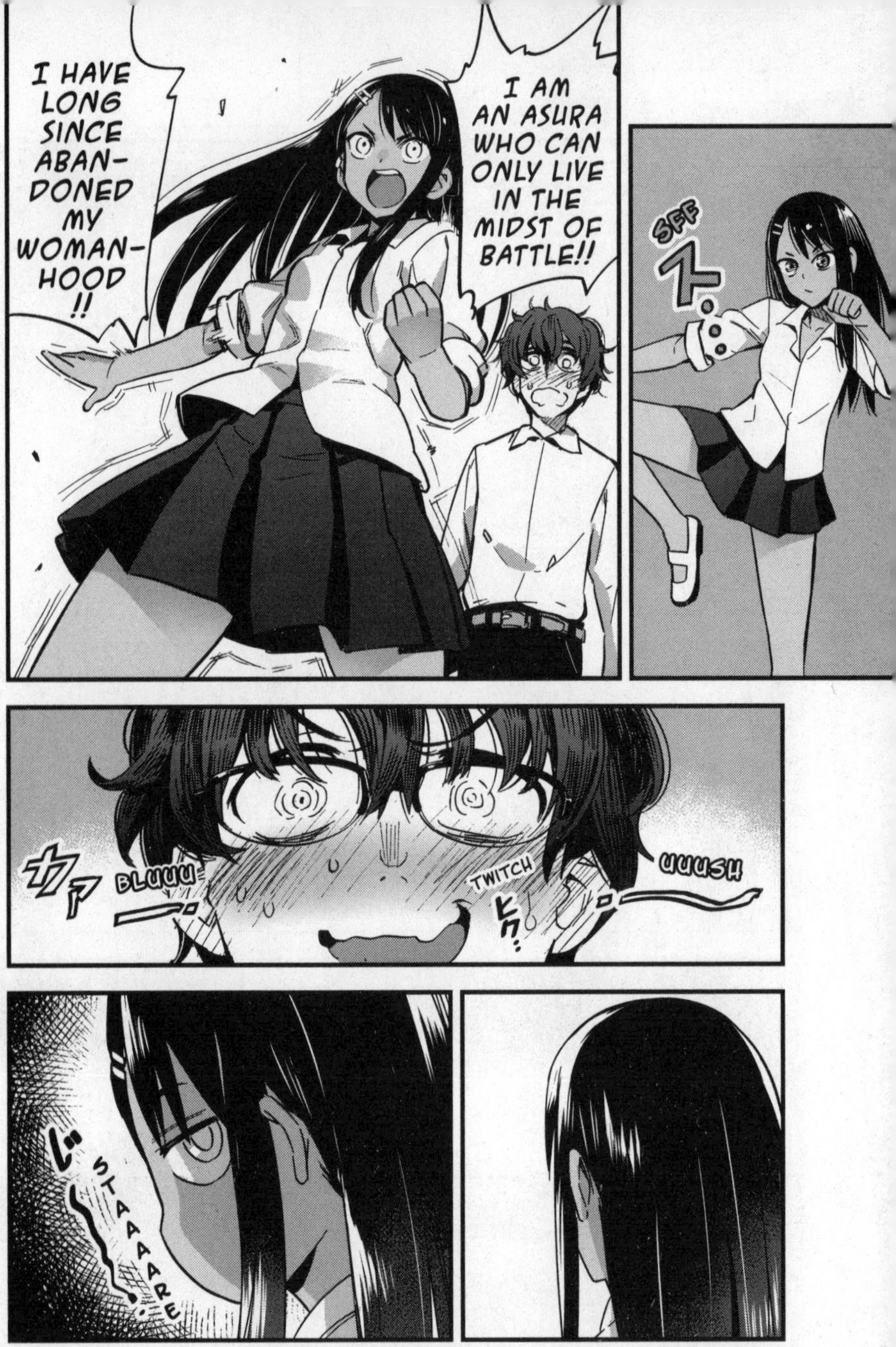
SFF
ス
I AM AN ASURA WHO CAN ONLY LIVE IN THE MIDST OF BATTLE!!
I HAVE LONG SINCE ABANDONED MY WOMANHOOD!!
UUUSH
TWITCH
ピク
BLUUU
カァ
STAAAARE
じー

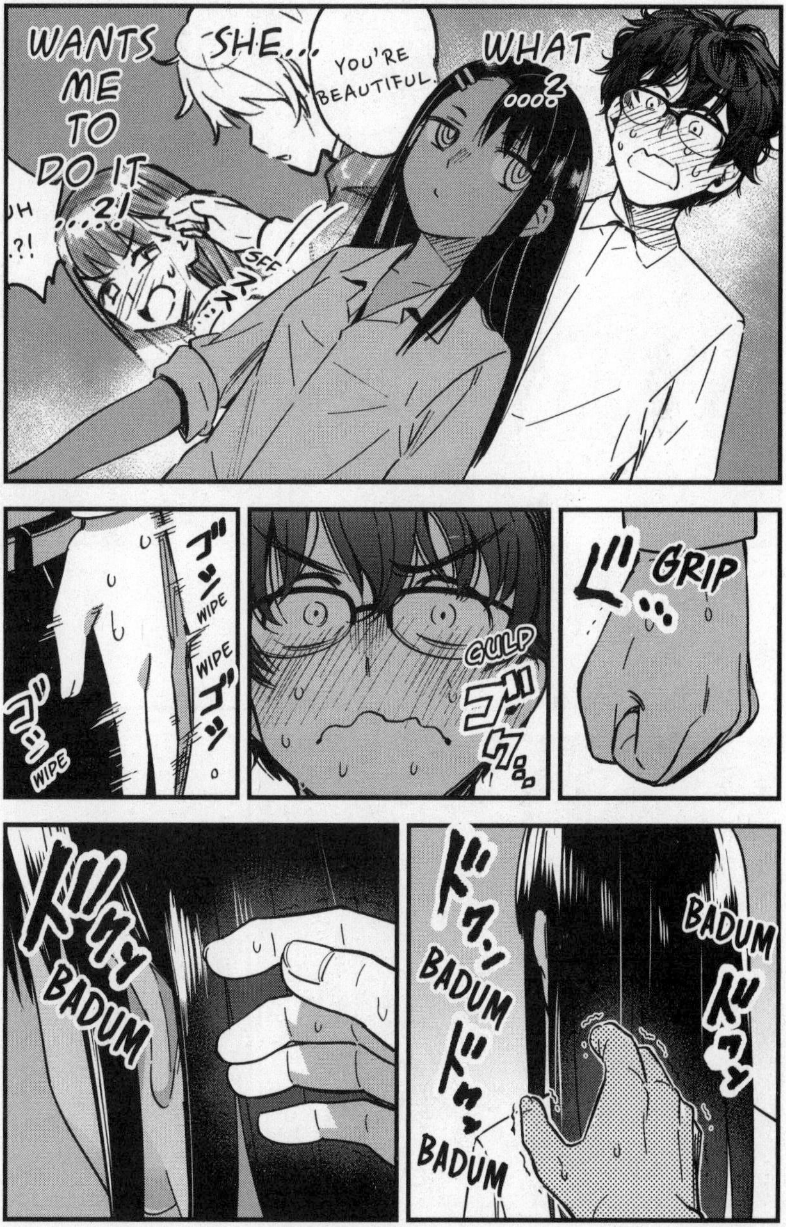
WHAT...?
YOU'RE BEAUTIFUL.
SHE...
WANTS ME TO DO IT...?!
SFF
GRIP
GULP
WIPE
WIPE
WIPE
BADUM
BADUM
BADUM
BADUM

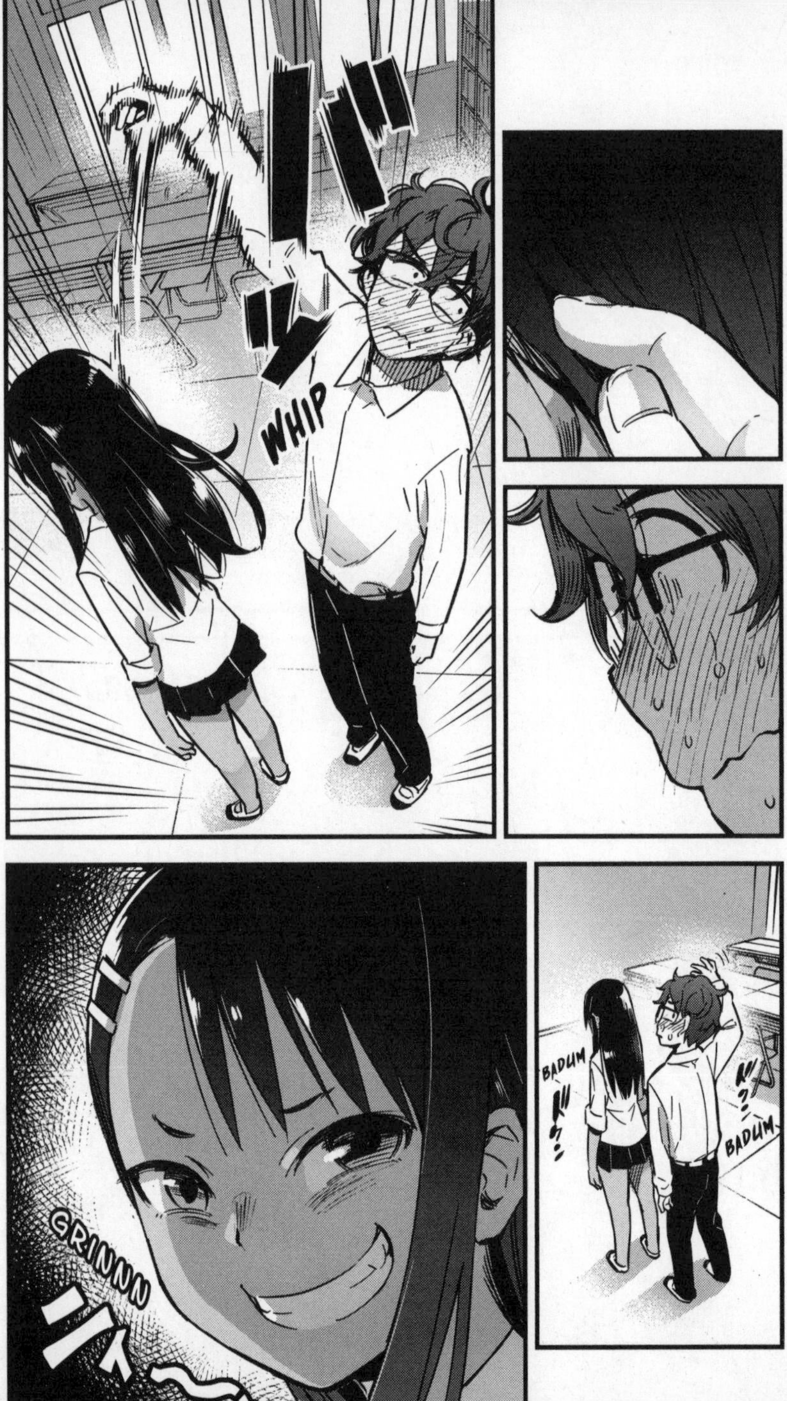
WHIP
BADUM
BADUM
GRINNN

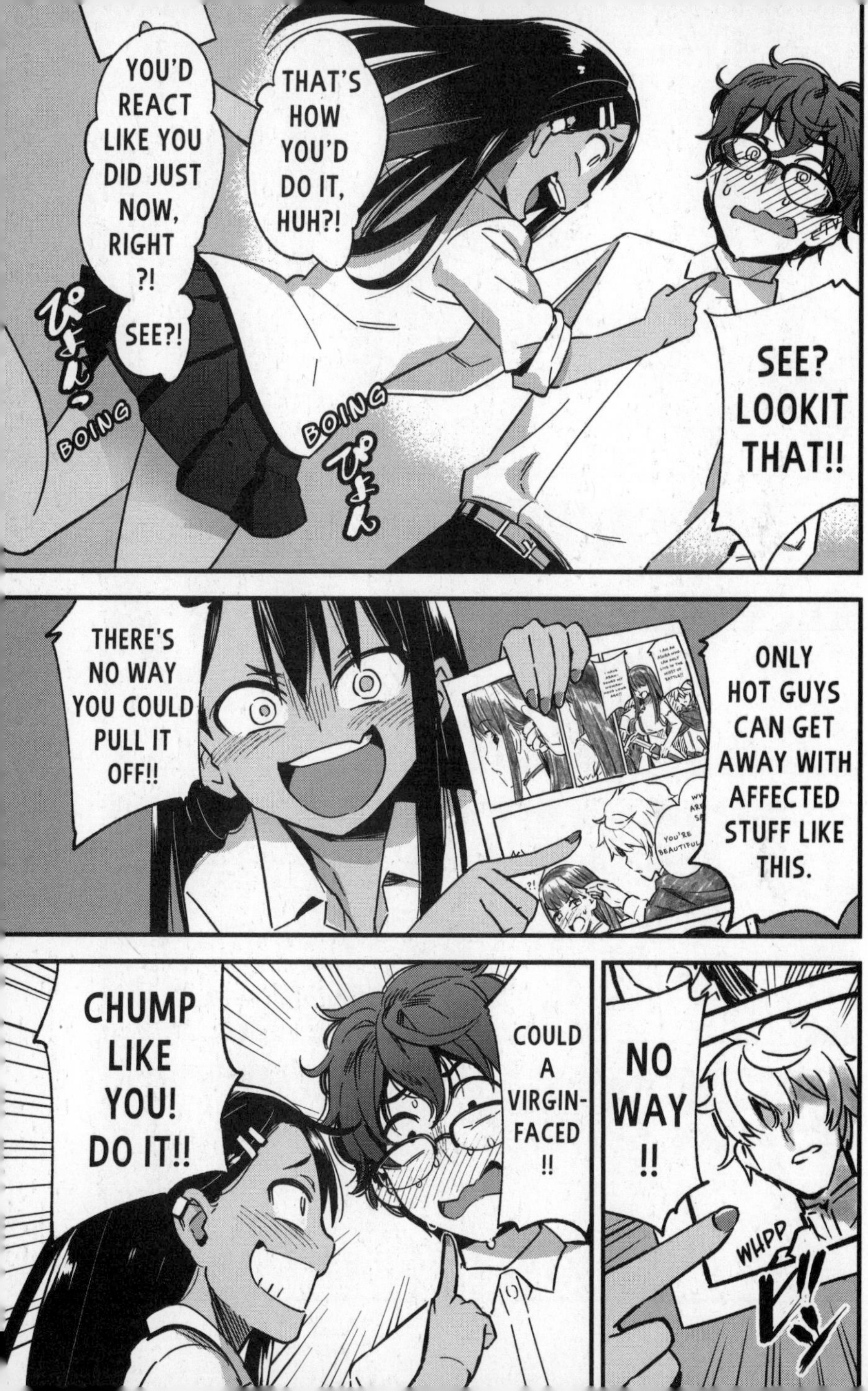
SEE? LOOKIT THAT!!
THAT'S HOW YOU'D DO IT, HUH?!
YOU'D REACT LIKE YOU DID JUST NOW, RIGHT?!
SEE?!
BOING ぴょん
BOING ぴょん
ONLY HOT GUYS CAN GET AWAY WITH AFFECTED STUFF LIKE THIS.
YOU'RE BEAUTIFUL
THERE'S NO WAY YOU COULD PULL IT OFF!!
NO WAY!!
WHPP
ビッ
COULD A VIRGIN-FACED!!
CHUMP LIKE YOU! DO IT!!

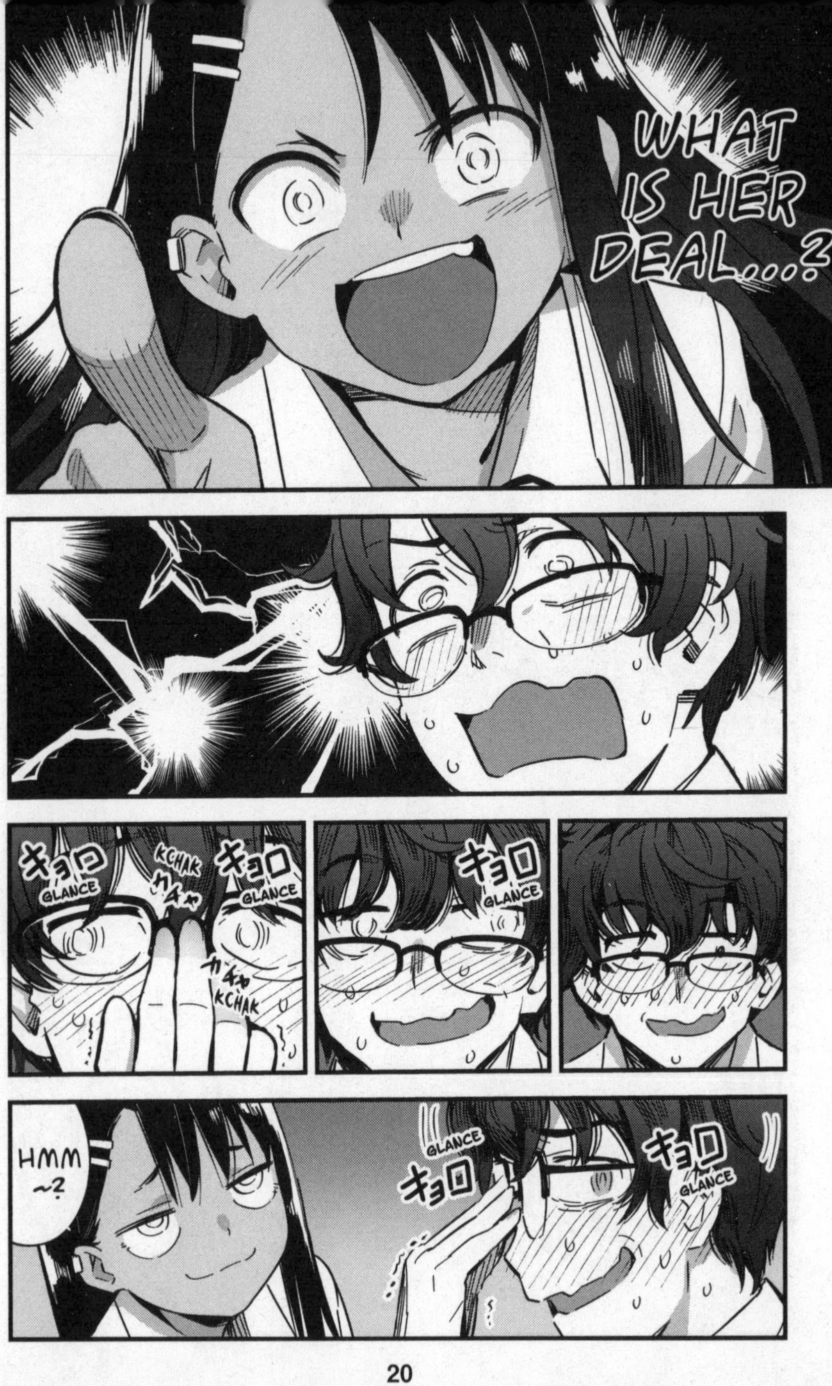
WHAT IS HER DEAL...?
キョロ
GLANCE
キョロ
GLANCE
KCHAK
カチャ
キョロ
GLANCE
カチャ
KCHAK
キョロ
GLANCE
GLANCE
キョロ
HMM ~?

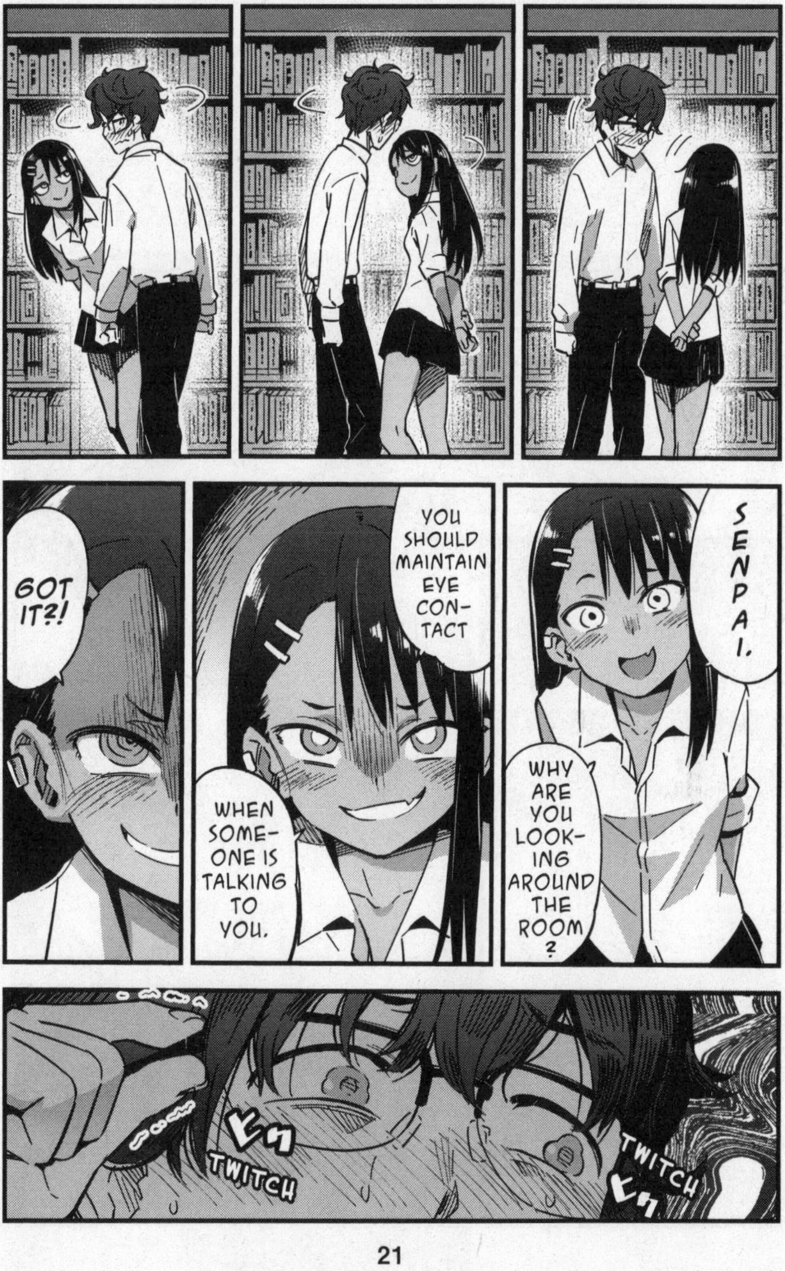
SENPAI.
WHY ARE YOU LOOKING AROUND THE ROOM?
YOU SHOULD MAINTAIN EYE CONTACT
WHEN SOMEONE IS TALKING TO YOU.
GOT IT?!
TWITCH
TWITCH

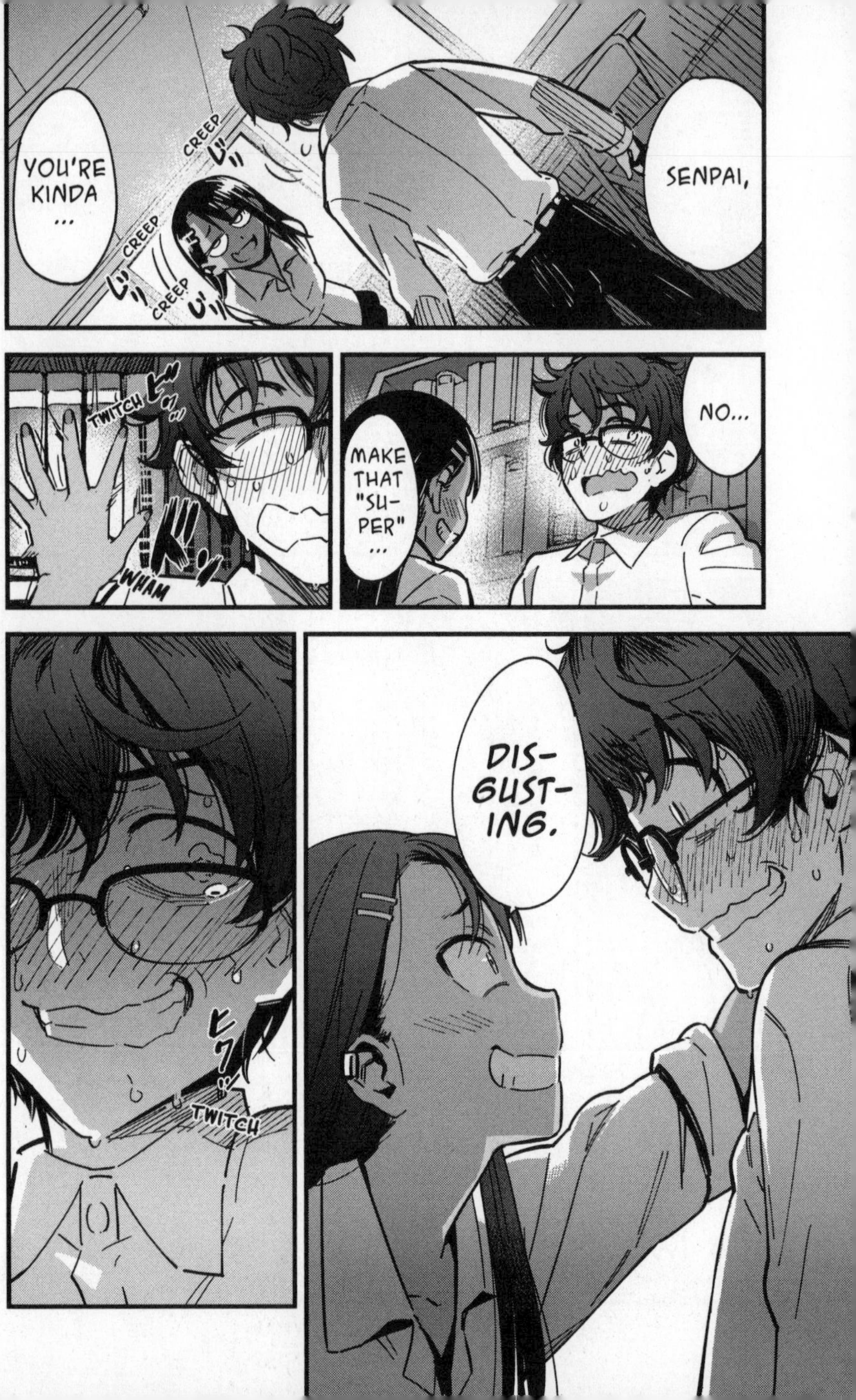
SENPAI,
CREEP
YOU'RE KINDA ...
CREEP
CREEP
NO...
MAKE THAT "SU-PER" ...
TWITCH
WHAM
DIS-GUST-ING.
TWITCH

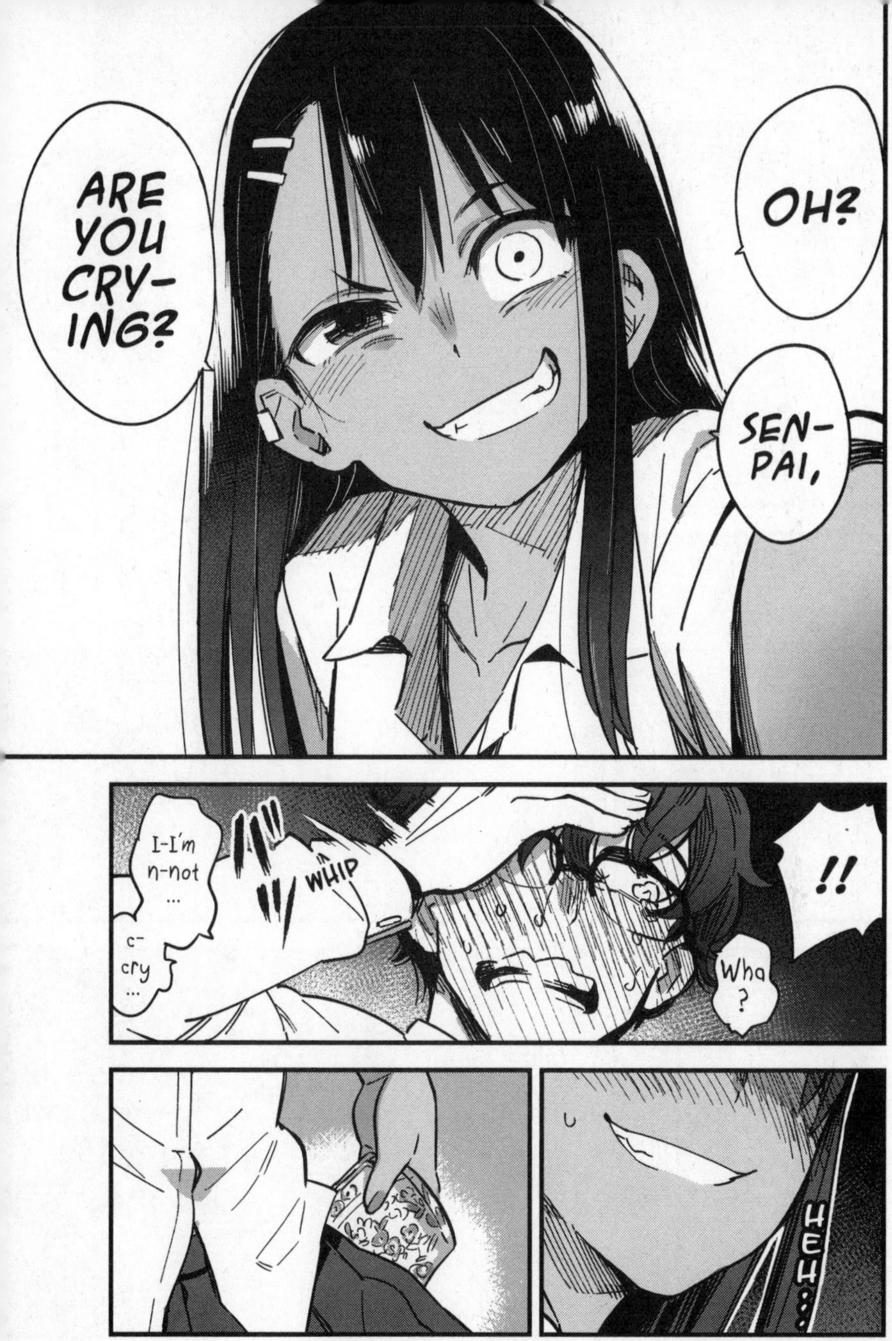
OH?
SEN-PAI,
ARE YOU CRY-ING?
!!
Wha ?
WHIP
I-I'm n-not ... c-cry ...
HEH...

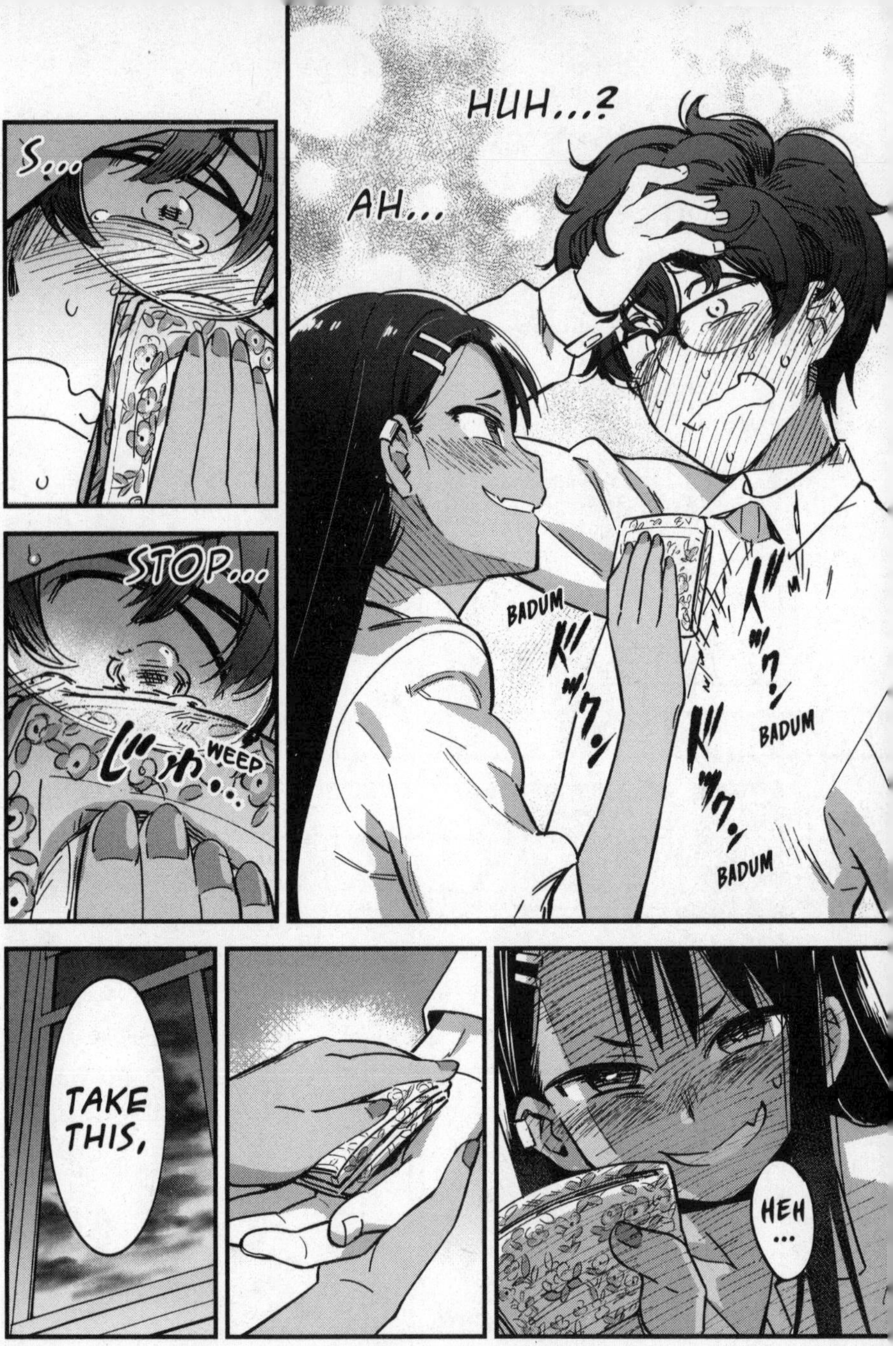
HUH...?
AH...
BADUM
BADUM
BADUM
S...
STOP...
WEEP...
HEH ...
TAKE THIS,

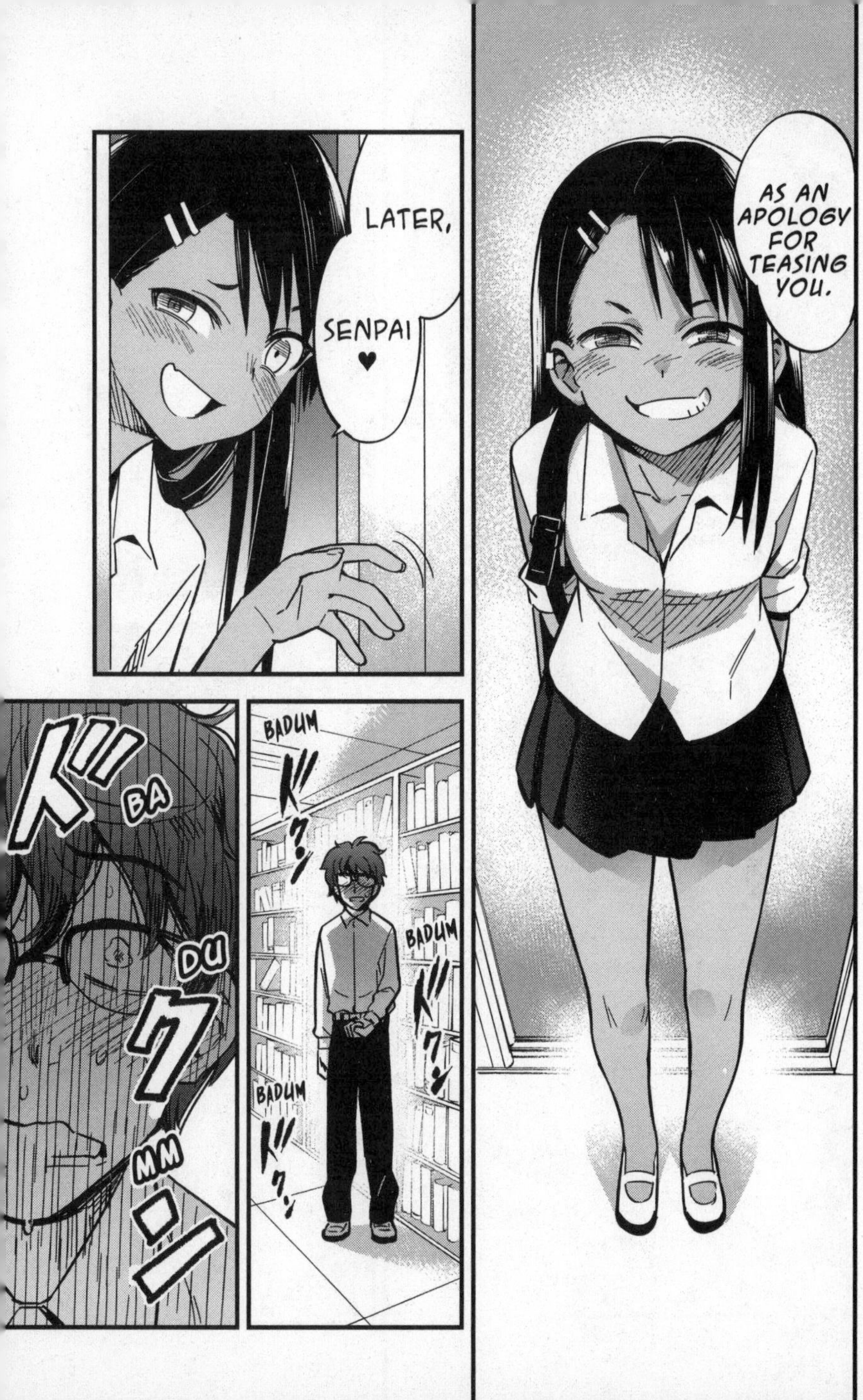
AS AN APOLOGY FOR TEASING YOU.
LATER,
SENPAI ♥
BADUM
BADUM
BADUM
BA
DU
MM

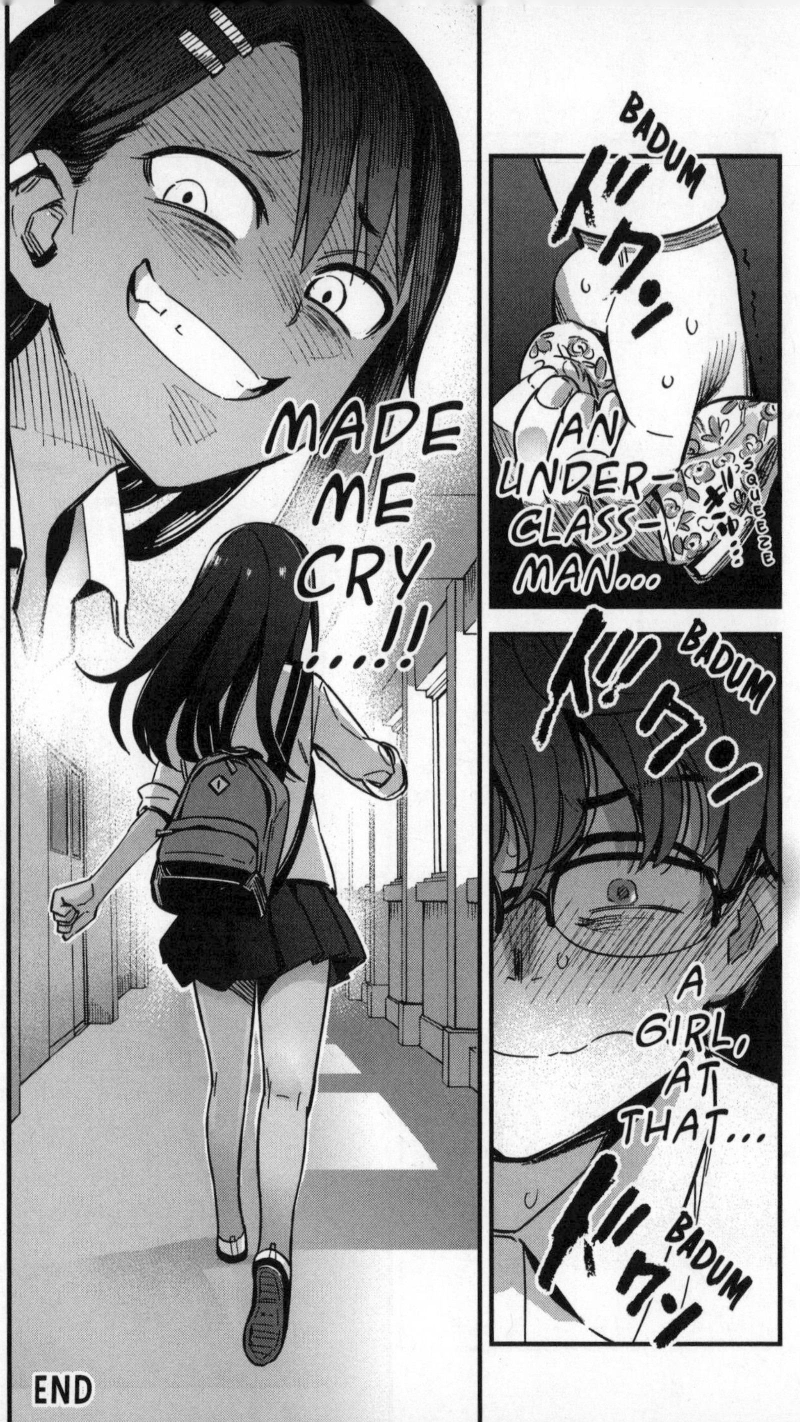
BADUM
AN UNDER-CLASS-MAN...
SQUEEZE
BADUM
A GIRL, AT THAT...
BADUM
MADE ME CRY ...!!
END

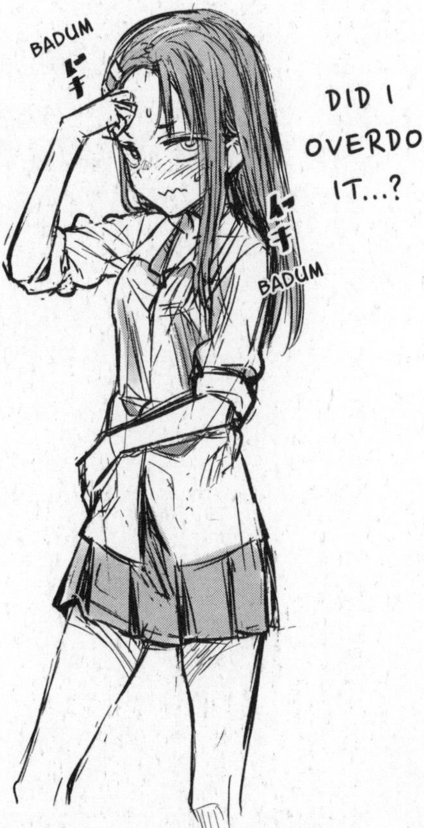
DID I OVERDO IT...?
ドキ
BADUM
BADUM
ドキ

DON'T TOY WITH ME, MISS NAGATORO

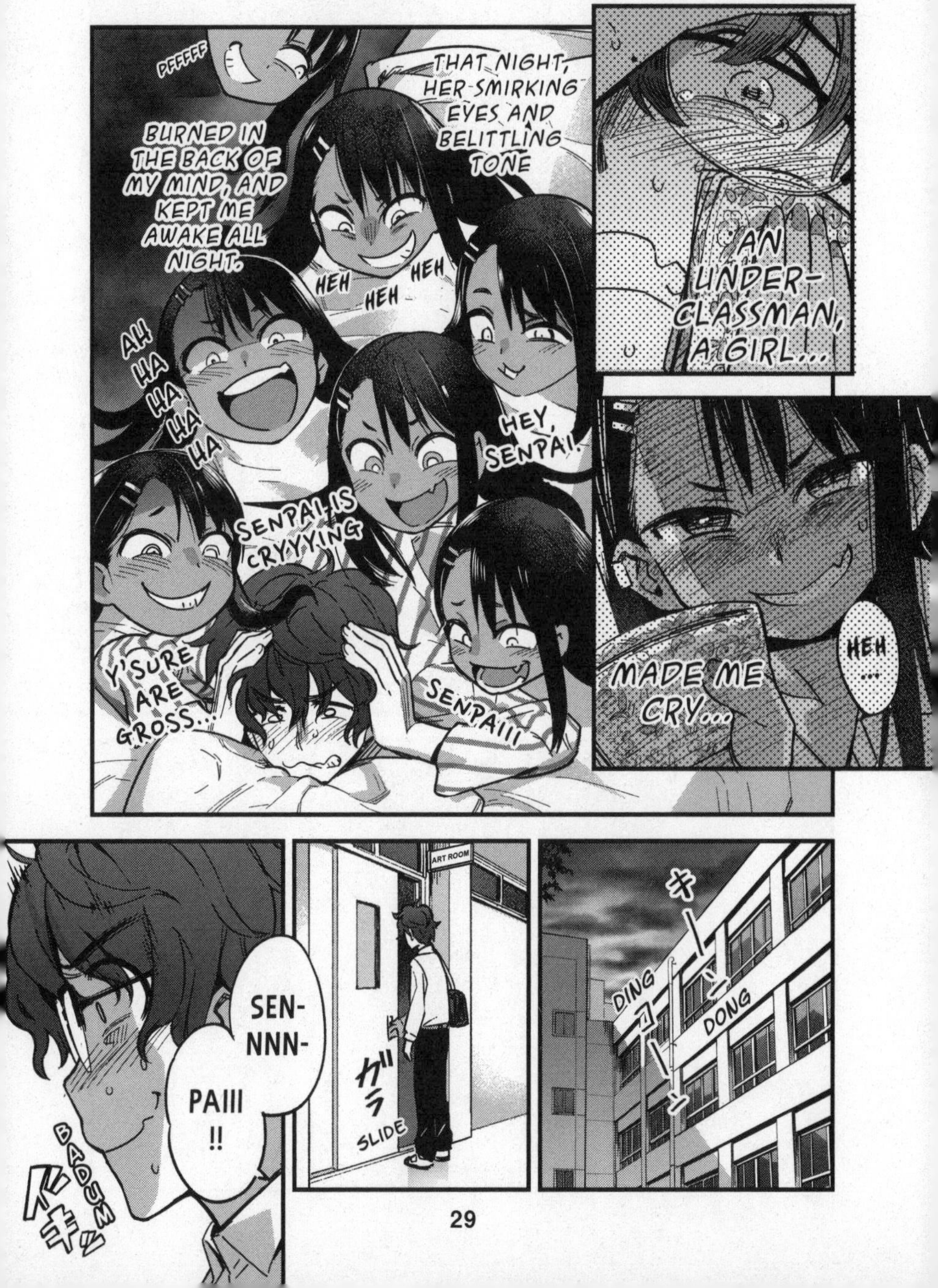
AN UNDER-CLASSMAN, A GIRL...
MADE ME CRY...
HEH...
THAT NIGHT, HER SMIRKING EYES AND BELITTLING TONE
BURNED IN THE BACK OF MY MIND, AND KEPT ME AWAKE ALL NIGHT.
PFFFFF
HEH HEH HEH
HEY, SENPAI!
AH HA HA HA HA
SENPAI IS CRYYYING
SENPAIII
Y'SURE ARE GROSS...
DING DONG
SLIDE
SEN-NNNN-PAIII!!
BADUM

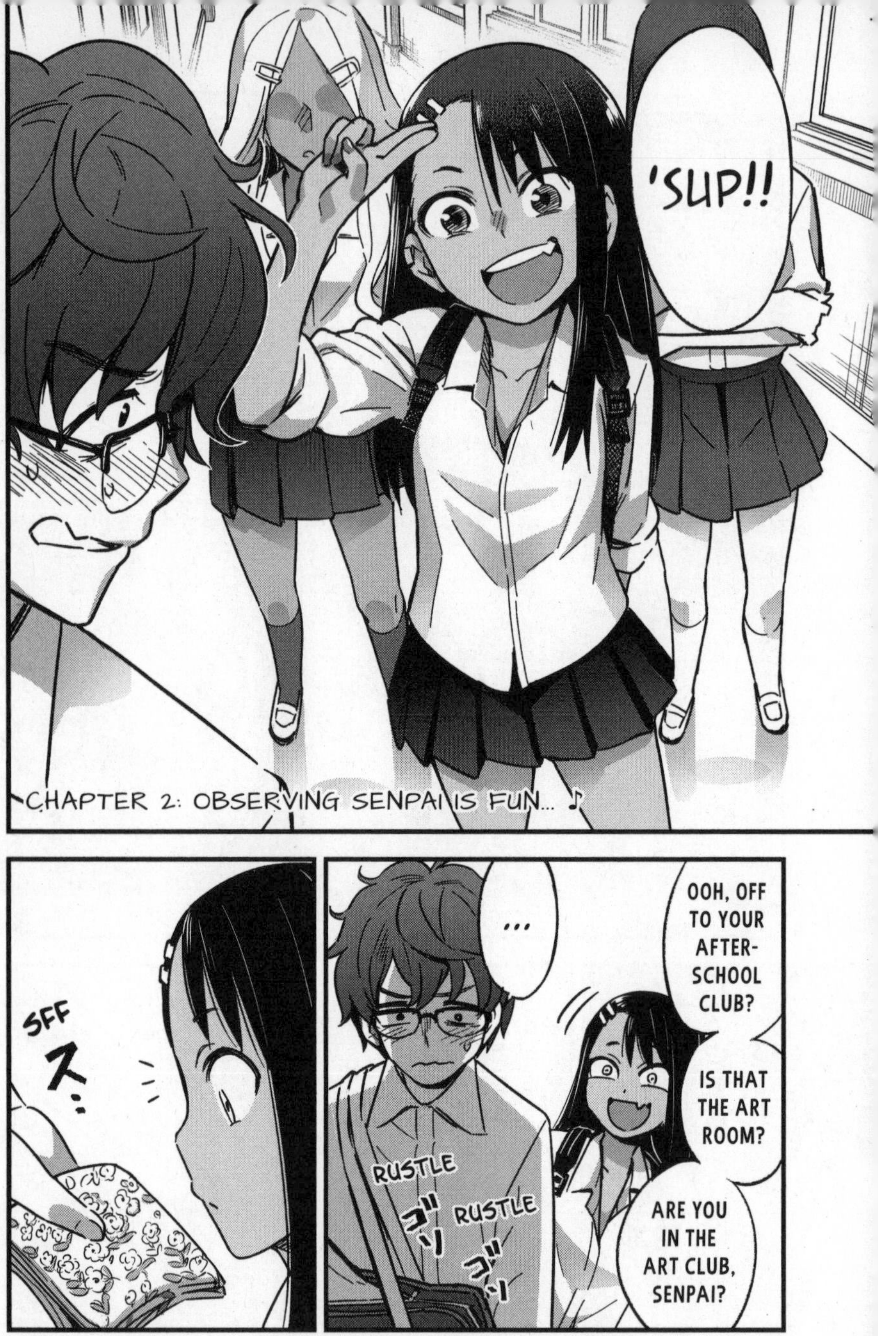
'SUP!!
CHAPTER 2: OBSERVING SENPAI IS FUN... ♪
OOH, OFF TO YOUR AFTER-SCHOOL CLUB?
IS THAT THE ART ROOM?
ARE YOU IN THE ART CLUB, SENPAI?
...
RUSTLE
ゴソ
RUSTLE
ゴソ
SFF
ス...

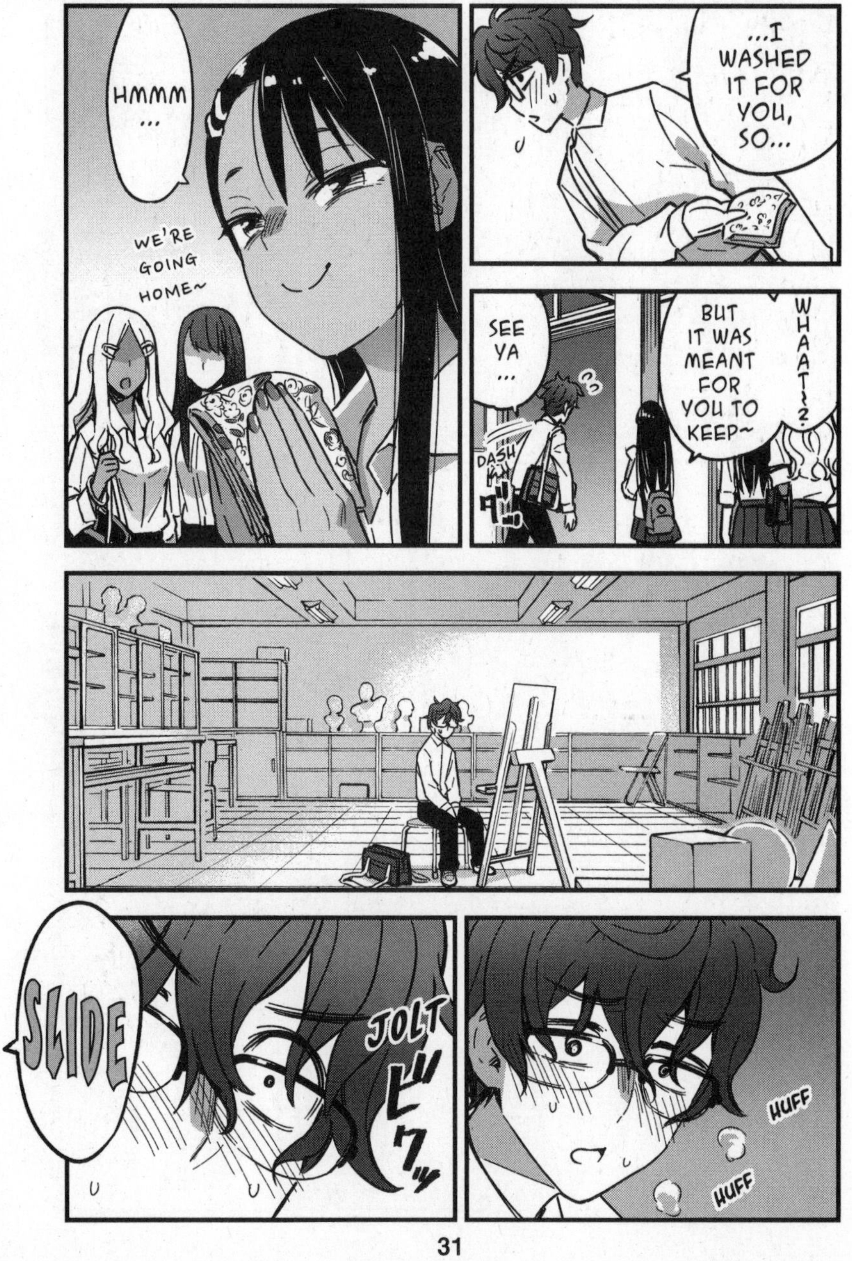
...I WASHED IT FOR YOU, SO...
WHAAT?!
BUT IT WAS MEANT FOR YOU TO KEEP~
SEE YA...
DASH
HMMM...
WE'RE GOING HOME~
HUFF
HUFF
SLIDE
JOLT

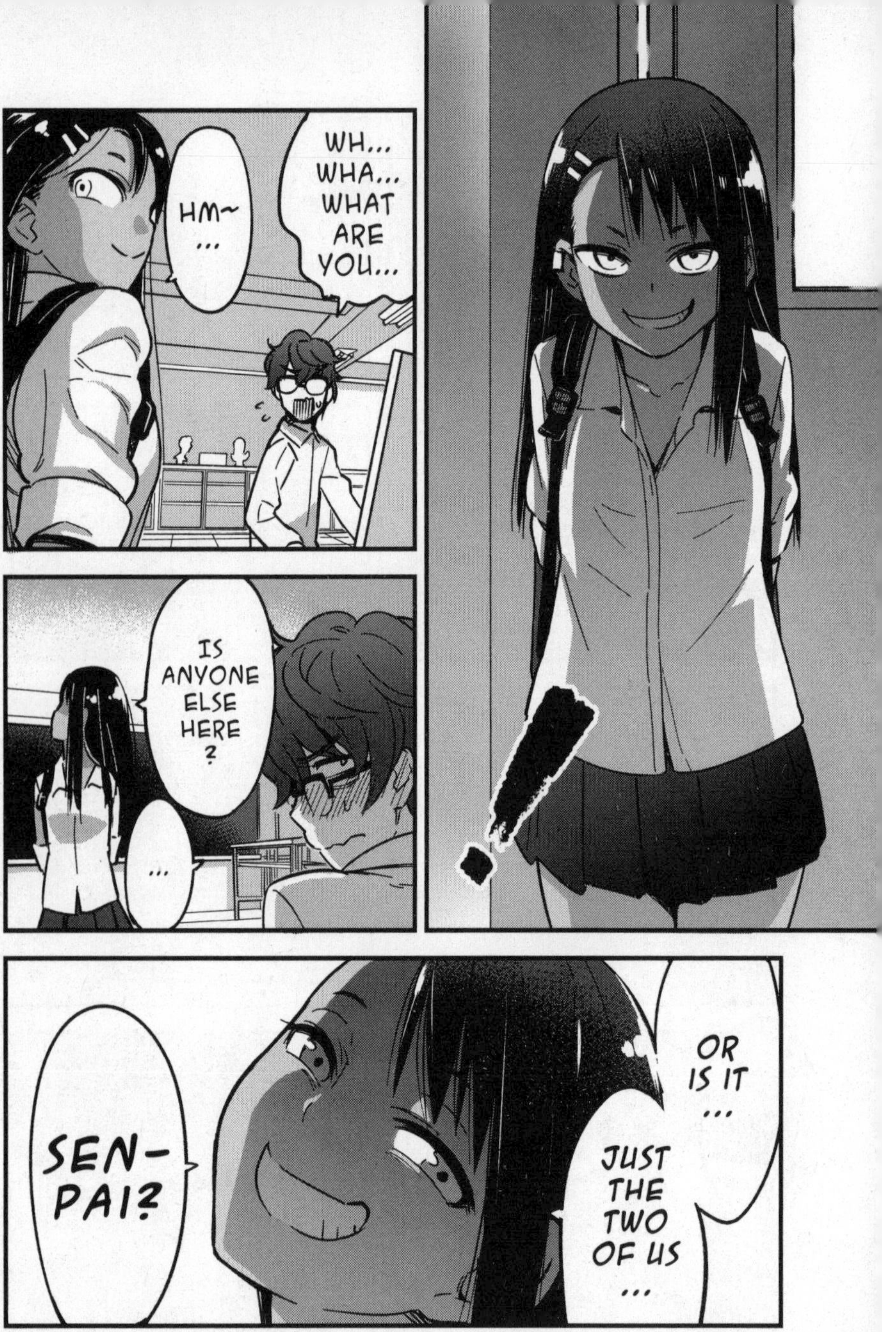
!
WH... WHA... WHAT ARE YOU...
HM~ ...
IS ANYONE ELSE HERE?
...
OR IS IT ... JUST THE TWO OF US ...
SEN-PAI?

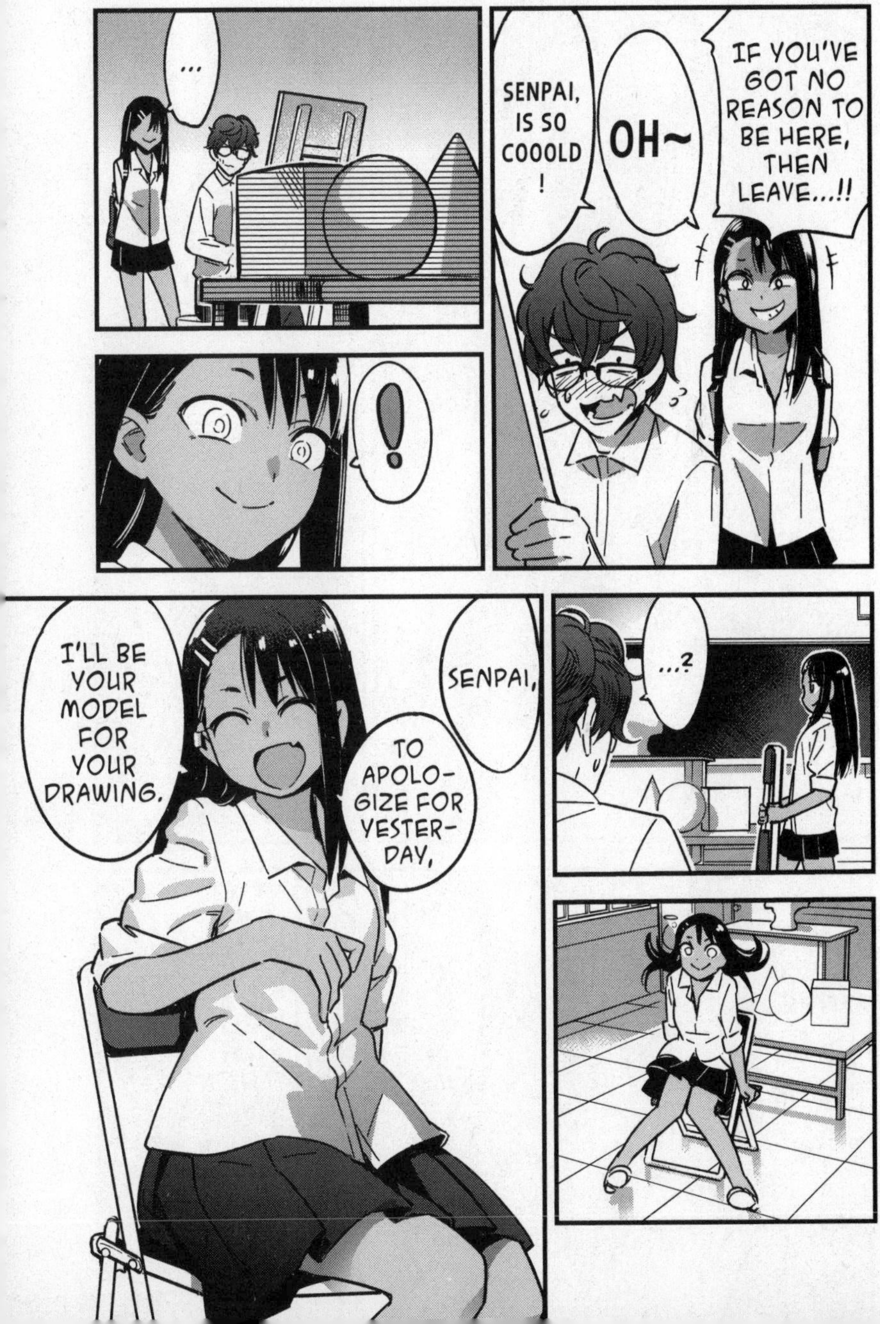
IF YOU'VE GOT NO REASON TO BE HERE, THEN LEAVE...!!
OH~
SENPAI, IS SO COOOLD !
...
!
...?
SENPAI,
TO APOLO-GIZE FOR YESTER-DAY,
I'LL BE YOUR MODEL FOR YOUR DRAWING.

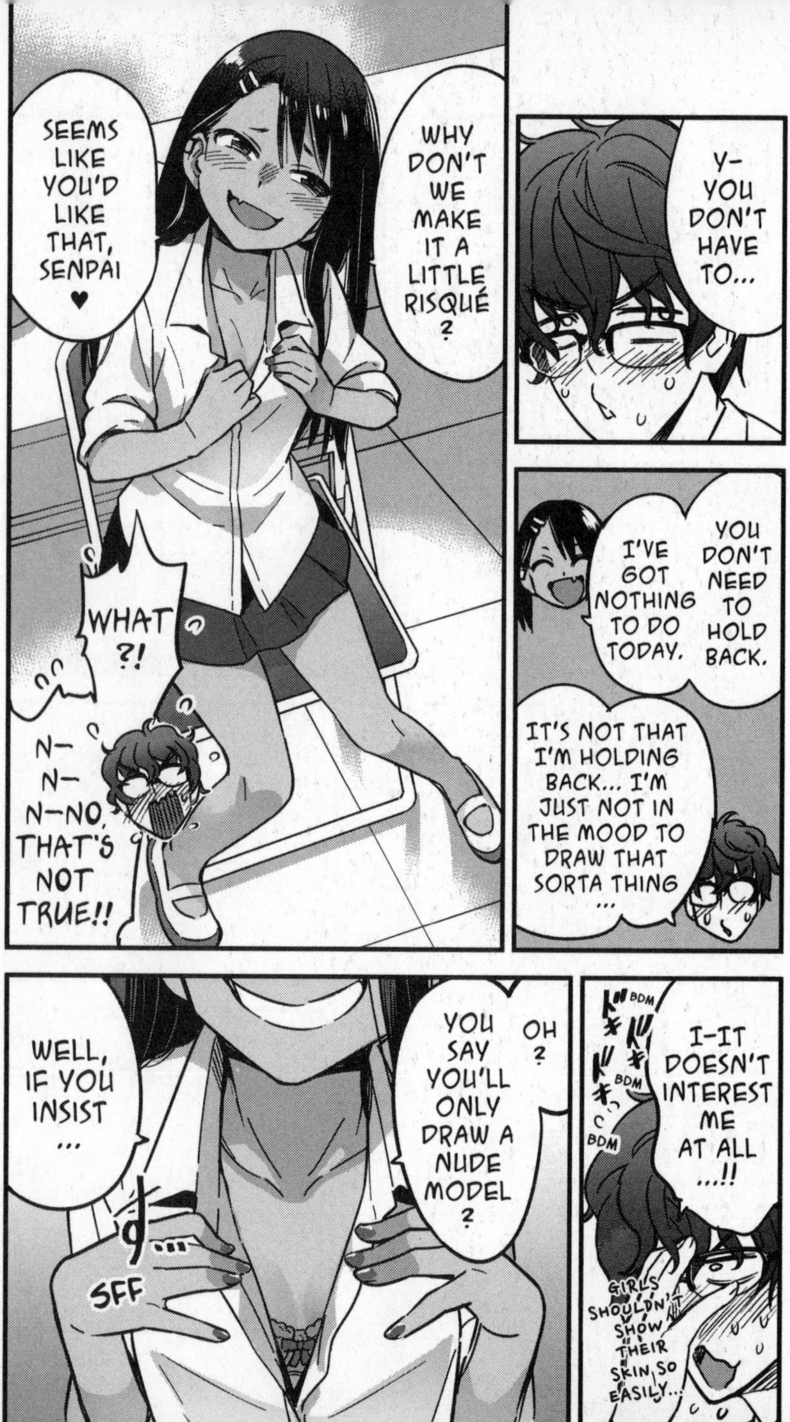
Y- YOU DON'T HAVE TO...
YOU DON'T NEED TO HOLD BACK.
I'VE GOT NOTHING TO DO TODAY.
IT'S NOT THAT I'M HOLDING BACK... I'M JUST NOT IN THE MOOD TO DRAW THAT SORTA THING...
WHY DON'T WE MAKE IT A LITTLE RISQUÉ?
SEEMS LIKE YOU'D LIKE THAT, SENPAI ♥
WHAT?!
N- N- N-NO, THAT'S NOT TRUE!!
BDM
BDM
BDM
I-IT DOESN'T INTEREST ME AT ALL...!!
GIRLS SHOULDN'T SHOW THEIR SKIN SO EASILY...
OH?
YOU SAY YOU'LL ONLY DRAW A NUDE MODEL?
WELL, IF YOU INSIST...
SFF

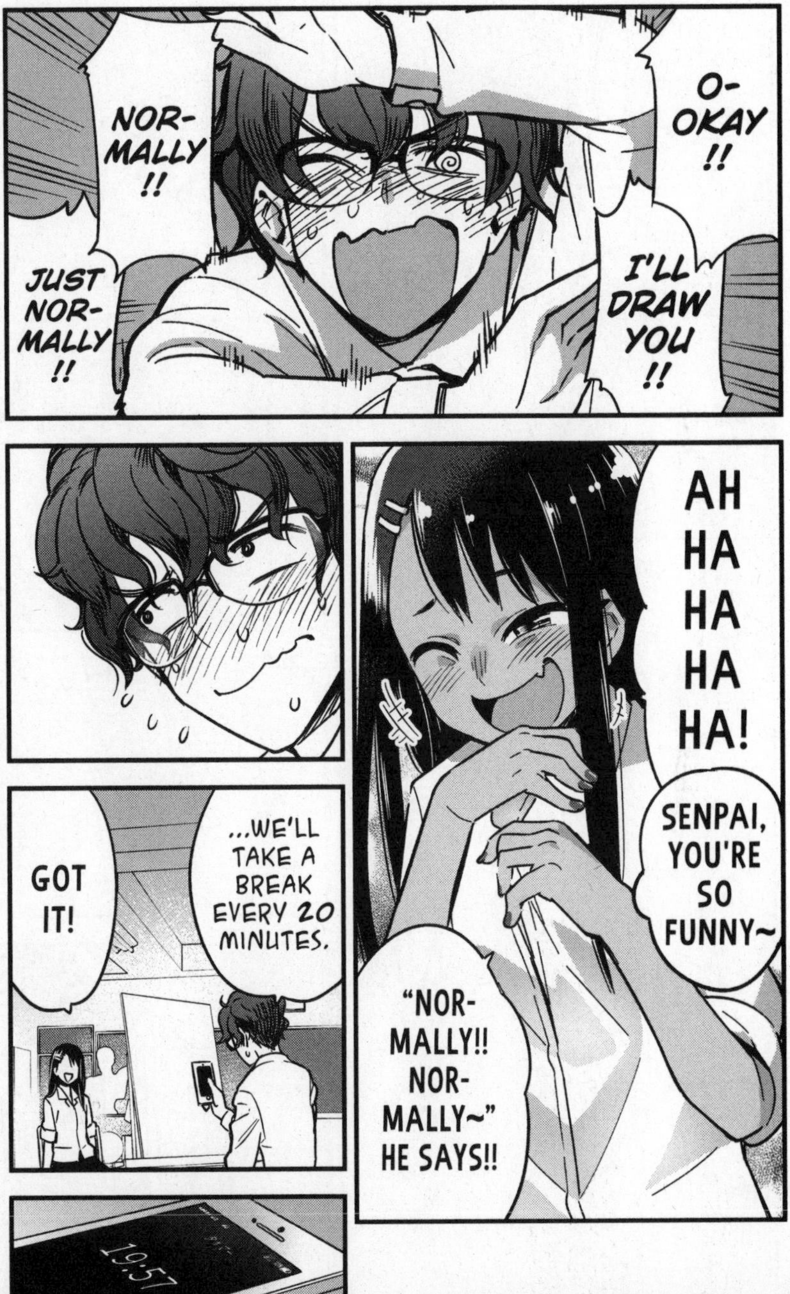
O-OKAY!!
I'LL DRAW YOU!!
NOR-MALLY!!
JUST NOR-MALLY!!
AH HA HA HA HA HA!
SENPAI, YOU'RE SO FUNNY~
"NOR-MALLY!! NOR-MALLY~" HE SAYS!!
...WE'LL TAKE A BREAK EVERY 20 MINUTES.
GOT IT!
19:57

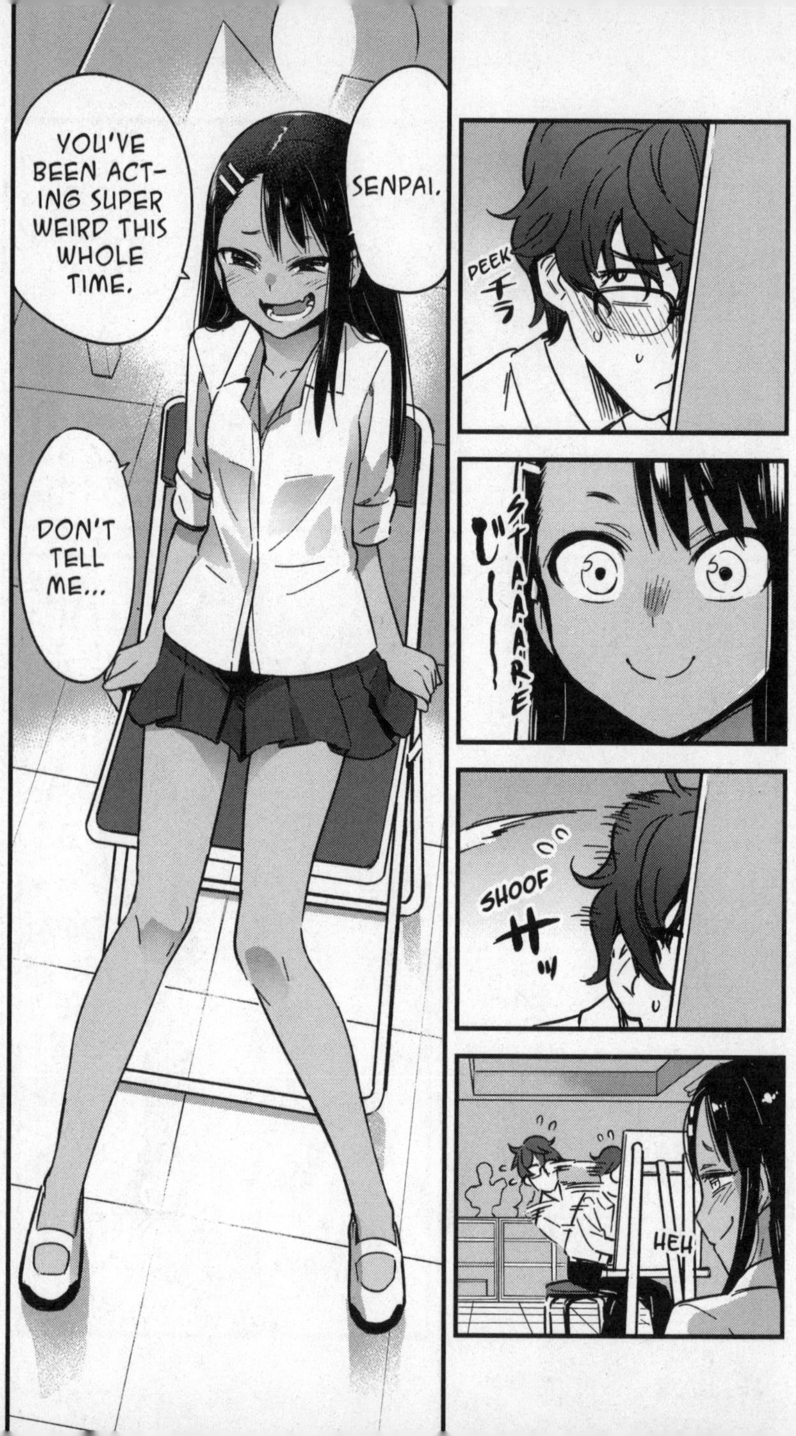
PEEK
チラ
STAAAARE
じー
SHOOF
サッ
HEH
SENPAI.
YOU'VE BEEN ACTING SUPER WEIRD THIS WHOLE TIME.
DON'T TELL ME...

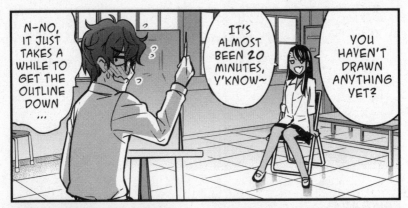

YOU HAVEN'T DRAWN ANYTHING YET?
IT'S ALMOST BEEN 20 MINUTES, Y'KNOW~
N-NO, IT JUST TAKES A WHILE TO GET THE OUTLINE DOWN ...
I CAN'T HELP IT...
AFTER ALL...
I'VE NEVER STARED AT A GIRL STRAIGHT-ON BEFORE IN MY LIFE.
NOT EVEN ONCE...

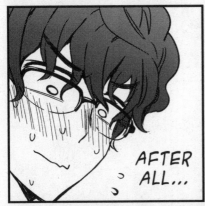

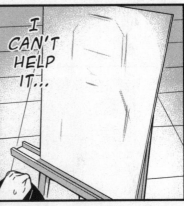

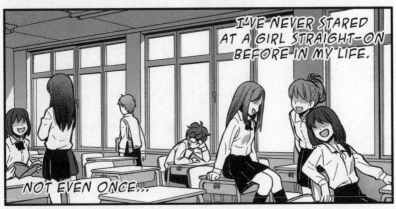

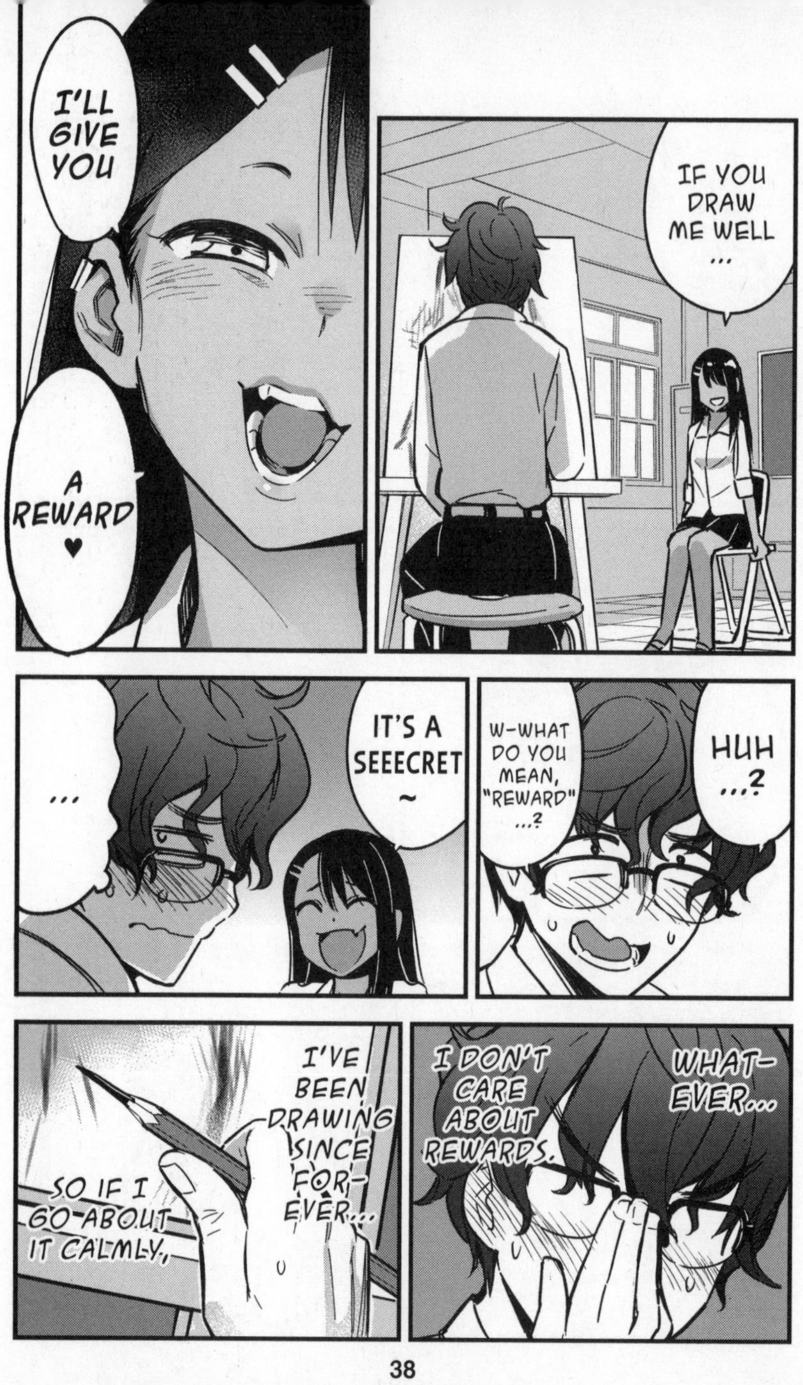
IF YOU DRAW ME WELL ...
I'LL GIVE YOU
A REWARD ♥
HUH ...?
W-WHAT DO YOU MEAN, "REWARD" ...?
IT'S A SEEECRET ~
...
WHAT-EVER...
I DON'T CARE ABOUT REWARDS.
I'VE BEEN DRAWING SINCE FOR-EVER...
SO IF I GO ABOUT IT CALMLY,

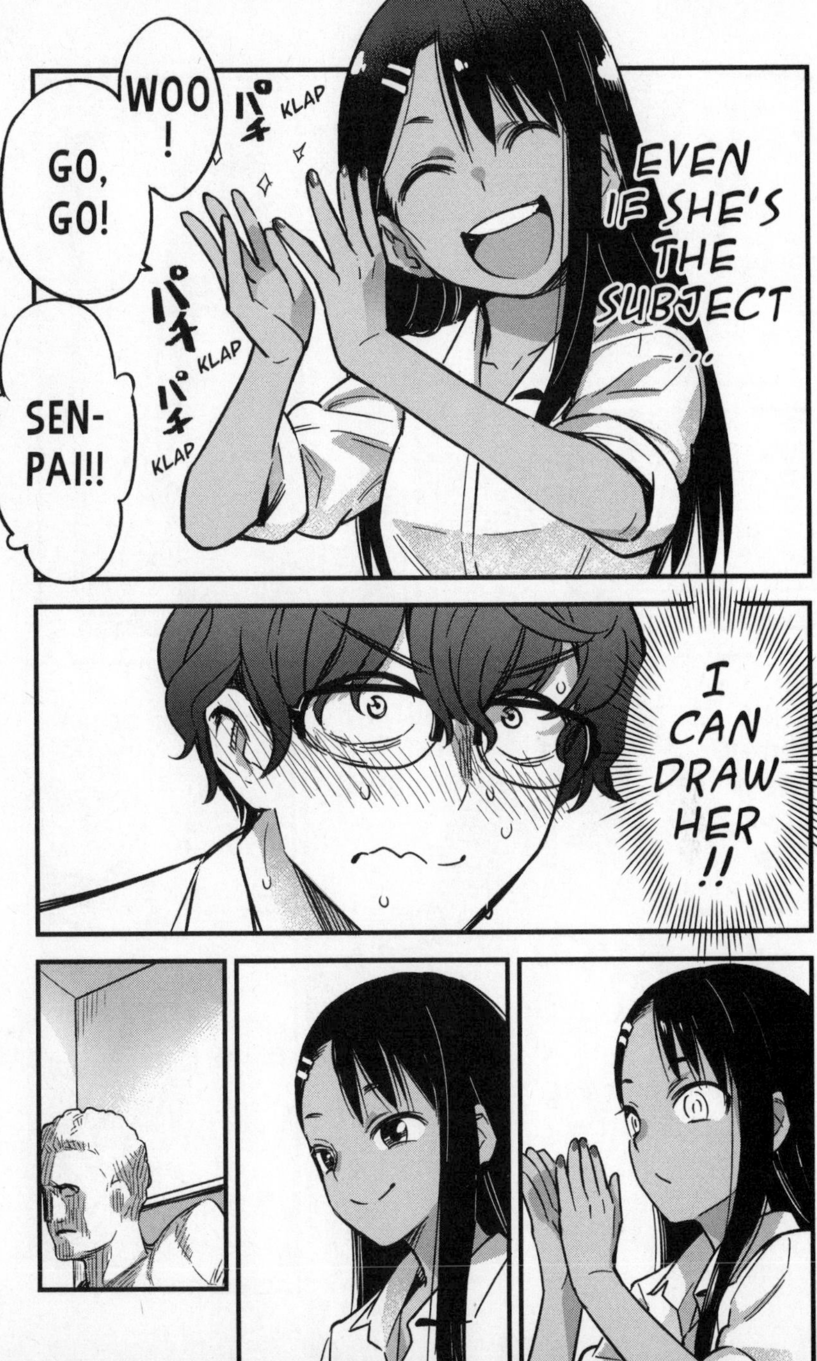
EVEN IF SHE'S THE SUBJECT...
WOO!
パチ KLAP
GO, GO!
パチ KLAP
SEN-PAI!!
パチ KLAP
I CAN DRAW HER!!

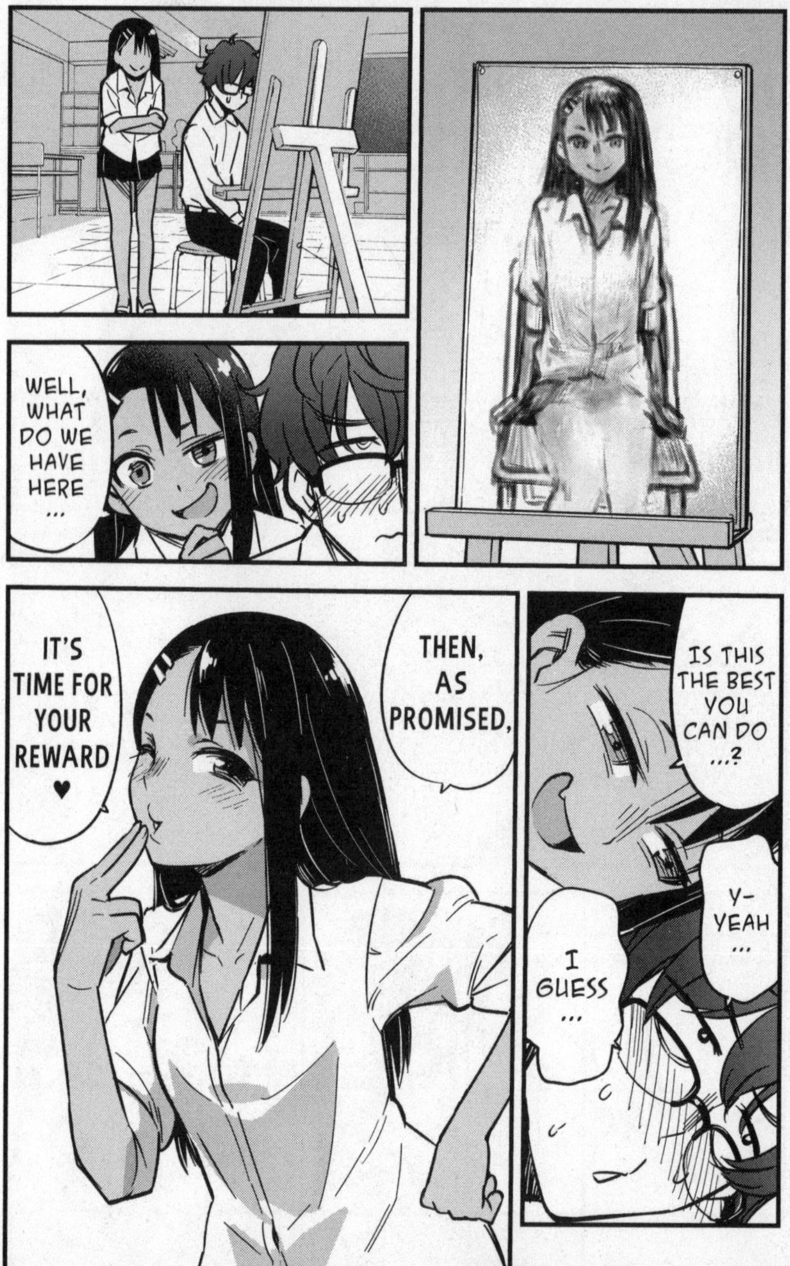
WELL, WHAT DO WE HAVE HERE ...
IS THIS THE BEST YOU CAN DO ...?
Y-YEAH ...
I GUESS ...
THEN, AS PROMISED,
IT'S TIME FOR YOUR REWARD ♥

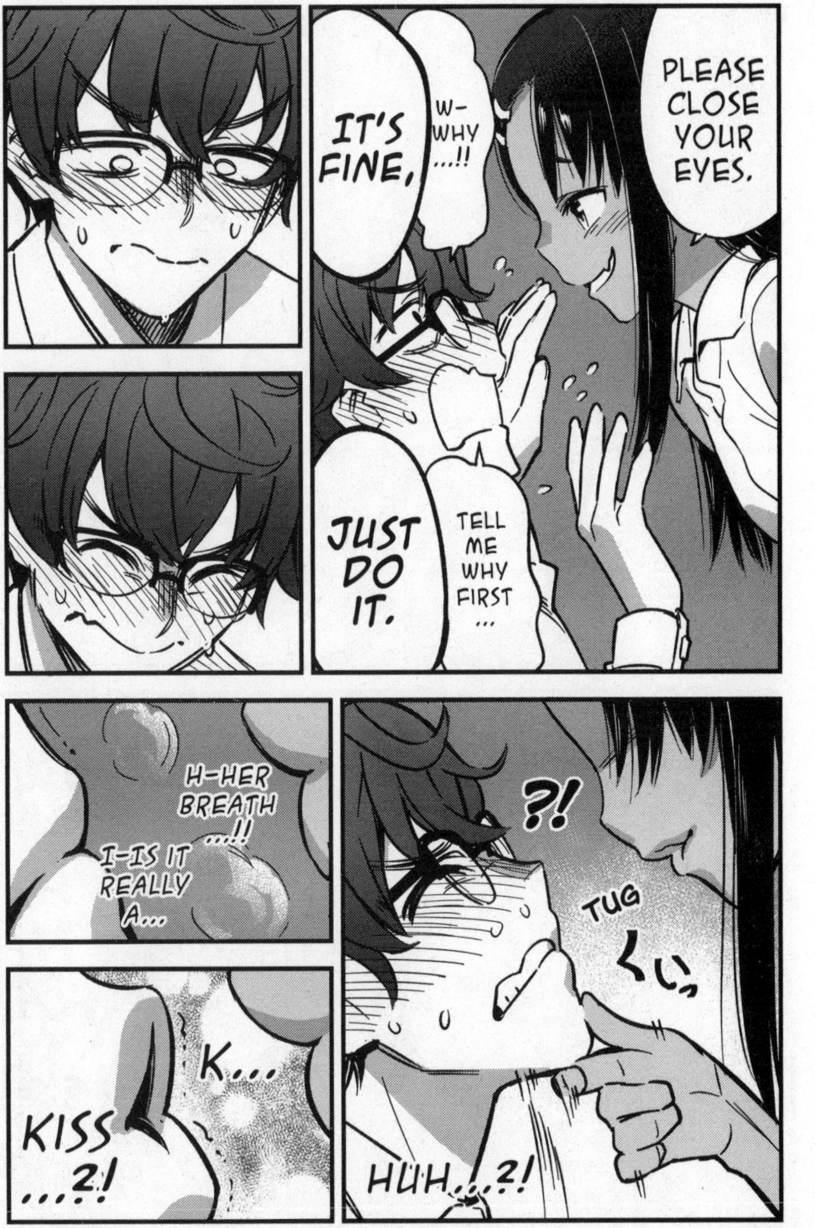
PLEASE CLOSE YOUR EYES.
W-WHY ...!!
IT'S FINE,
TELL ME WHY FIRST ...
JUST DO IT.
?!
TUG
くいっ
HUH...?!
H-HER BREATH ...!!
I-IS IT REALLY A...
K...
KISS ...?!

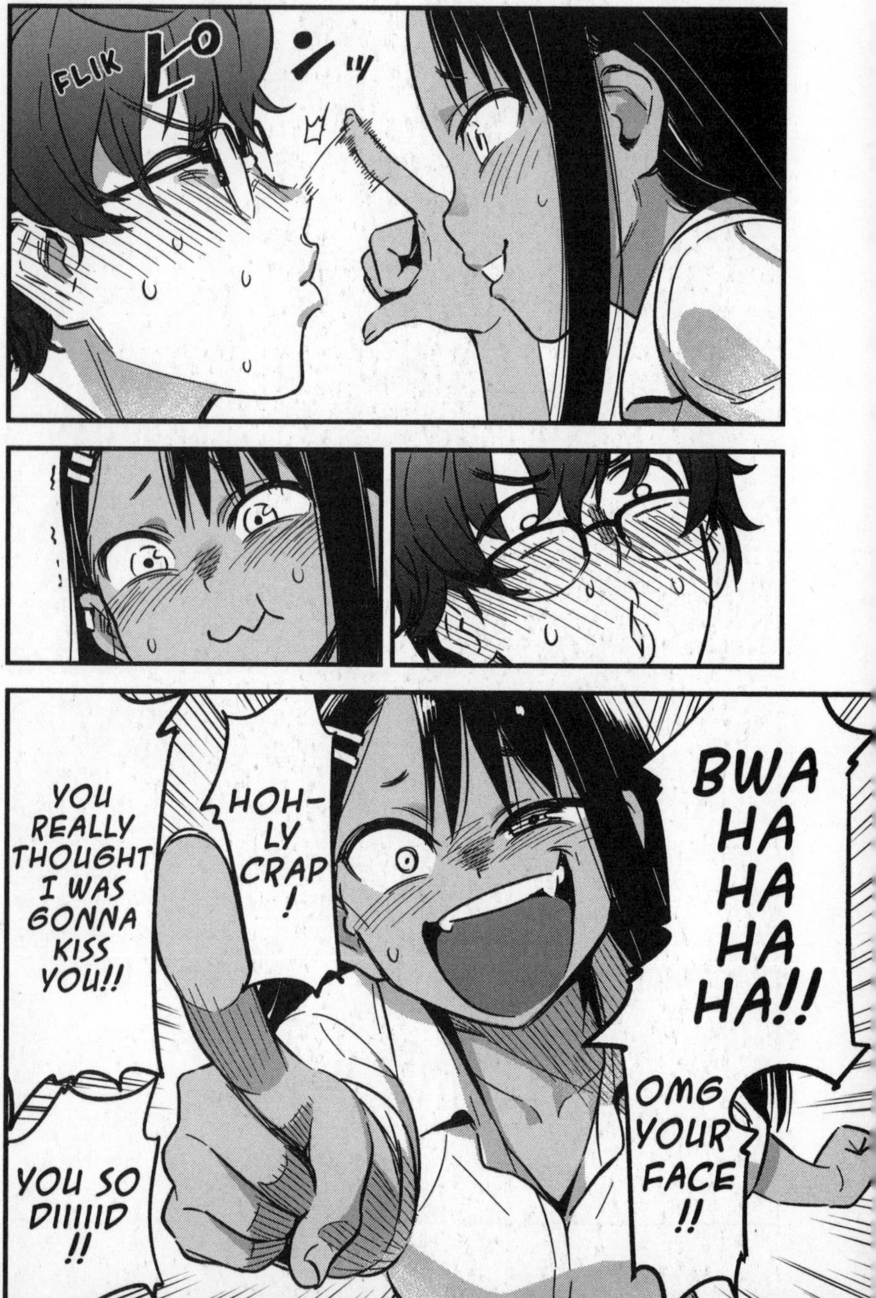
ピシッ
FLIK
BWA HA HA HA HA HA!!
OMG YOUR FACE!!
HOH-LY CRAP!
YOU REALLY THOUGHT I WAS GONNA KISS YOU!!
YOU SO DIIIIID!!

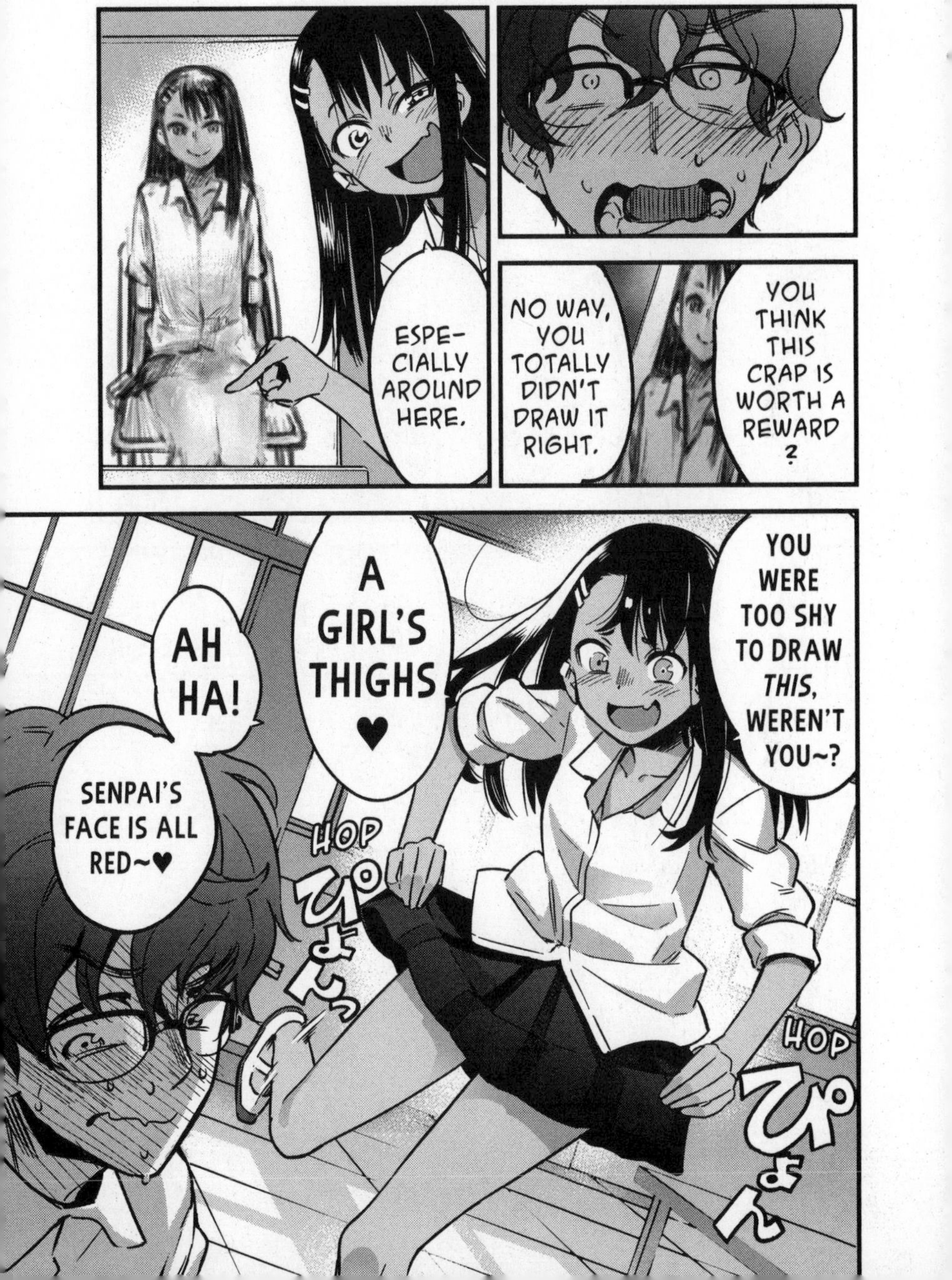
YOU THINK THIS CRAP IS WORTH A REWARD?
NO WAY, YOU TOTALLY DIDN'T DRAW IT RIGHT.
ESPE-CIALLY AROUND HERE.
YOU WERE TOO SHY TO DRAW *THIS*, WEREN'T YOU~?
A GIRL'S THIGHS ♥
AH HA!
SENPAI'S FACE IS ALL RED~♥
HOP ぴょんっ
HOP ぴょん

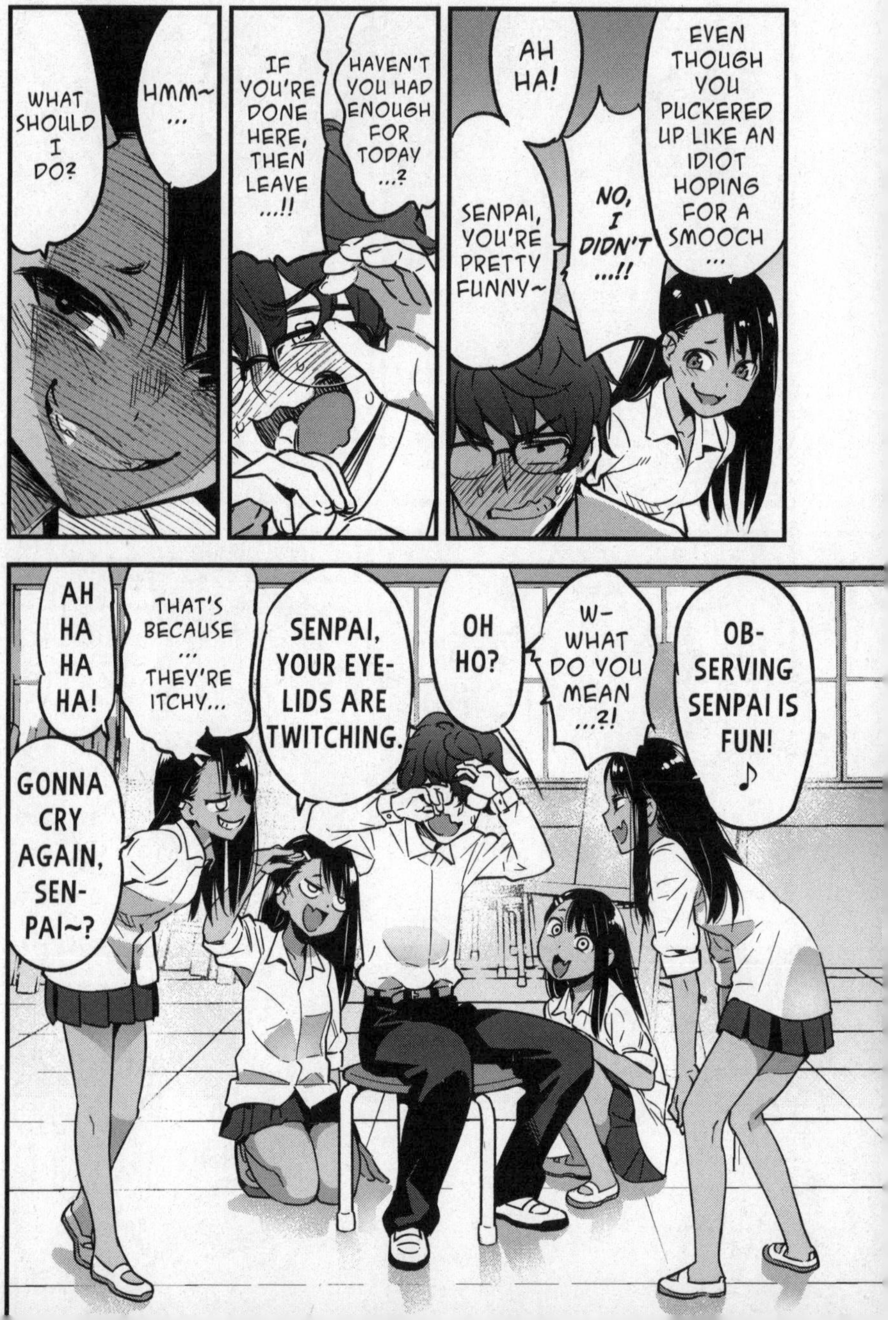
EVEN THOUGH YOU PUCKERED UP LIKE AN IDIOT HOPING FOR A SMOOCH ...
AH HA!
NO, I DIDN'T ...!!
SENPAI, YOU'RE PRETTY FUNNY~
HAVEN'T YOU HAD ENOUGH FOR TODAY ...?
IF YOU'RE DONE HERE, THEN LEAVE ...!!
HMM~ ...
WHAT SHOULD I DO?
OBSERVING SENPAI IS FUN! ♪
W-WHAT DO YOU MEAN ...?!
OH HO?
SENPAI, YOUR EYELIDS ARE TWITCHING.
THAT'S BECAUSE ... THEY'RE ITCHY...
AH HA HA HA!
GONNA CRY AGAIN, SENPAI~?

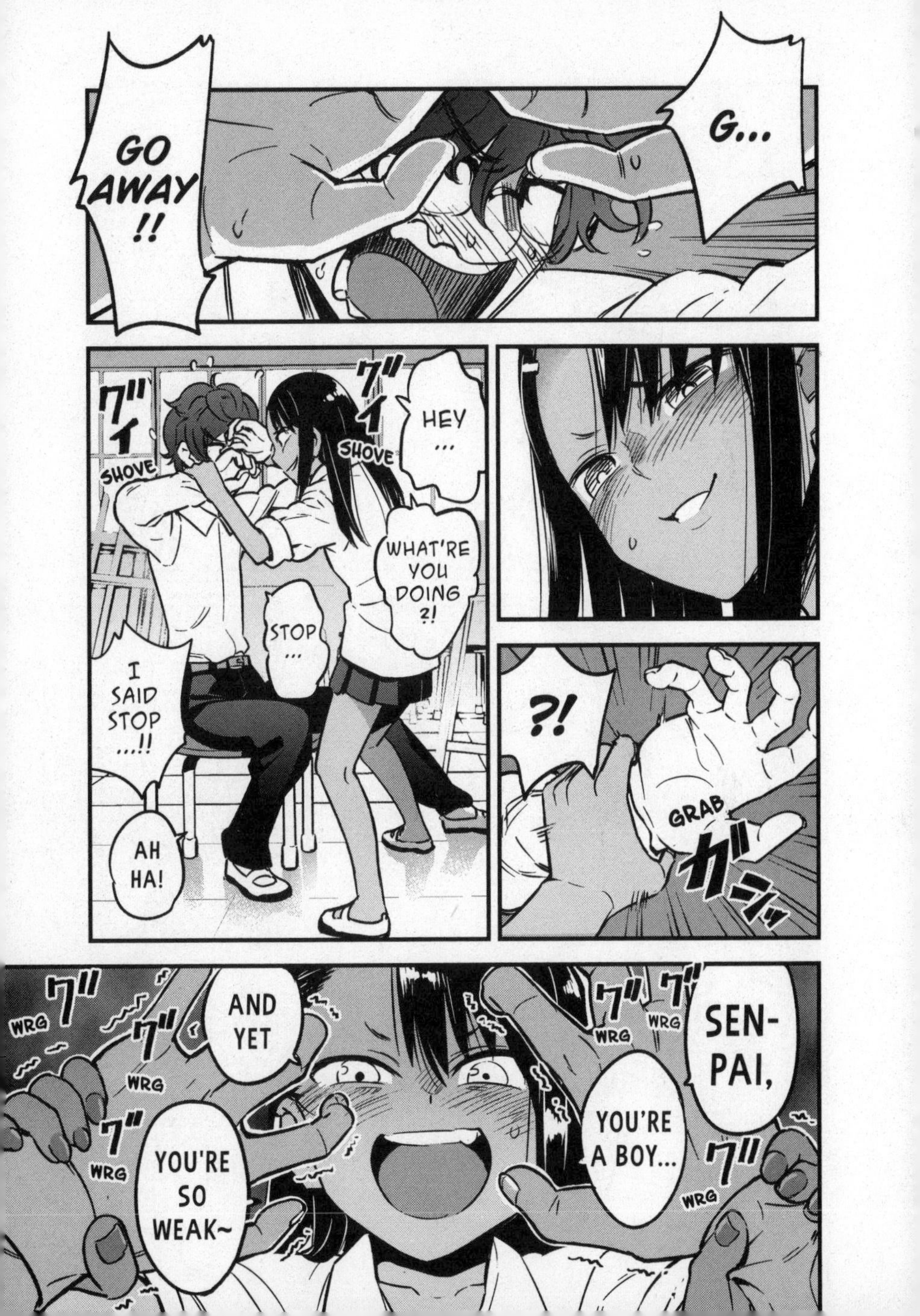
G...
GO AWAY !!
?!
GRAB
ガシッ
グイ
SHOVE
HEY ...
WHAT'RE YOU DOING ?!
グイ
SHOVE
STOP ...
I SAID STOP ...!!
AH HA!
SEN-PAI,
YOU'RE A BOY...
グ
WRG
AND YET
YOU'RE SO WEAK~
グ
WRG

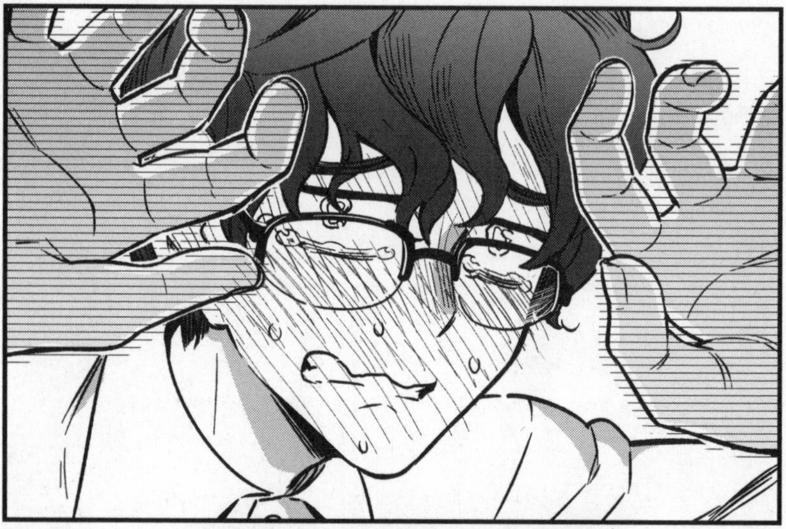

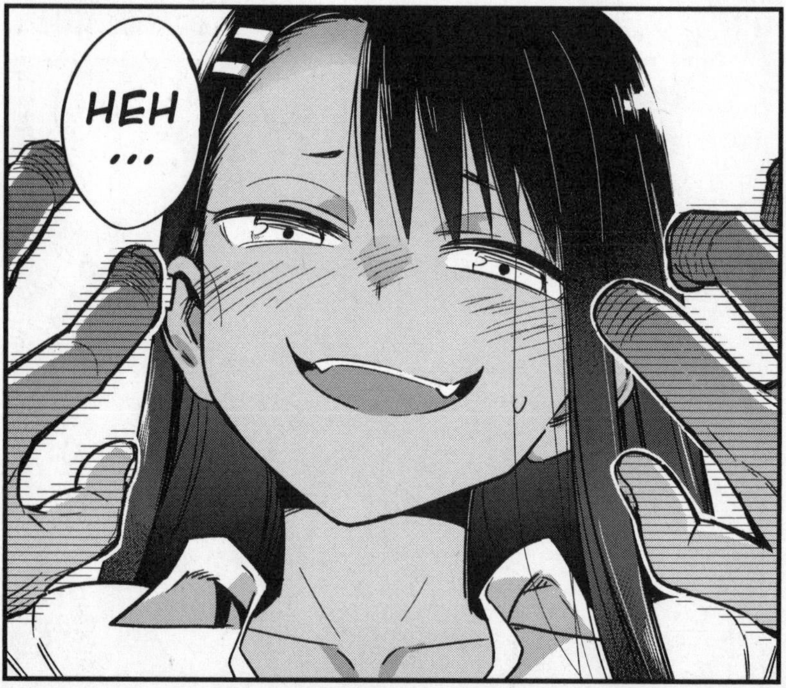
HEH ...

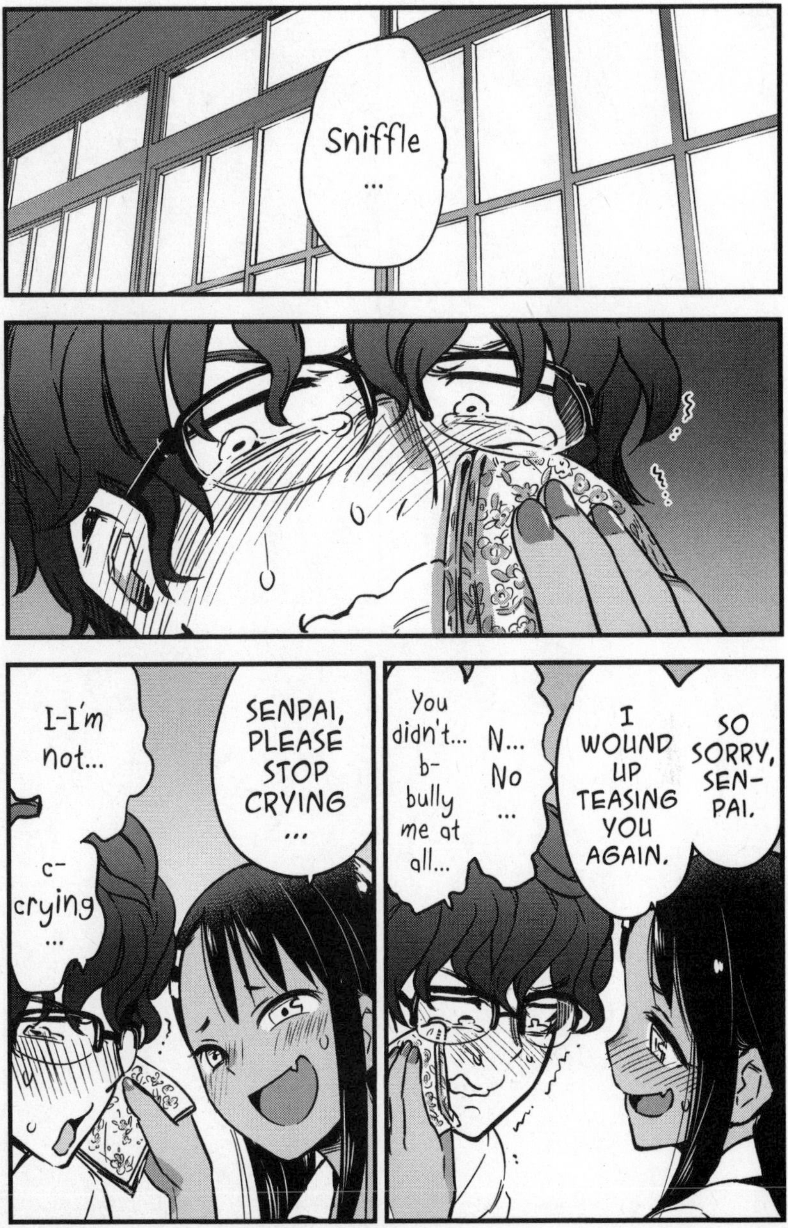
Sniffle ...
SO SORRY, SEN-PAI.
I WOUND UP TEASING YOU AGAIN.
N... No ...
You didn't... b-bully me at all...
SENPAI, PLEASE STOP CRYING ...
I-I'm not... c-crying ...

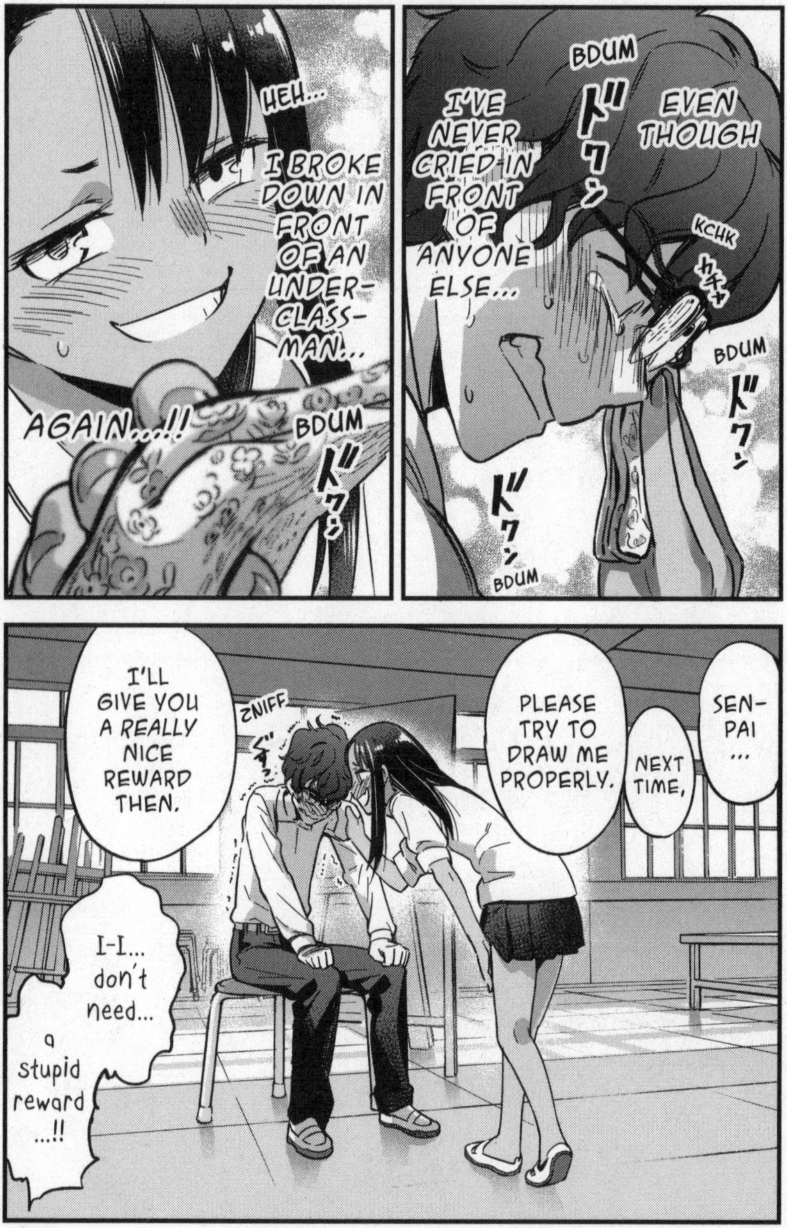
BDUM
ドクン
EVEN THOUGH
I'VE NEVER CRIED IN FRONT OF ANYONE ELSE...
KCHK
カチャ
BDUM
ドクン
ドクン
BDUM
HEH...
I BROKE DOWN IN FRONT OF AN UNDER-CLASSMAN...
AGAIN...!!
BDUM
ドクン
SEN-PAI...
NEXT TIME,
PLEASE TRY TO DRAW ME PROPERLY.
I'LL GIVE YOU A REALLY NICE REWARD THEN.
SNIFF
I-I... don't need... a stupid reward...!!

END

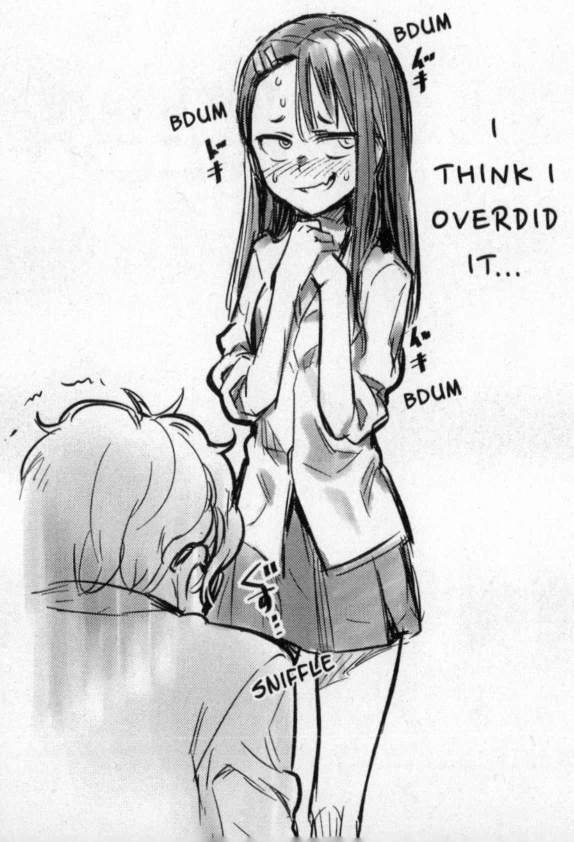

I THINK I OVERDID IT...
BDUM
BDUM
BDUM
SNIFFLE

DON'T TOY WITH ME,
MISS NAGATORO

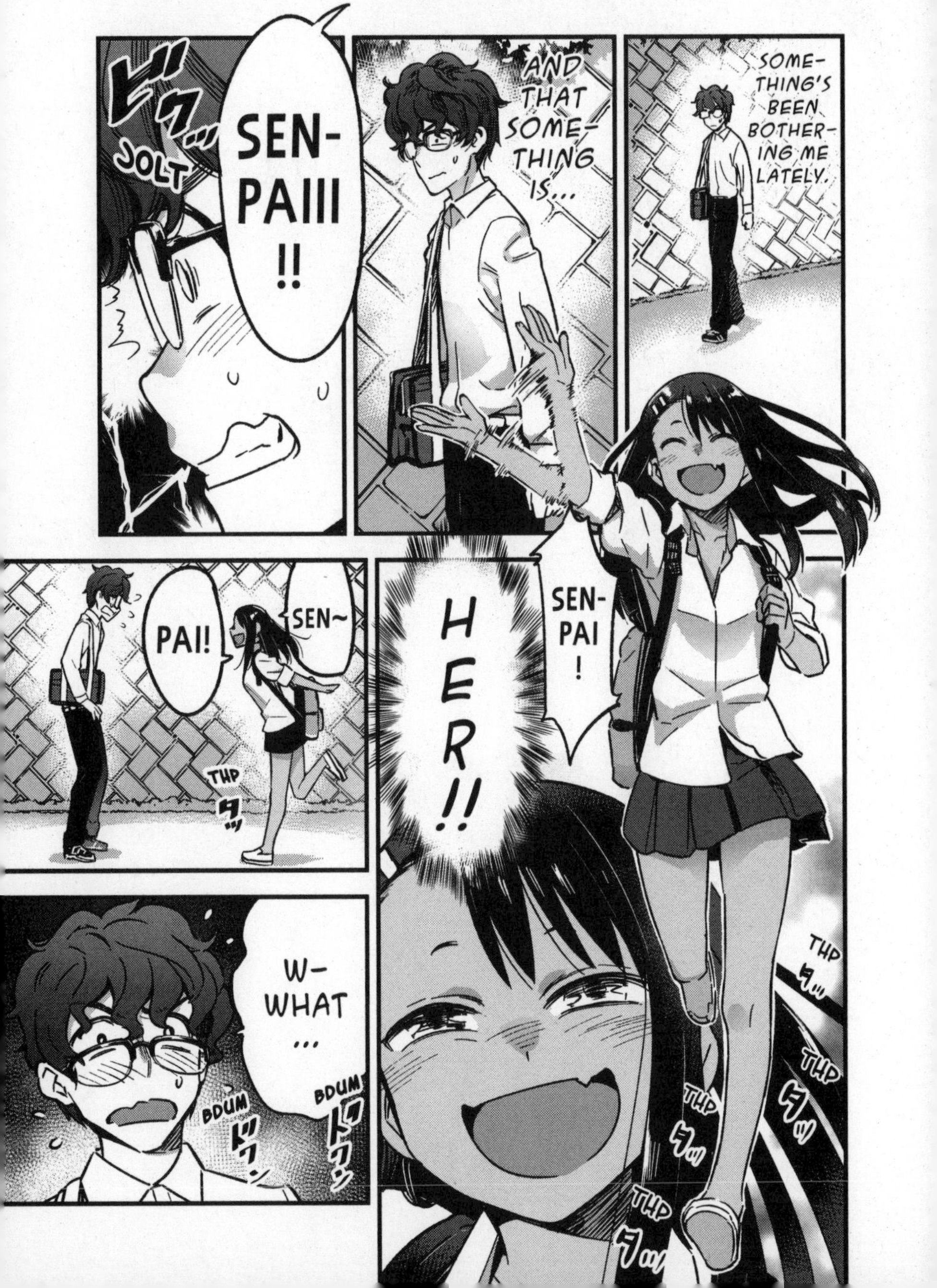

SOME-THING'S BEEN BOTHER-ING ME LATELY.
AND THAT SOME-THING IS...
JOLT
SEN-PAIII!!
SEN-PAI!
HER!!
THP
THP
THP
THP
SEN~
PAI!
THP
W-WHAT...
BDUM
BDUM

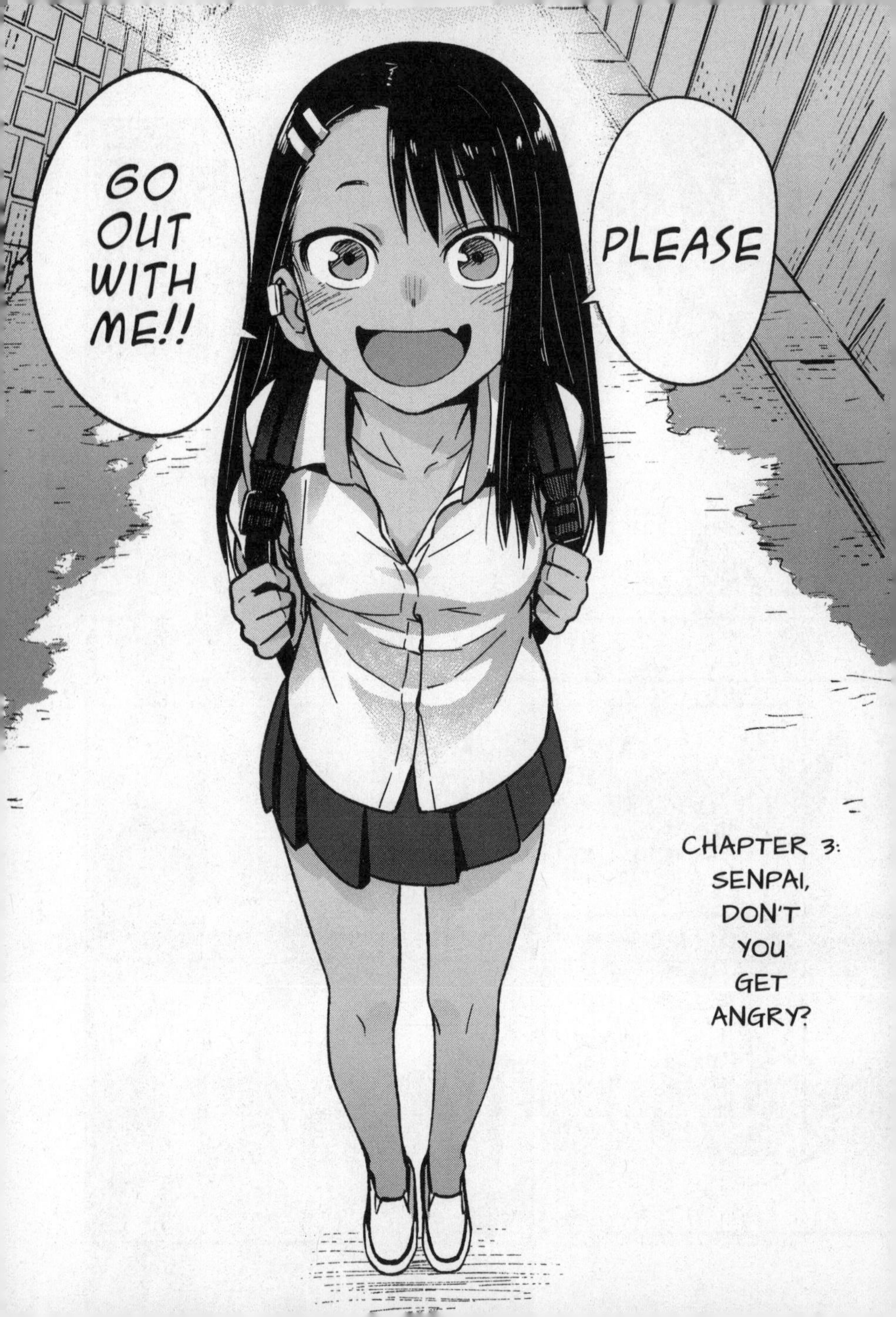
PLEASE
GO OUT WITH ME!!

CHAPTER 3: SENPAI, DON'T YOU GET ANGRY?

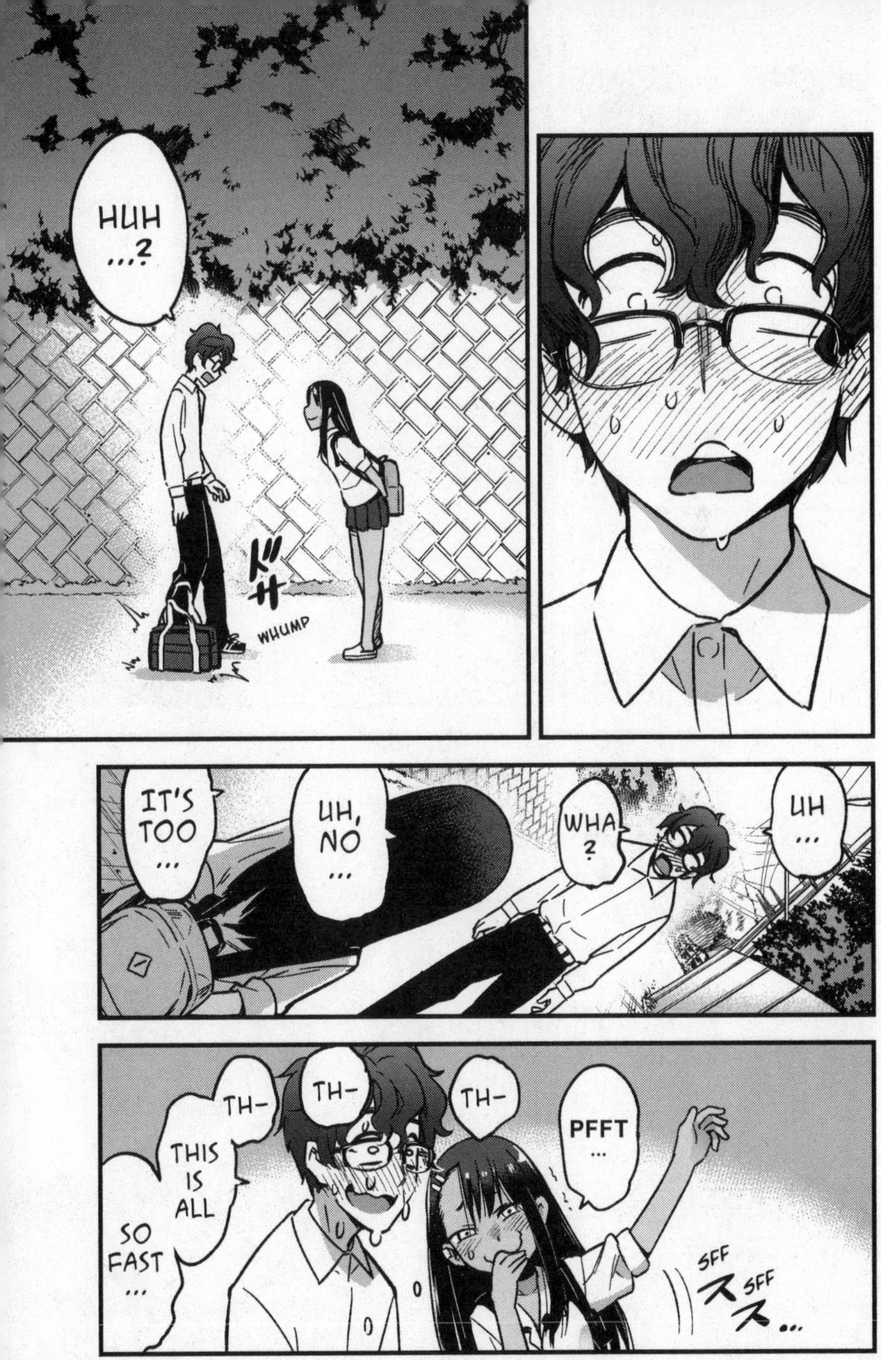
HUH ...?
ドサ
WHUMP
UH ...
WHA ?
UH, NO ...
IT'S TOO ...
PFFT ...
TH-
TH-
TH-
THIS IS ALL SO FAST ...
SFF SFF
スス...

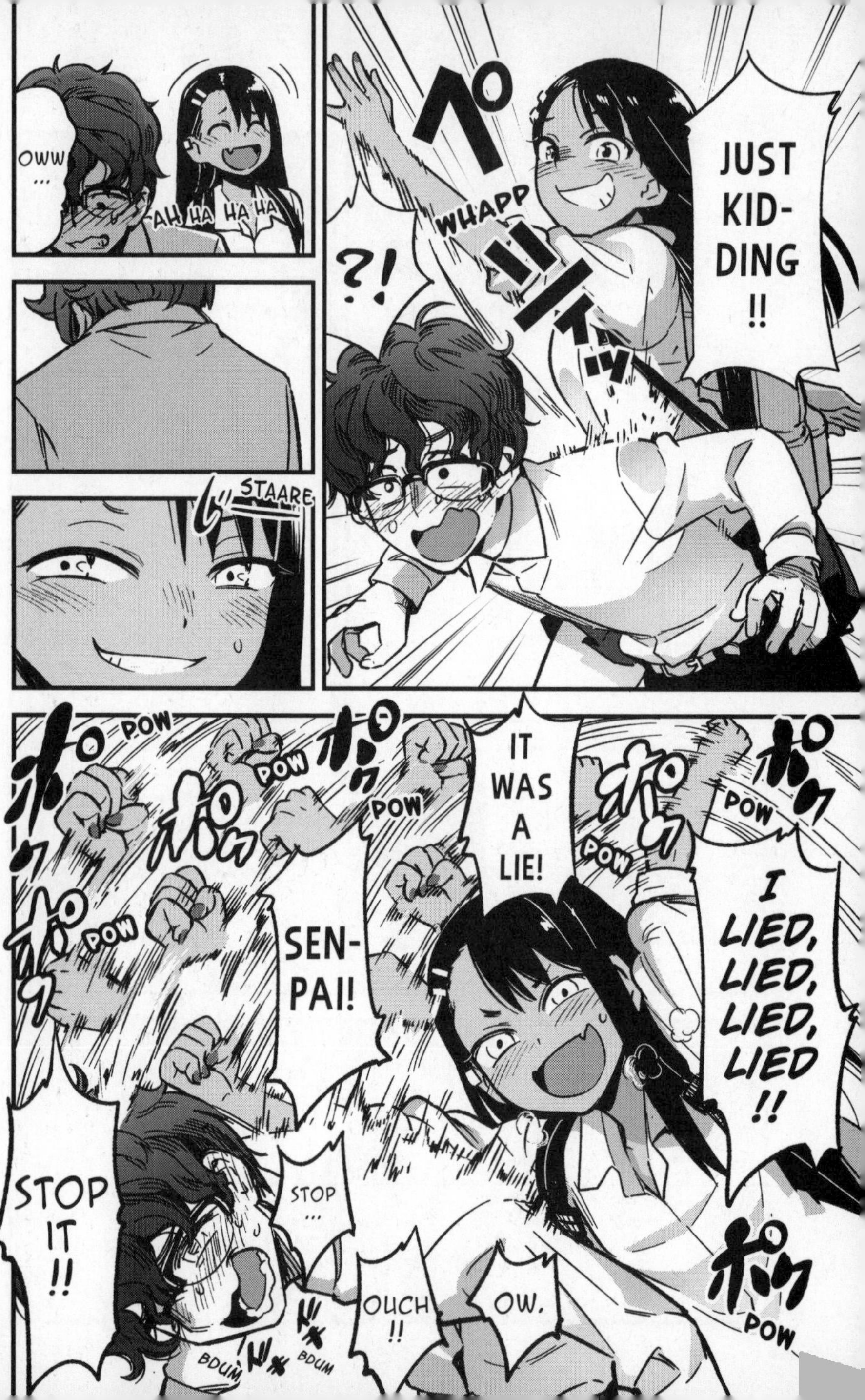
JUST KID-DING!!
WHAPP
?!
OWW...
AH HA HA HA
STAARE
POW
POW
POW
POW
IT WAS A LIE!
POW
POW
I LIED, LIED, LIED, LIED!!
SENPAI!
STOP IT!!
STOP...
OUCH!!
OW.
BDUM
BDUM
POW

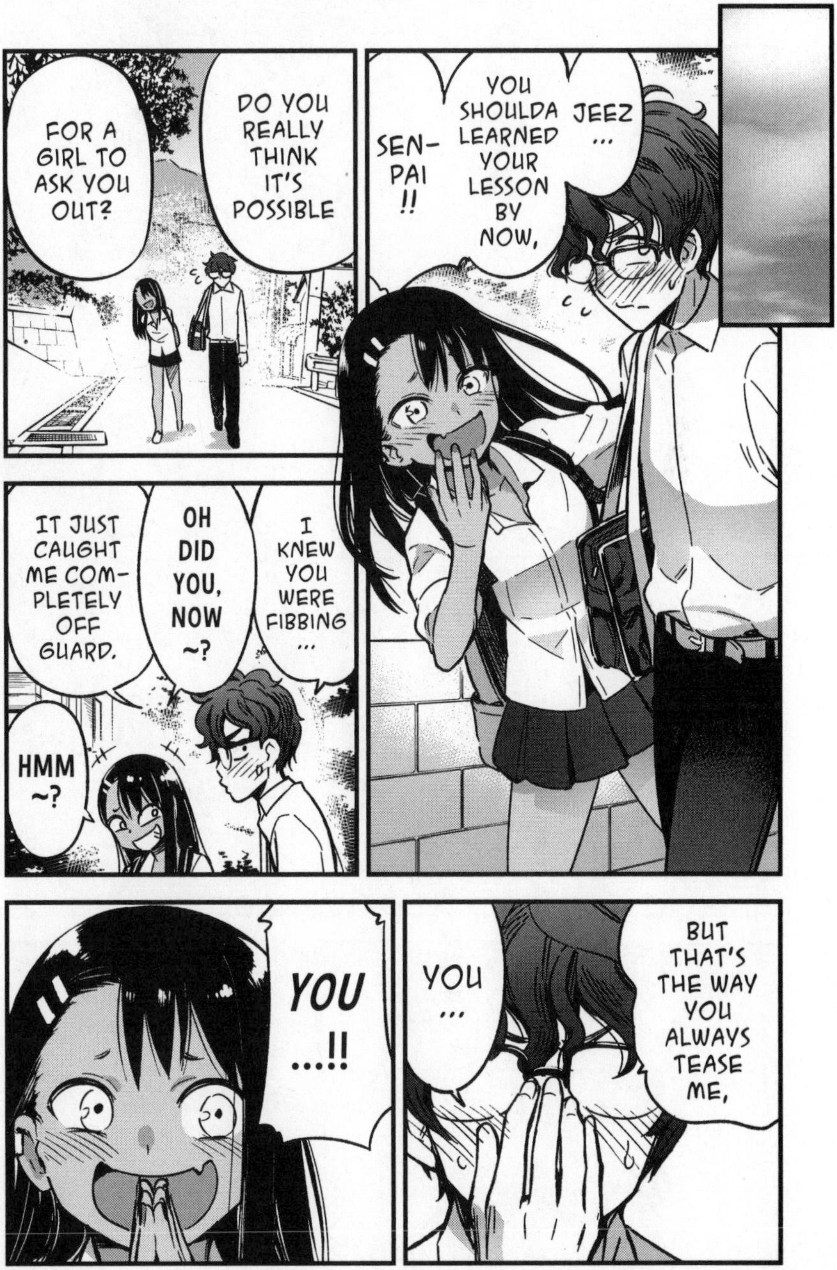

JEEZ ...
YOU SHOULDA LEARNED YOUR LESSON BY NOW,
SEN-PAI !!
DO YOU REALLY THINK IT'S POSSIBLE
FOR A GIRL TO ASK YOU OUT?
I KNEW YOU WERE FIBBING ...
OH DID YOU, NOW ~?
IT JUST CAUGHT ME COM-PLETELY OFF GUARD.
HMM ~?
BUT THAT'S THE WAY YOU ALWAYS TEASE ME,
YOU ...
YOU ...!!

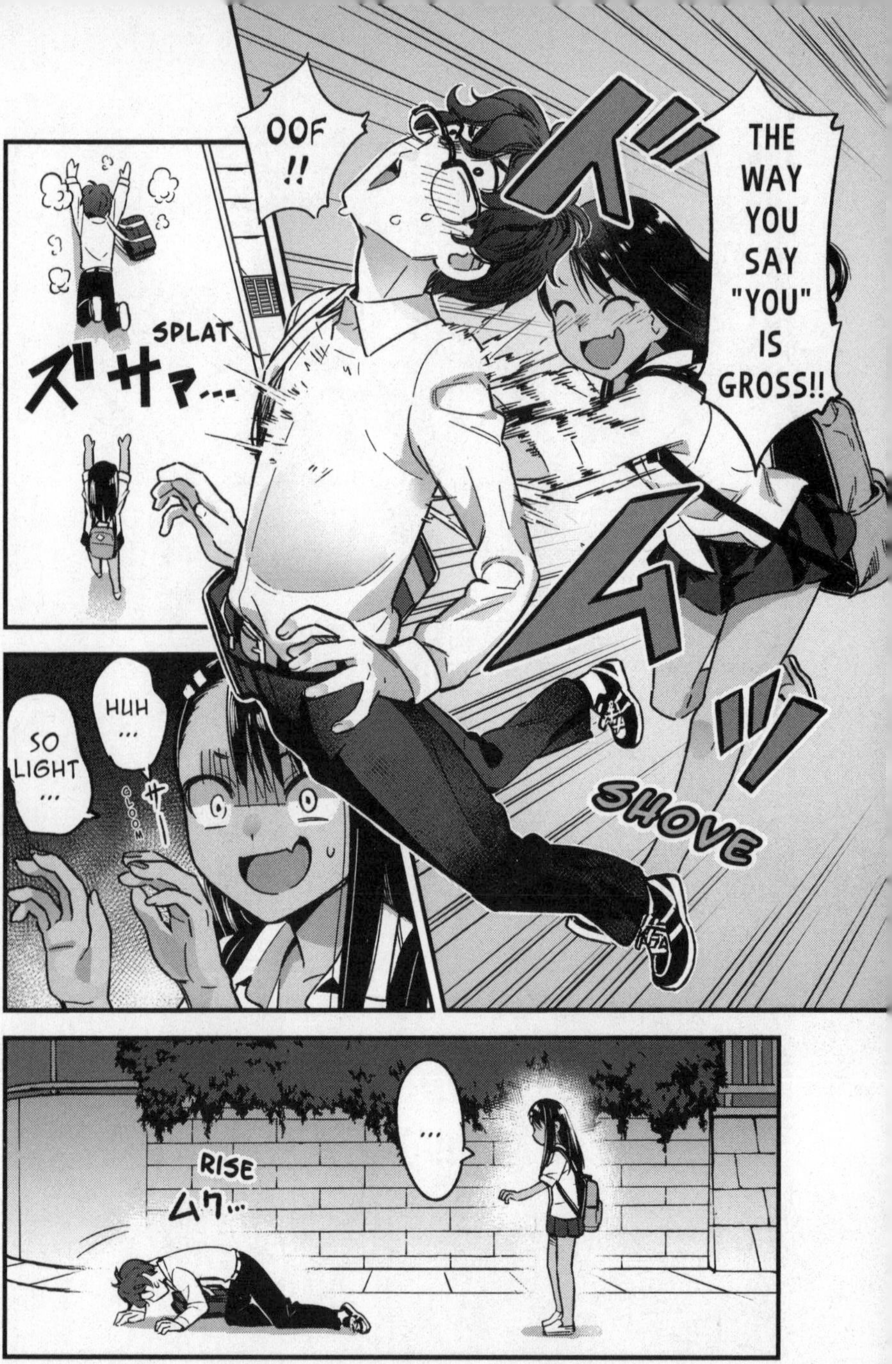
THE WAY YOU SAY "YOU" IS GROSS!!
OOF !!
SHOVE
SPLAT
ズサァ...
HUH ...
SO LIGHT ...
GLOOM
サー
...
RISE
ムク...

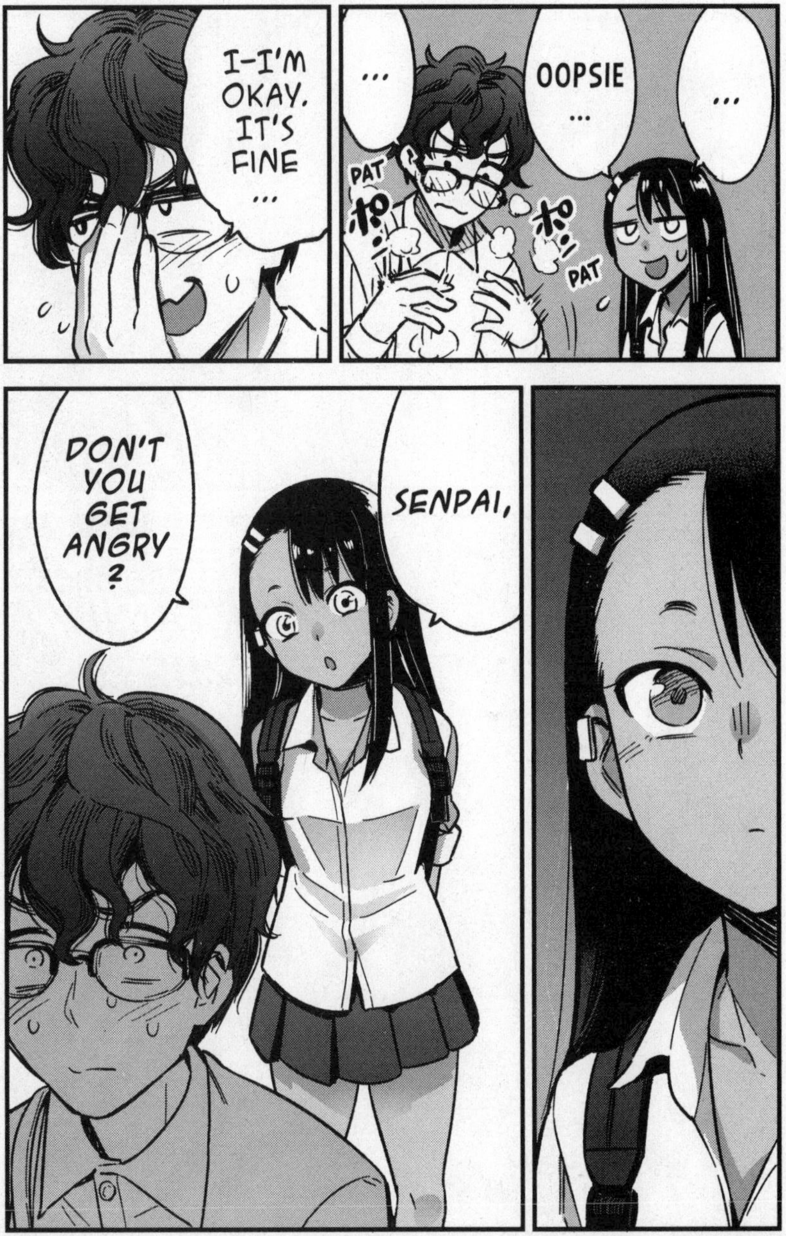
...
OOPSIE ...
...
PAT
PAT
I-I'M OKAY. IT'S FINE ...
SENPAI,
DON'T YOU GET ANGRY?

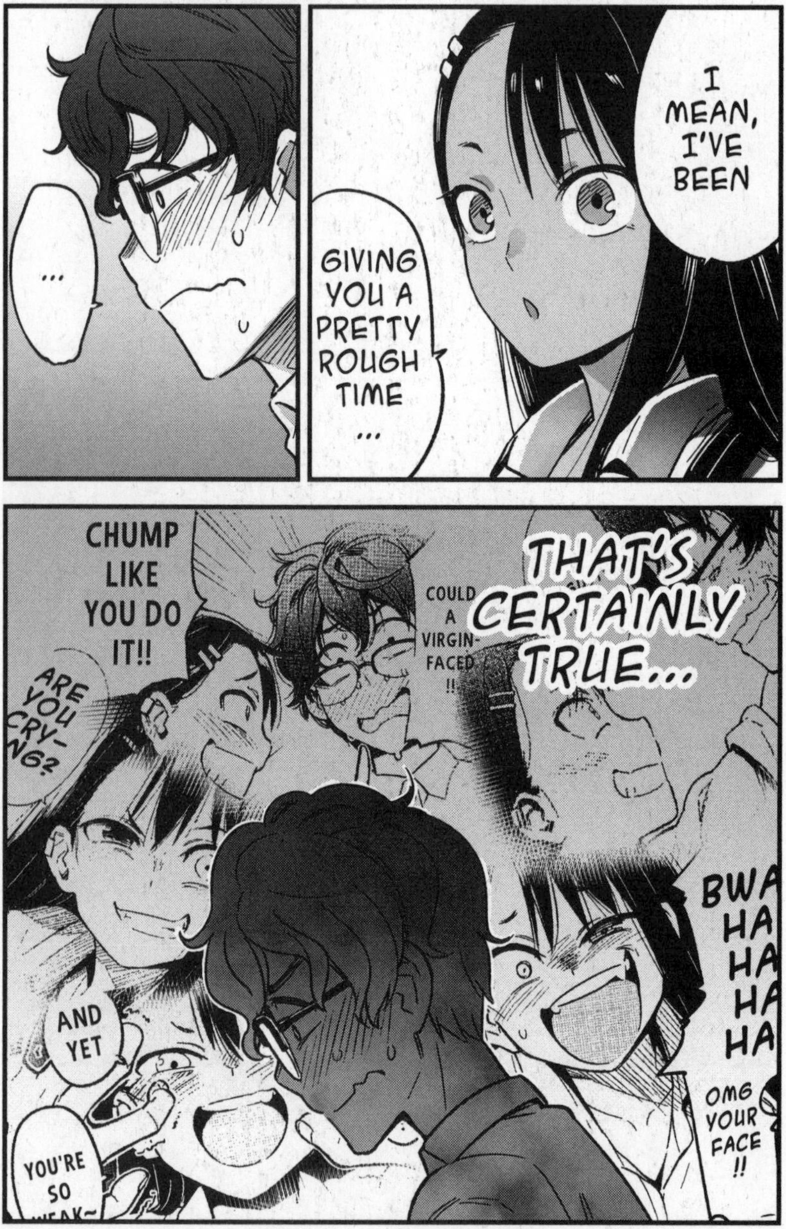
I MEAN, I'VE BEEN
GIVING YOU A PRETTY ROUGH TIME ...
...
THAT'S CERTAINLY TRUE...
COULD A VIRGIN-FACED !!
CHUMP LIKE YOU DO IT!!
ARE YOU CRYING?
BWA HA HA HA HA HA
OMG YOUR FACE !!
AND YET
YOU'RE SO

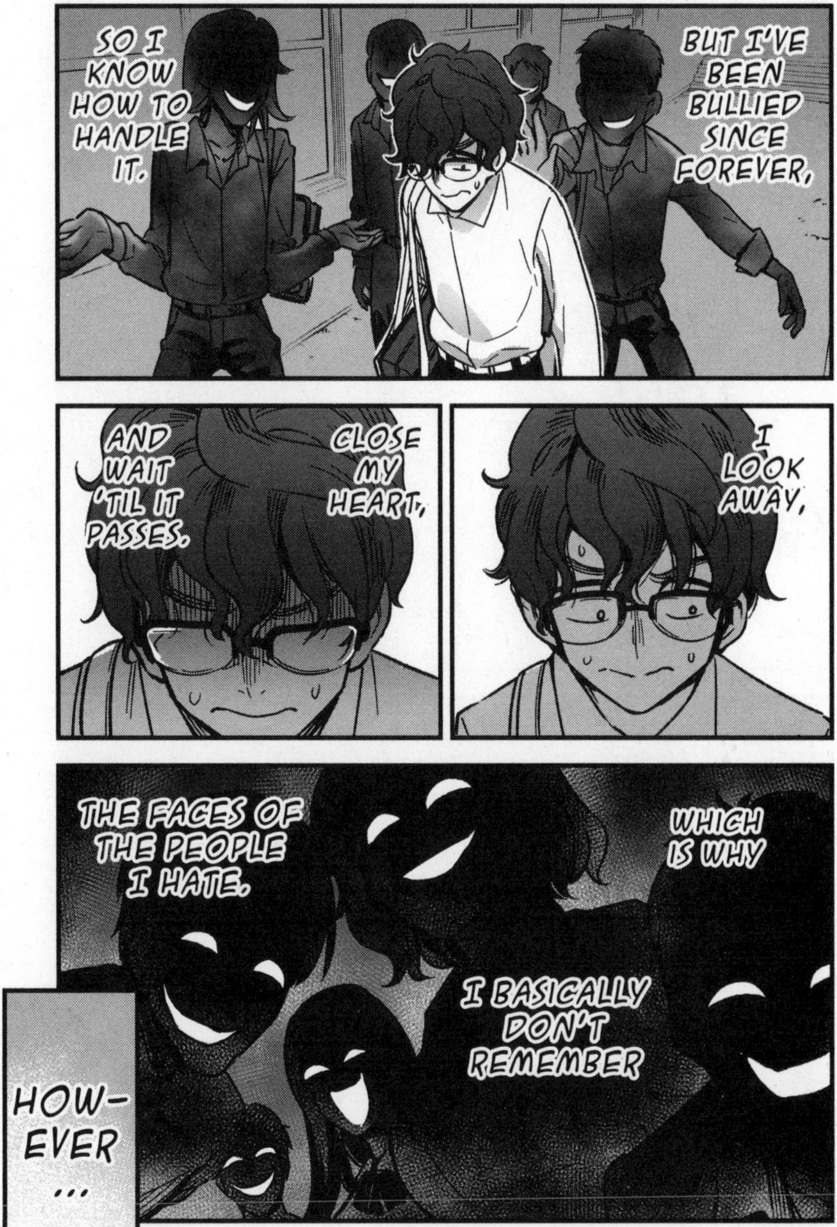
BUT I'VE BEEN BULLIED SINCE FOREVER,
SO I KNOW HOW TO HANDLE IT.
I LOOK AWAY,
CLOSE MY HEART,
AND WAIT 'TIL IT PASSES.
WHICH IS WHY
I BASICALLY DON'T REMEMBER
THE FACES OF THE PEOPLE I HATE.
HOW-EVER ...

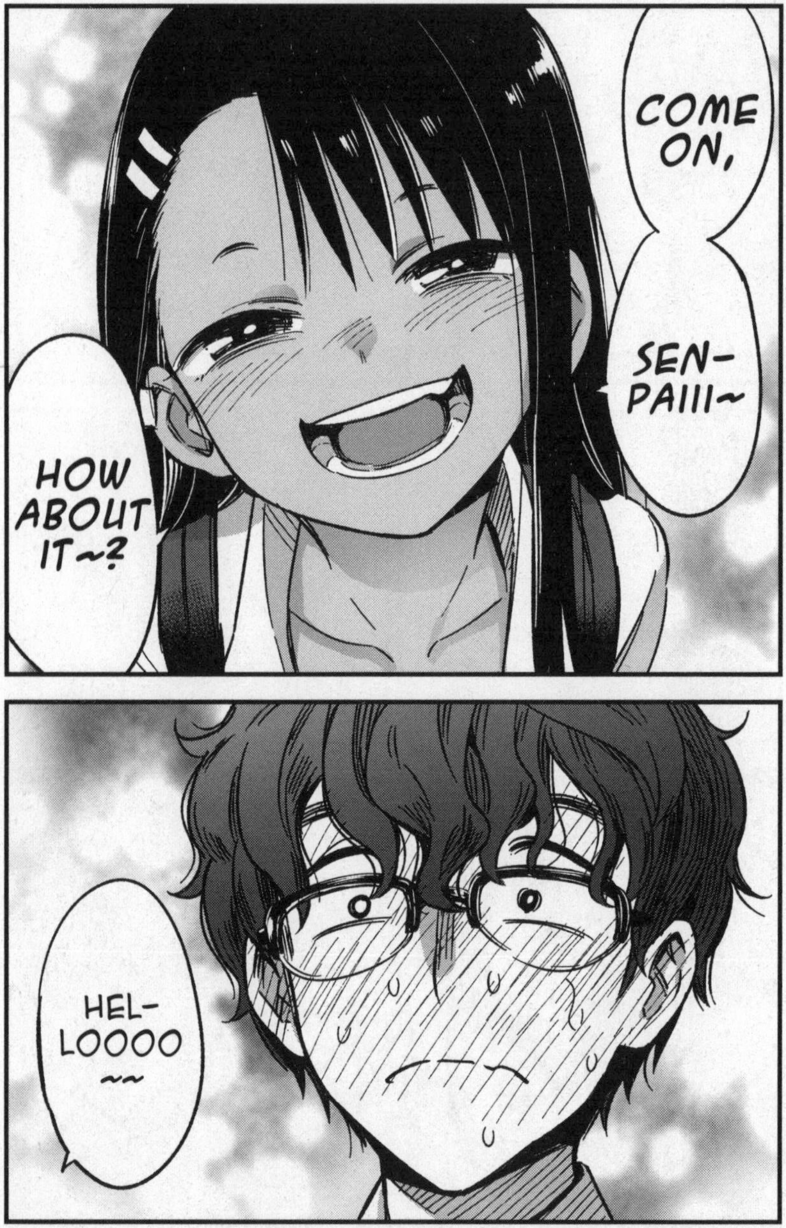
COME ON,
SEN-PAIII~
HOW ABOUT IT~?
HEL-LOOOO ~~

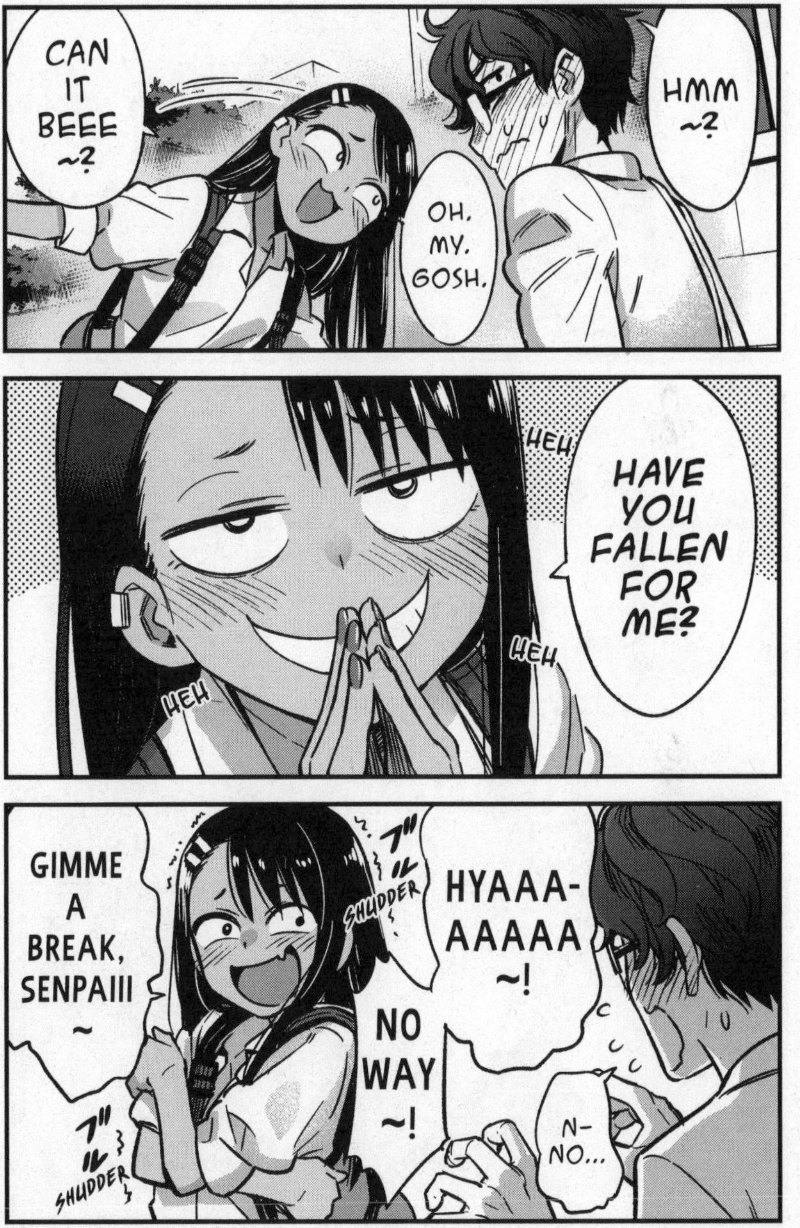
HMM ~?
OH. MY. GOSH.
CAN IT BEEE ~?
HEH
HAVE YOU FALLEN FOR ME?
HEH
HEH
HYAAA-AAAAA ~!
NO WAY ~!
ブル
SHUDDER
GIMME A BREAK, SENPAIII ~
ブル
SHUDDER
N-NO...

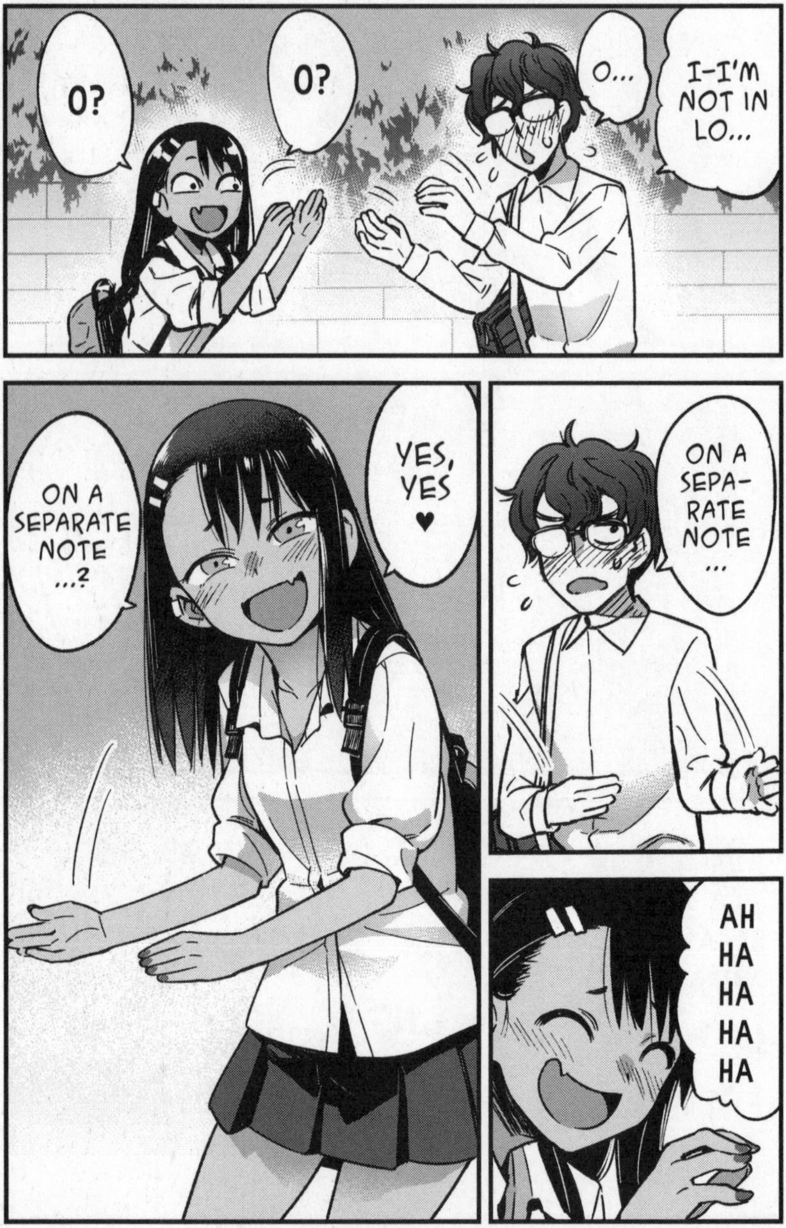
I-I'M NOT IN LO...
O...
O?
O?
ON A SEPA-RATE NOTE ...
AH HA HA HA HA HA
YES, YES ♥
ON A SEPARATE NOTE ...?

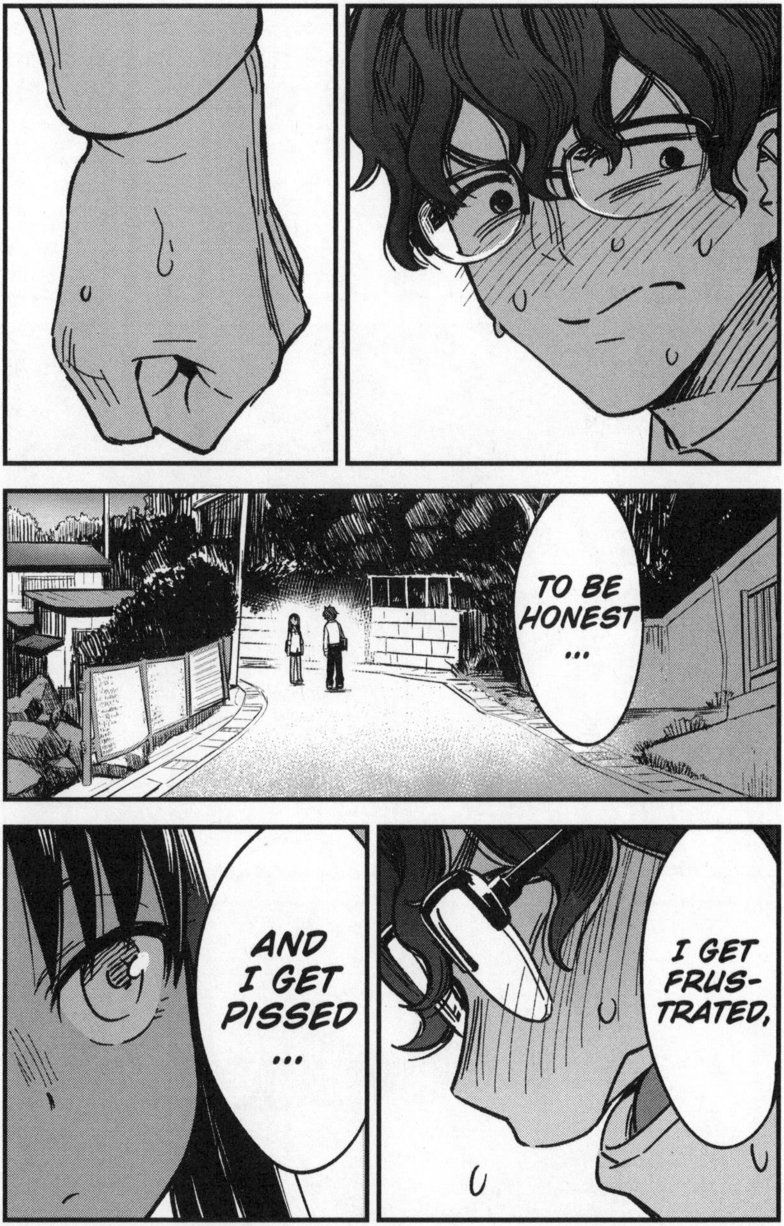
TO BE HONEST ...
I GET FRUS-TRATED,
AND I GET PISSED ...

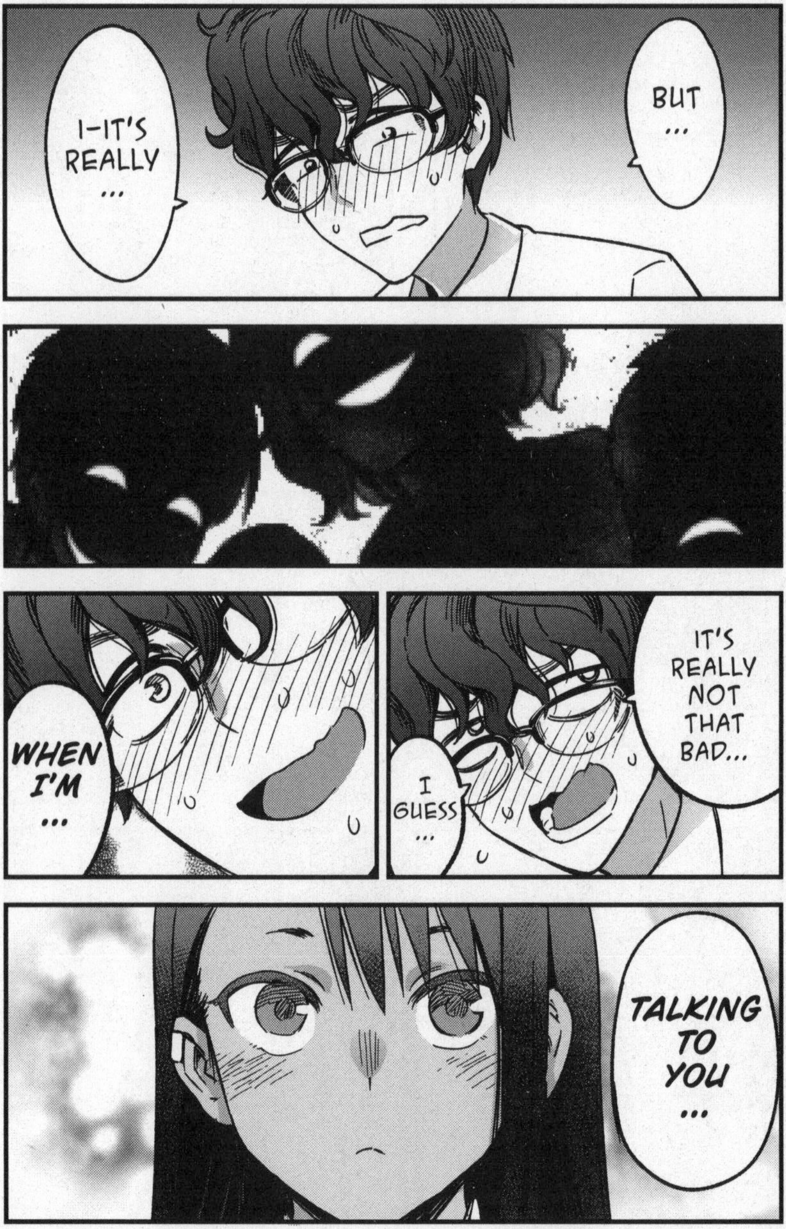
BUT ...
I-IT'S REALLY ...
IT'S REALLY NOT THAT BAD...
I GUESS ...
WHEN I'M ...
TALKING TO YOU ...

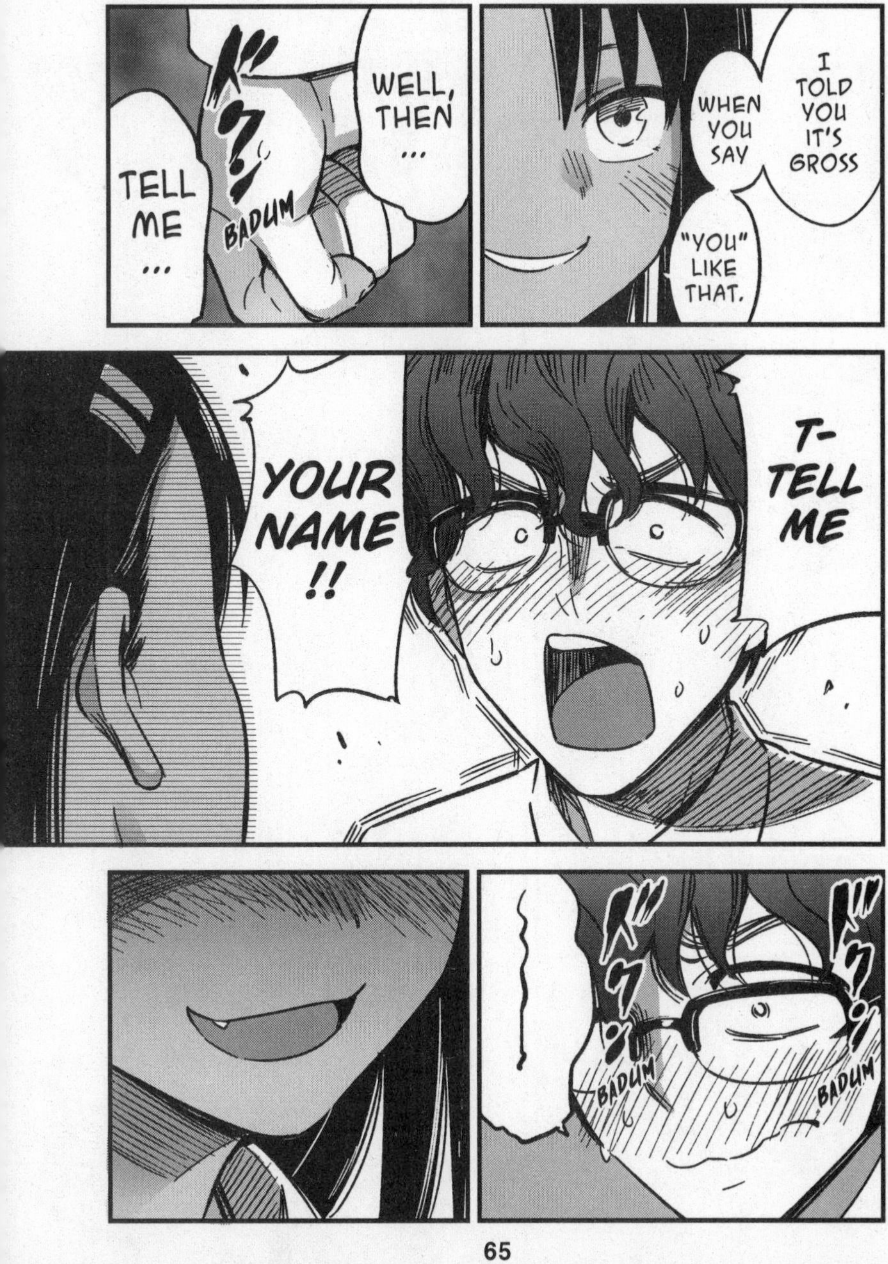
I TOLD YOU IT'S GROSS
WHEN YOU SAY
"YOU" LIKE THAT.
WELL, THEN ...
BADUM
TELL ME ...
T-TELL ME
YOUR NAME!!
BADUM
BADUM

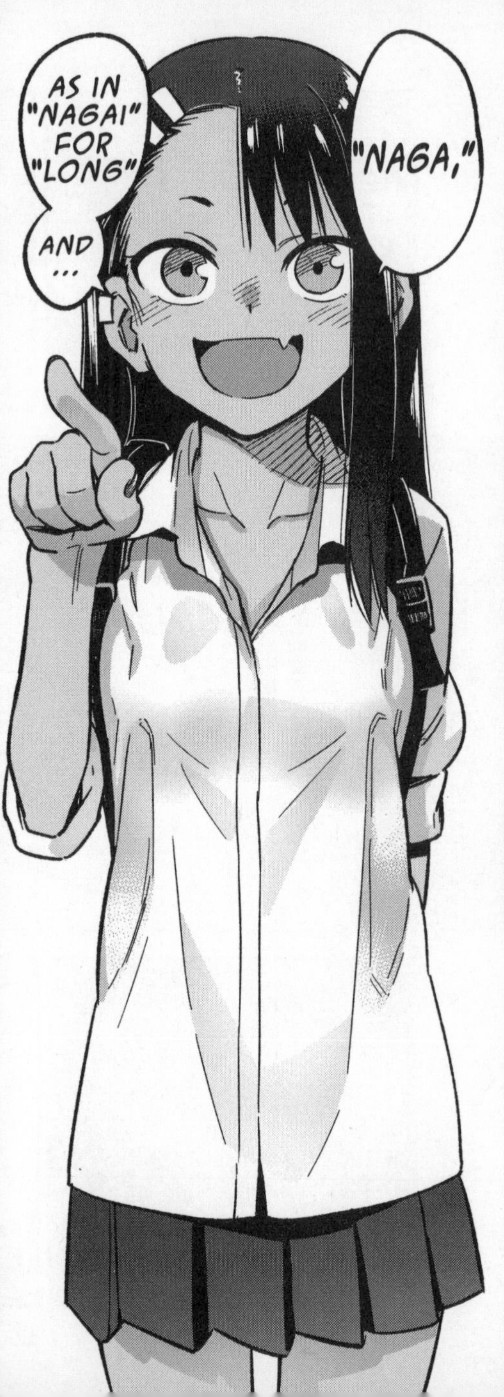
"NAGA,"
AS IN "NAGAI" FOR "LONG"
AND ...
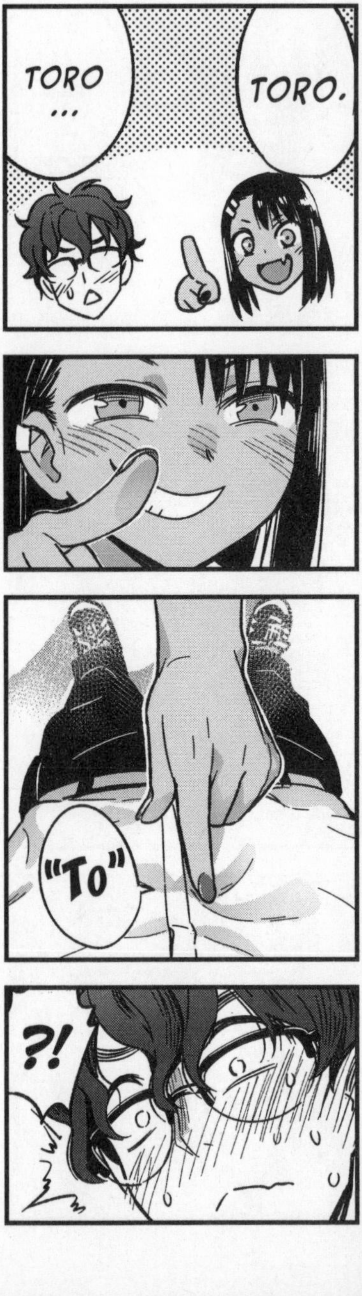
TORO.
TORO ...
"To"
?!

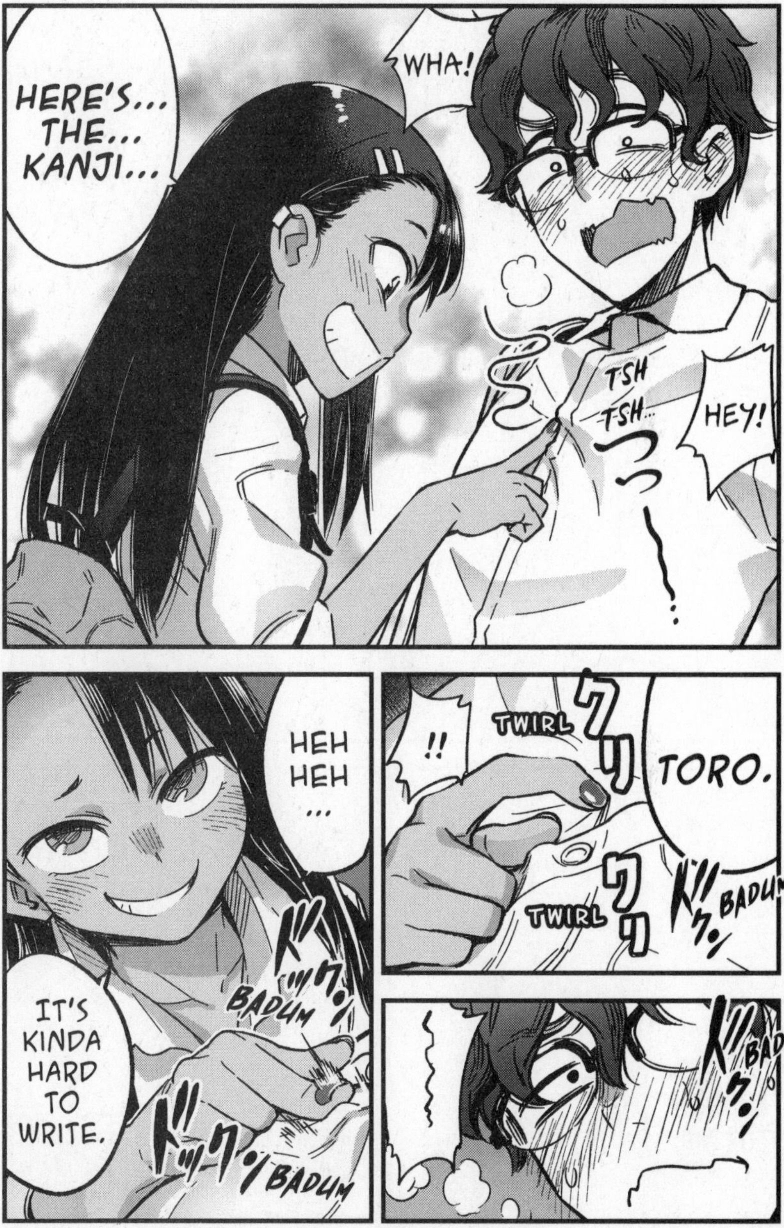
WHA!
HERE'S... THE... KANJI...
HEY!
TSH TSH...
TORO.
!!
TWIRL
TWIRL
BADUM
BADUM
HEH HEH ...
BADUM
IT'S KINDA HARD TO WRITE.
BADUM

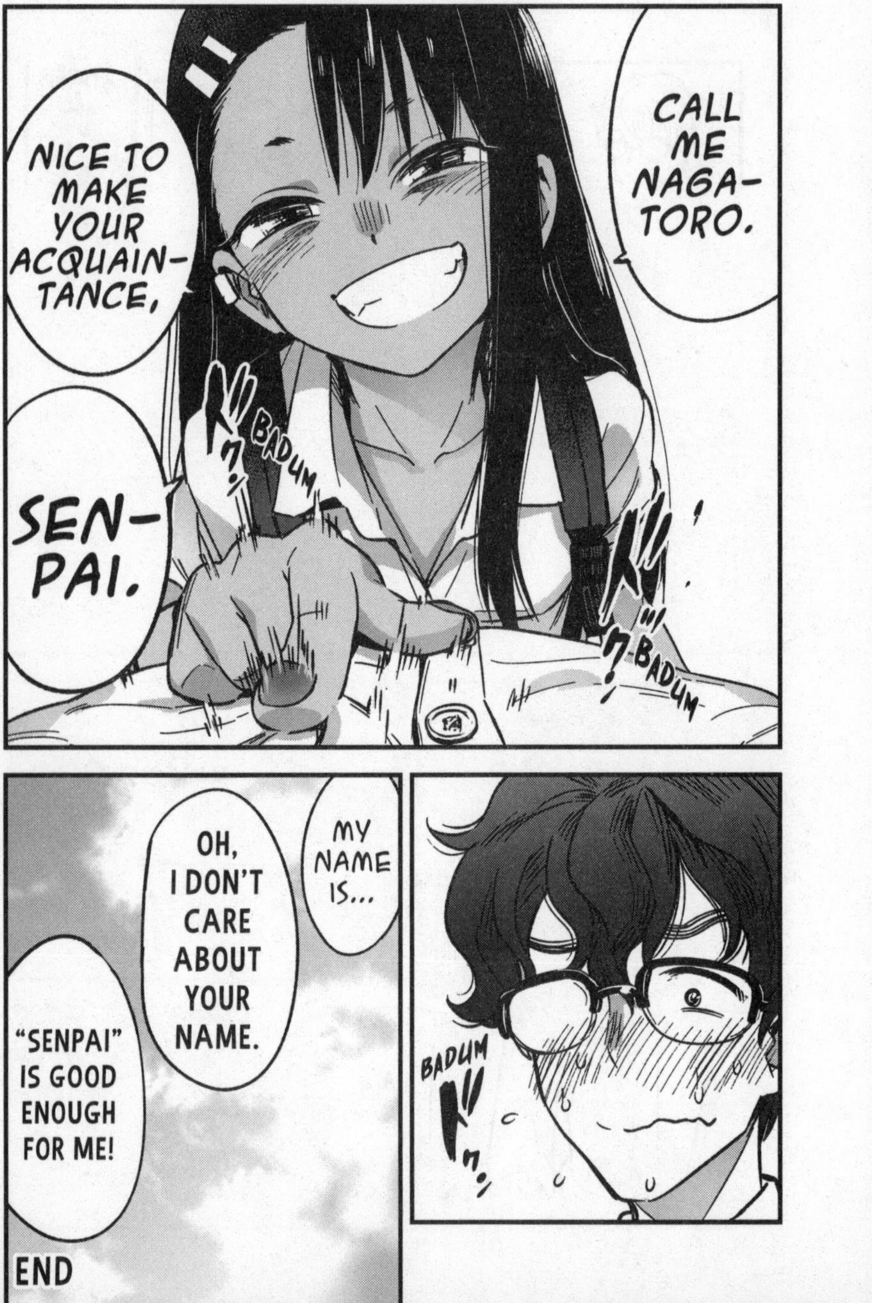
CALL ME NAGA-TORO.
NICE TO MAKE YOUR ACQUAIN-TANCE,
SEN-PAI.
BADUM
BADUM
BADUM
MY NAME IS...
OH, I DON'T CARE ABOUT YOUR NAME.
"SENPAI" IS GOOD ENOUGH FOR ME!
END

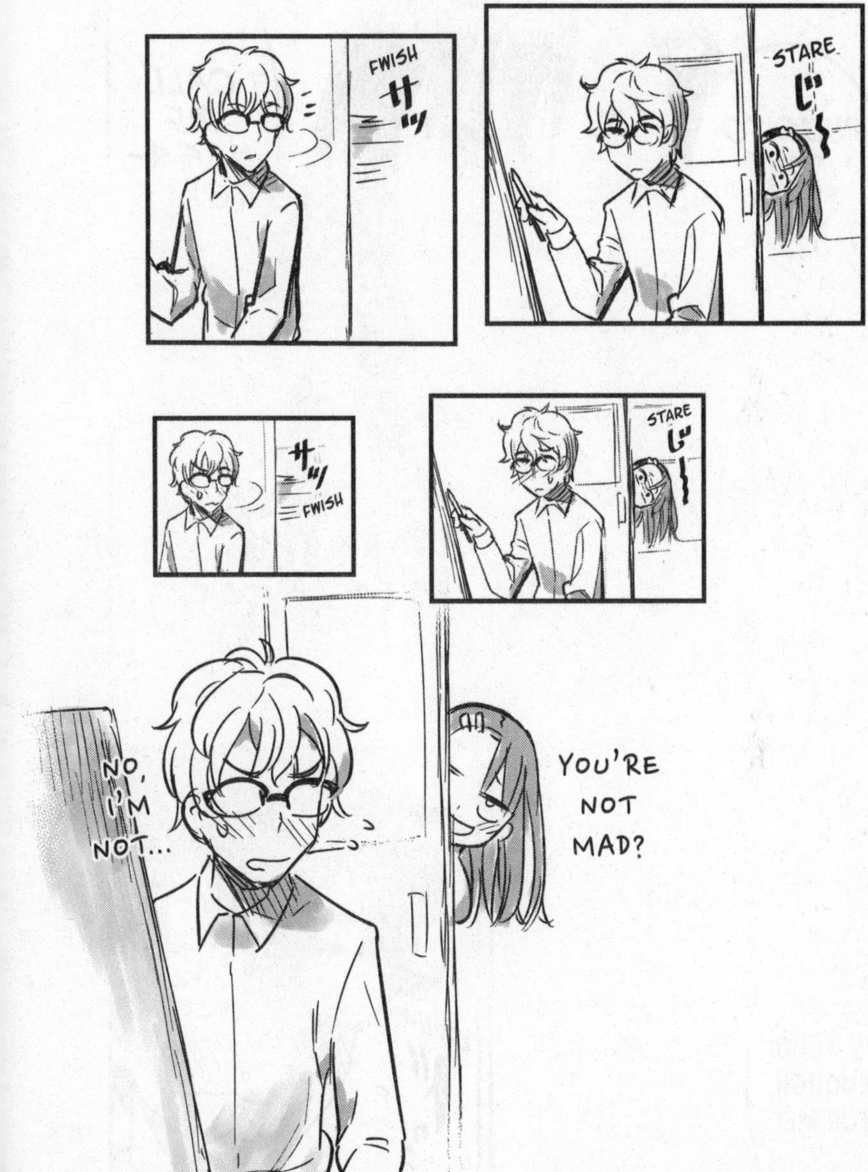
STARE
じ～
FWISH
サッ
STARE
じー
サッ
FWISH
YOU'RE NOT MAD?
NO, I'M NOT...

DON'T TOY WITH ME,
MISS NAGATORO

CHAPTER 4: SENPAI'S WISH JUST CAME TRUE!!

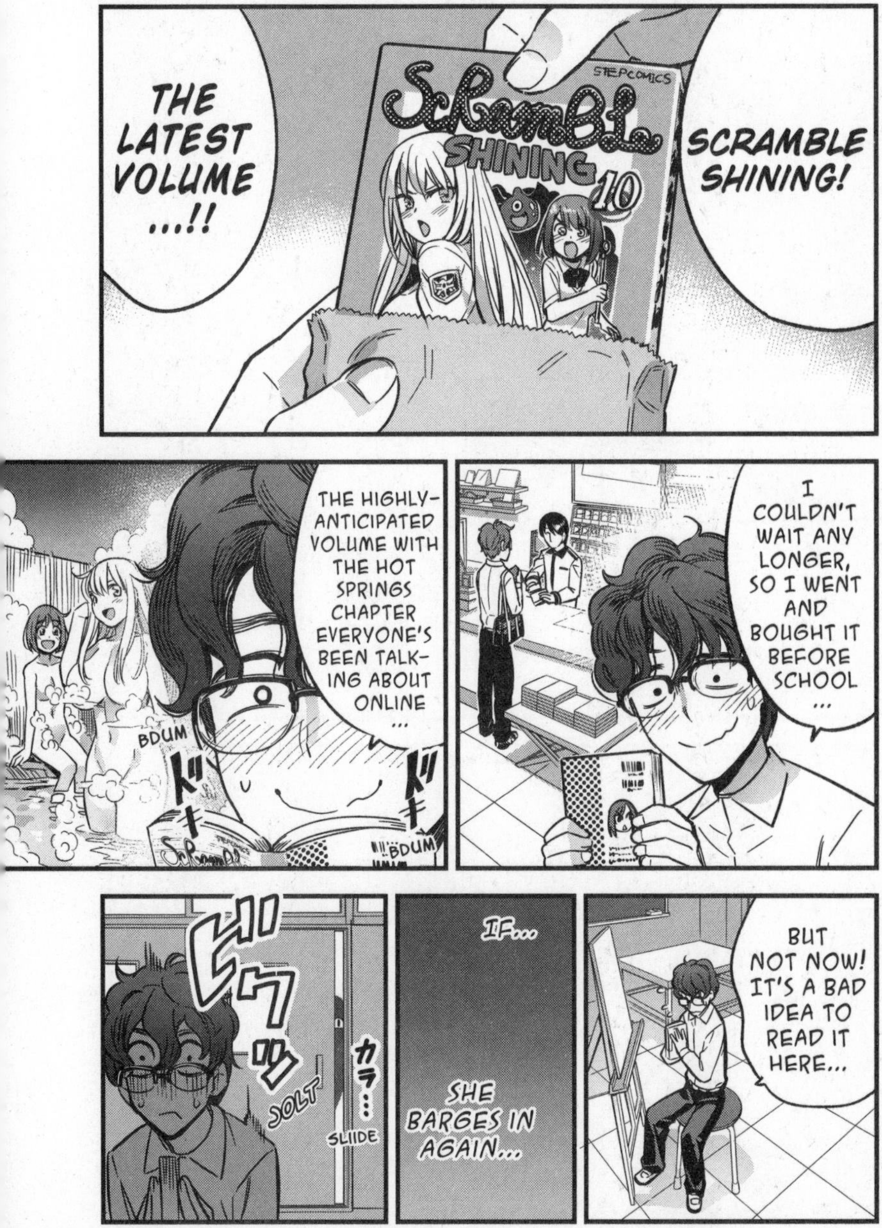
SCRAMBLE SHINING!
THE LATEST VOLUME ...!!
STEPCOMICS
SHINING
10
I COULDN'T WAIT ANY LONGER, SO I WENT AND BOUGHT IT BEFORE SCHOOL ...
THE HIGHLY-ANTICIPATED VOLUME WITH THE HOT SPRINGS CHAPTER EVERYONE'S BEEN TALKING ABOUT ONLINE ...
ドキ
BDUM
ドキ
BDUM
BUT NOT NOW! IT'S A BAD IDEA TO READ IT HERE...
IF...
SHE BARGES IN AGAIN...
カラ…
SLIIDE
ビクッ
JOLT

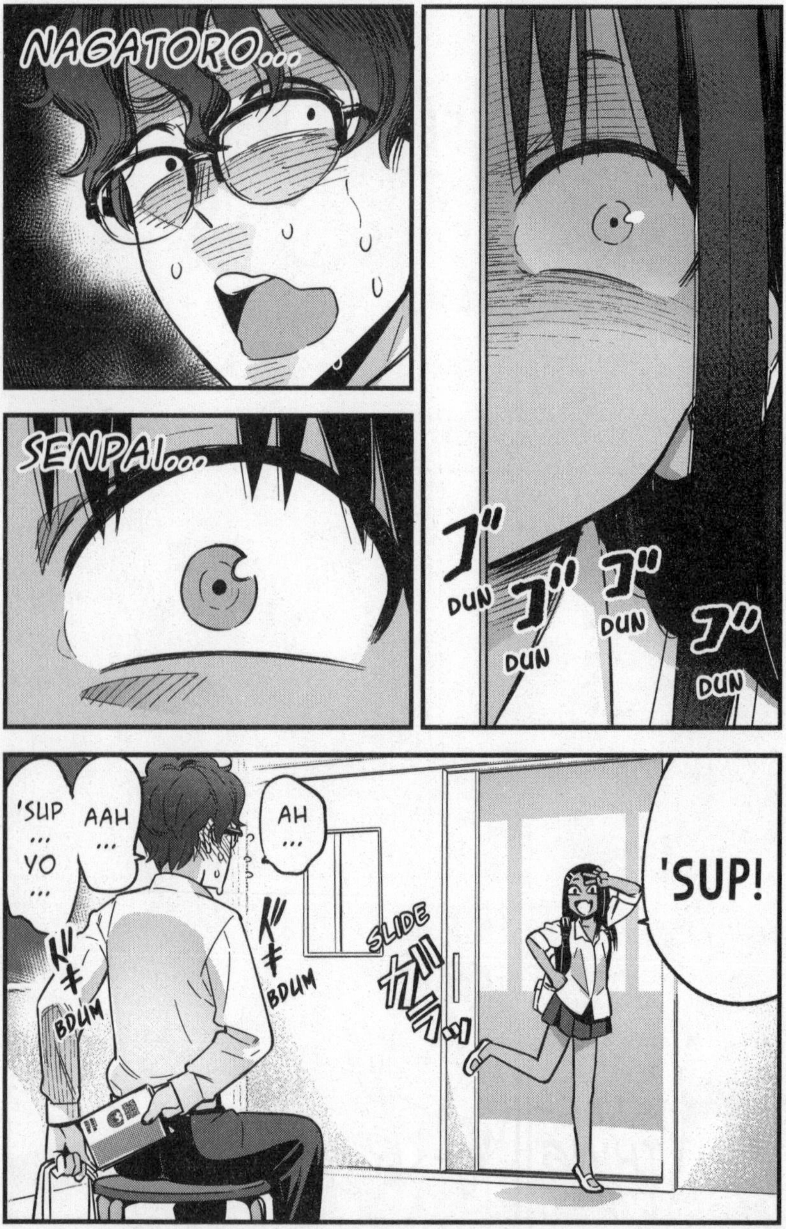
ゴ DUN
ゴ DUN
ゴ DUN
ゴ DUN
NAGATORO...
SENPAI...
'SUP!
SLIDE
ガラッ
ドキ BDUM
AH ...
AAH ...
'SUP ... YO ...
ドキ BDUM

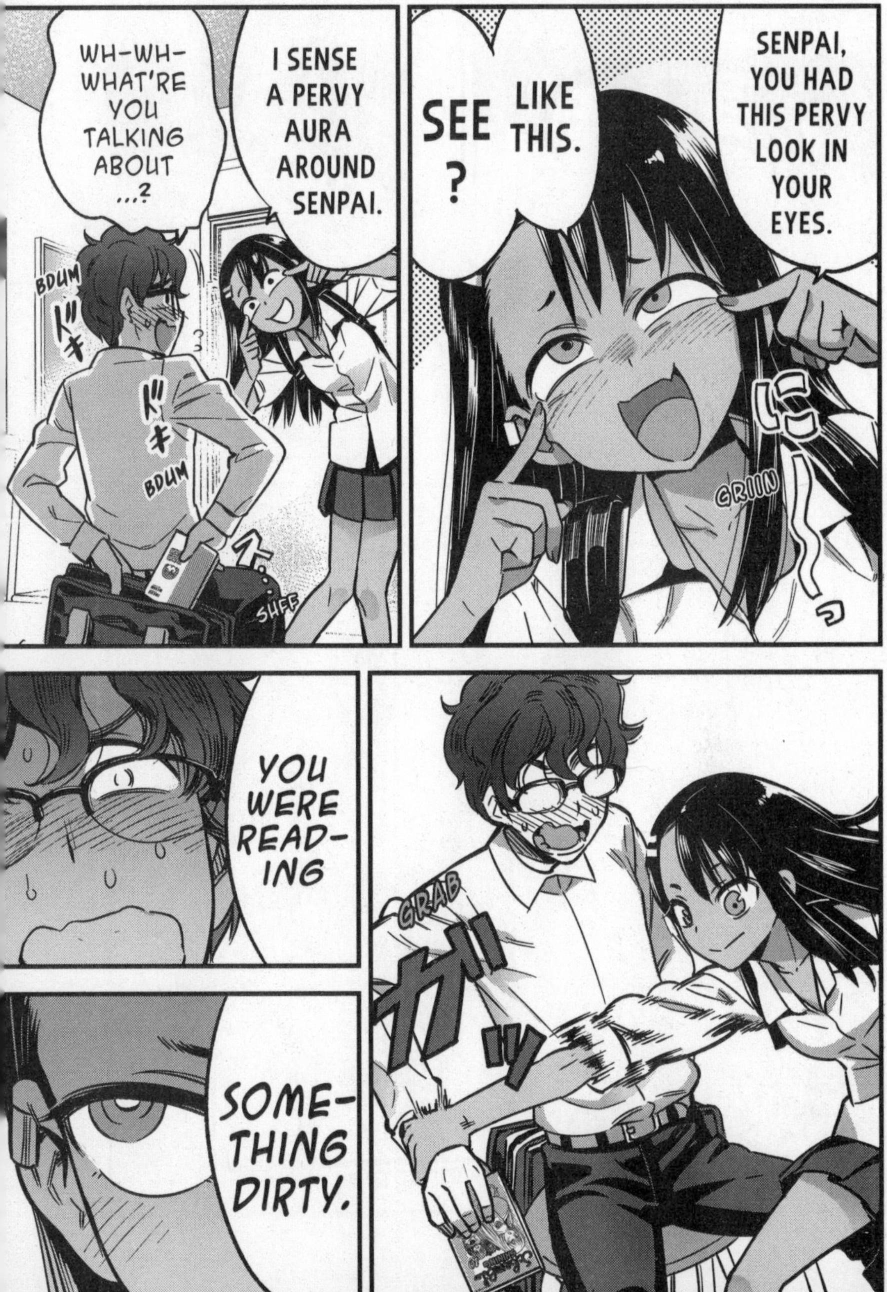
SENPAI, YOU HAD THIS PERVY LOOK IN YOUR EYES.
LIKE THIS.
SEE ?
GRIIN
I SENSE A PERVY AURA AROUND SENPAI.
WH-WH-WHAT'RE YOU TALKING ABOUT ...?
BDUM
BDUM
SHFF
GRAB
YOU WERE READING
SOMETHING DIRTY.

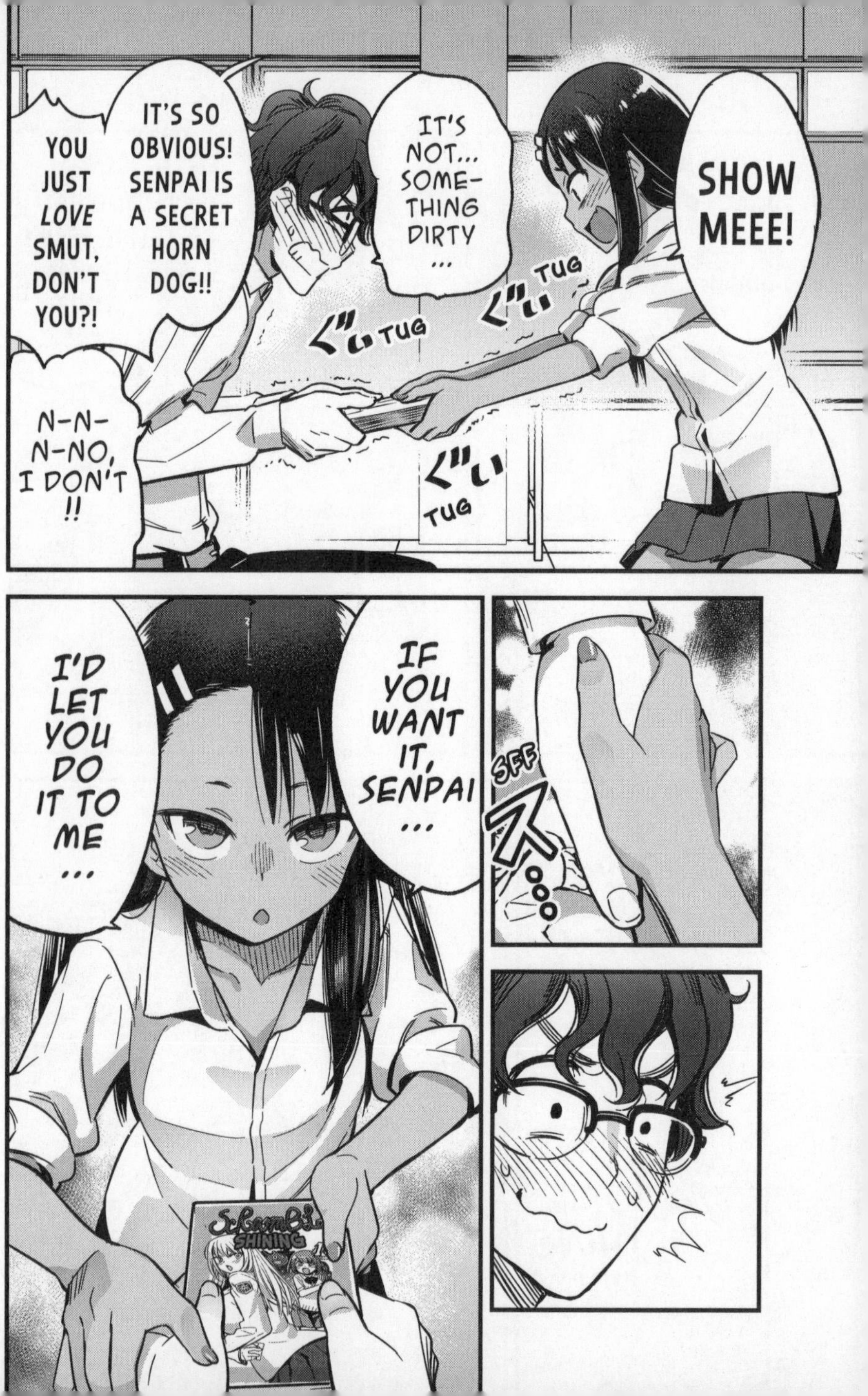
SHOW MEEE!
IT'S NOT... SOMETHING DIRTY ...
IT'S SO OBVIOUS! SENPAI IS A SECRET HORN DOG!!
YOU JUST *LOVE* SMUT, DON'T YOU?!
TUG
TUG
TUG
TUG
N-N-N-NO, I DON'T!!
SFF
IF YOU WANT IT, SENPAI ...
I'D LET YOU DO IT TO ME ...

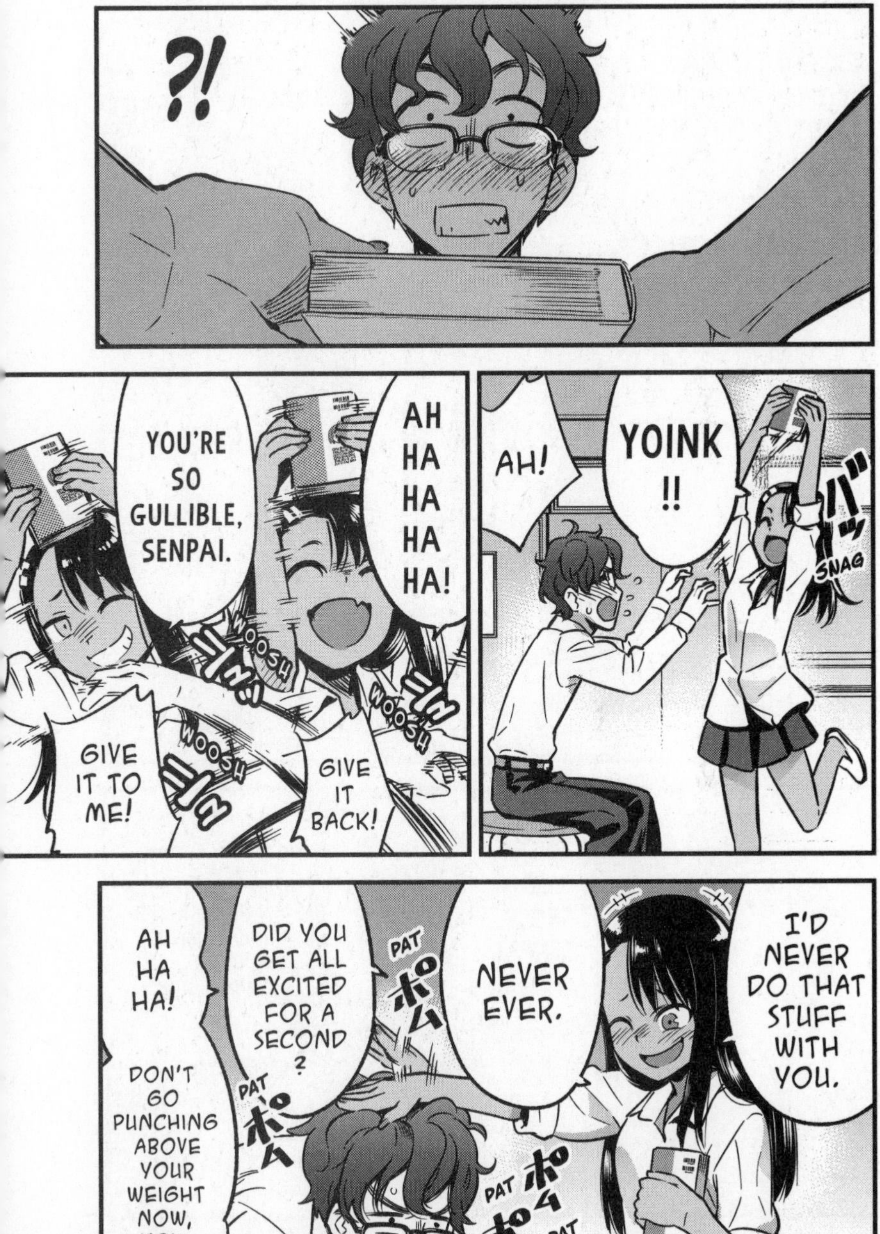
?!
YOINK!!
AH!
SNAG
AH HA HA HA HA!
YOU'RE SO GULLIBLE, SENPAI.
WOOSH
WOOSH
GIVE IT BACK!
WOOSH
GIVE IT TO ME!
I'D NEVER DO THAT STUFF WITH YOU.
NEVER EVER.
PAT
DID YOU GET ALL EXCITED FOR A SECOND?
AH HA HA!
PAT
DON'T GO PUNCHING ABOVE YOUR WEIGHT NOW, YOU CREEP!!
PAT
PAT

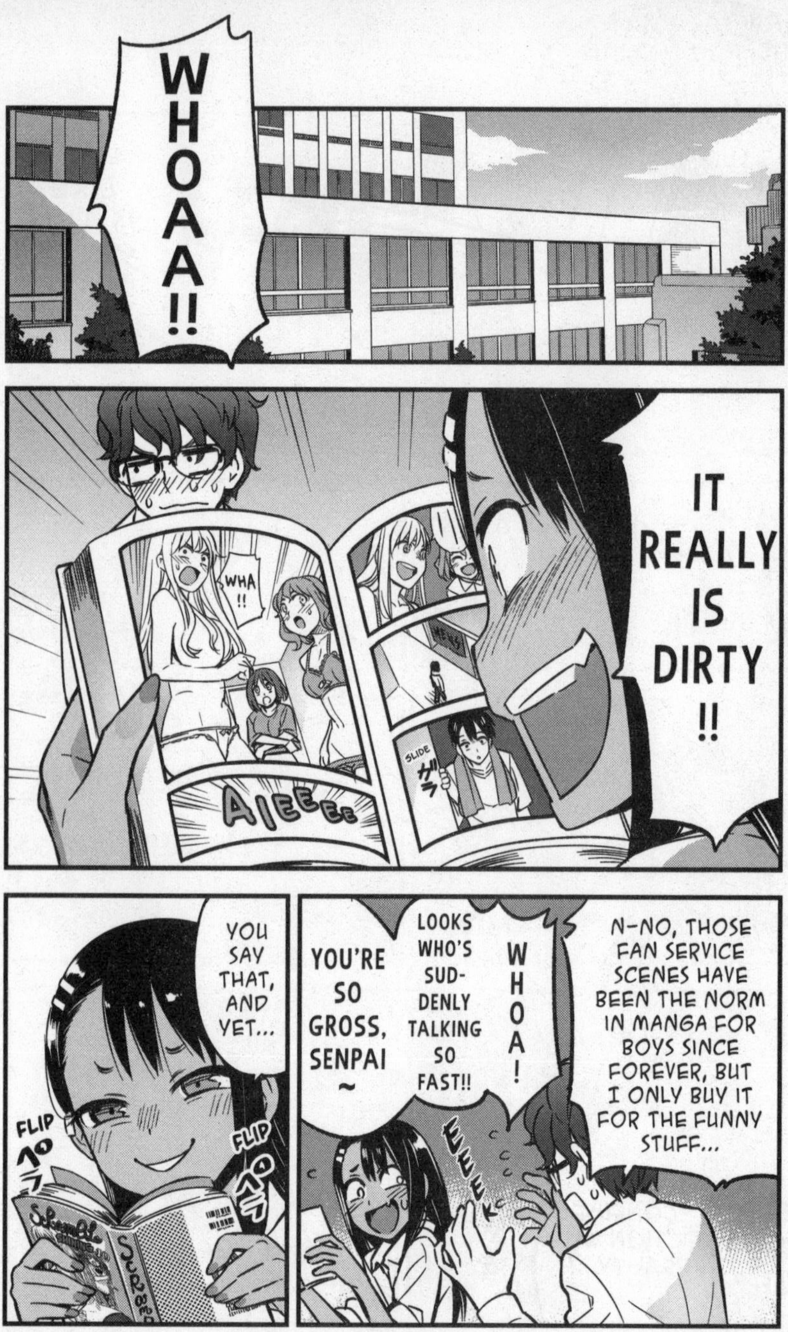
WHOAA!!
IT REALLY IS DIRTY!!
WHA!!
SLIDE
AIEEEEE
N-NO, THOSE FAN SERVICE SCENES HAVE BEEN THE NORM IN MANGA FOR BOYS SINCE FOREVER, BUT I ONLY BUY IT FOR THE FUNNY STUFF...
WHOA!
LOOKS WHO'S SUD-DENLY TALKING SO FAST!!
YOU'RE SO GROSS, SENPAI ~
EEEEK
YOU SAY THAT, AND YET...
FLIP
FLIP

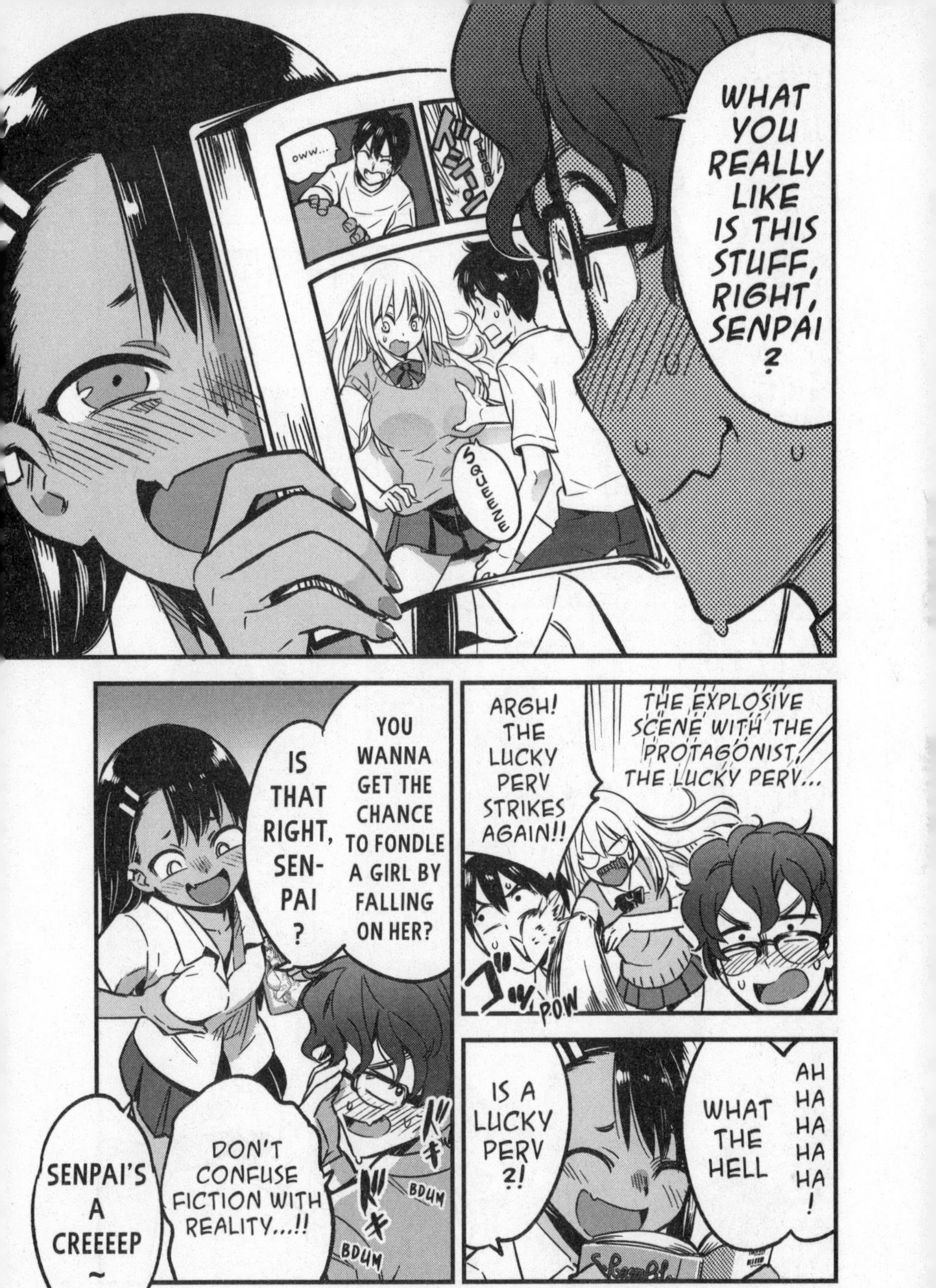
OWW...
THUD
WHAT YOU REALLY LIKE IS THIS STUFF, RIGHT, SENPAI?
SQUEEZE
THE EXPLOSIVE SCENE WITH THE PROTAGONIST, THE LUCKY PERV...
ARGH! THE LUCKY PERV STRIKES AGAIN!!
POW
AH HA HA HA HA HA!
WHAT THE HELL
IS A LUCKY PERV?!
YOU WANNA GET THE CHANCE TO FONDLE A GIRL BY FALLING ON HER?
IS THAT RIGHT, SEN-PAI?
DON'T CONFUSE FICTION WITH REALITY...!!
BDUM
BDUM
SENPAI'S A CREEEEP ~

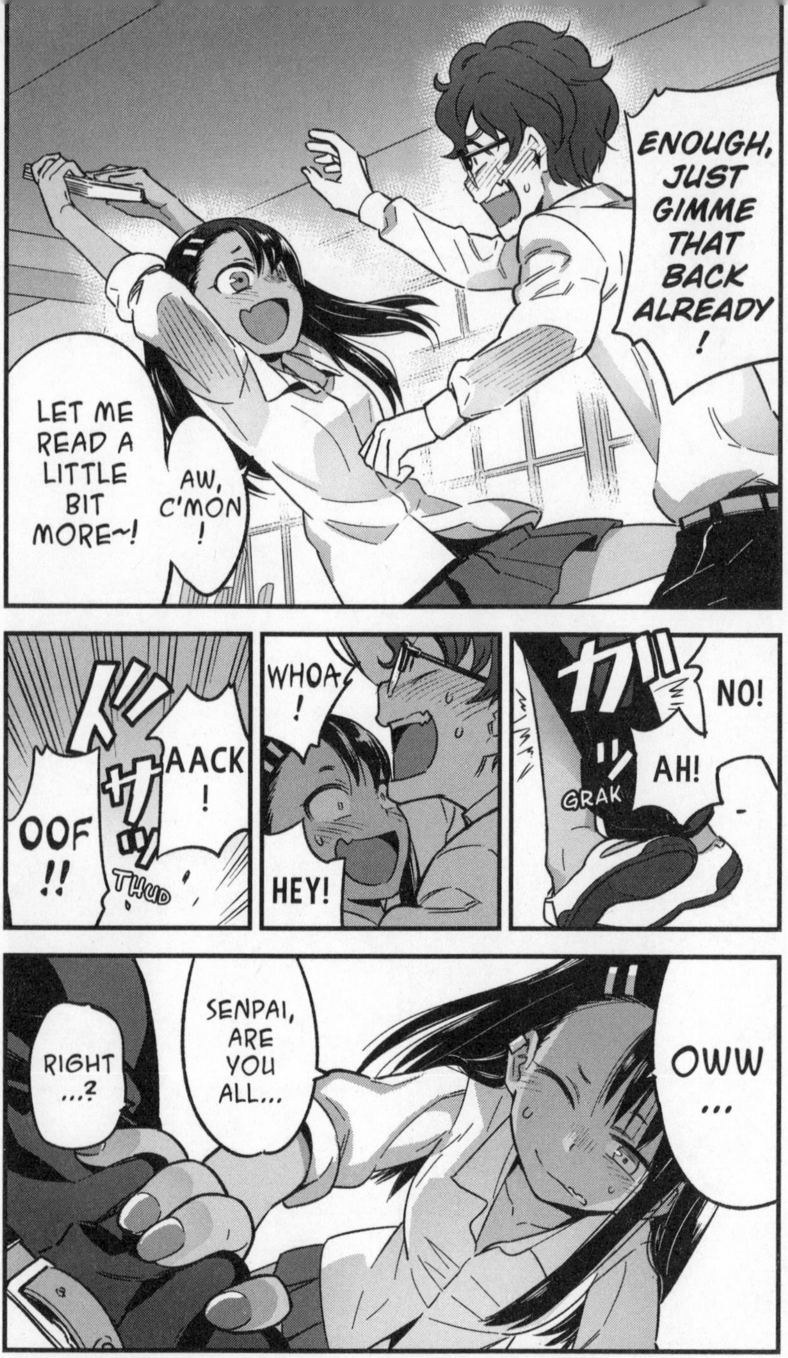

ENOUGH, JUST GIMME THAT BACK ALREADY!
AW, C'MON!
LET ME READ A LITTLE BIT MORE~!
NO!
AH!
GRAK
WHOA!
HEY!
AACK!
OOF!!
THUD
OWW...
SENPAI, ARE YOU ALL...
RIGHT...?

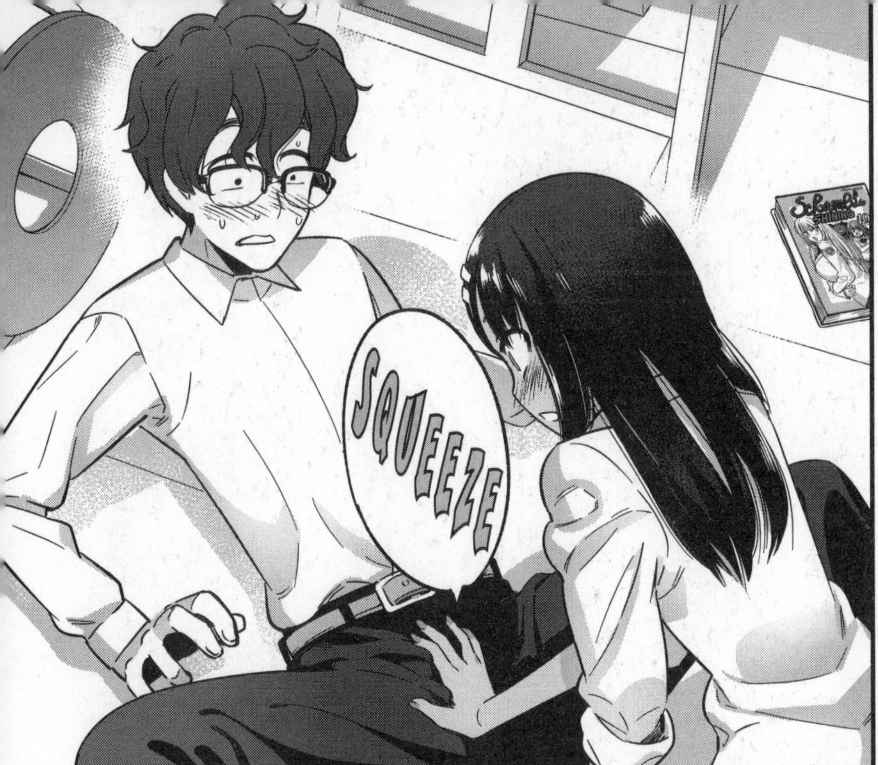
SQUEEZE

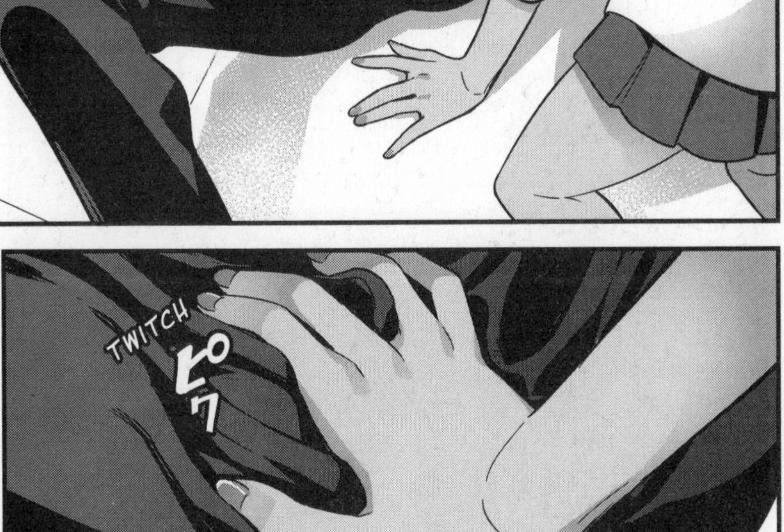
TWITCH
ピク

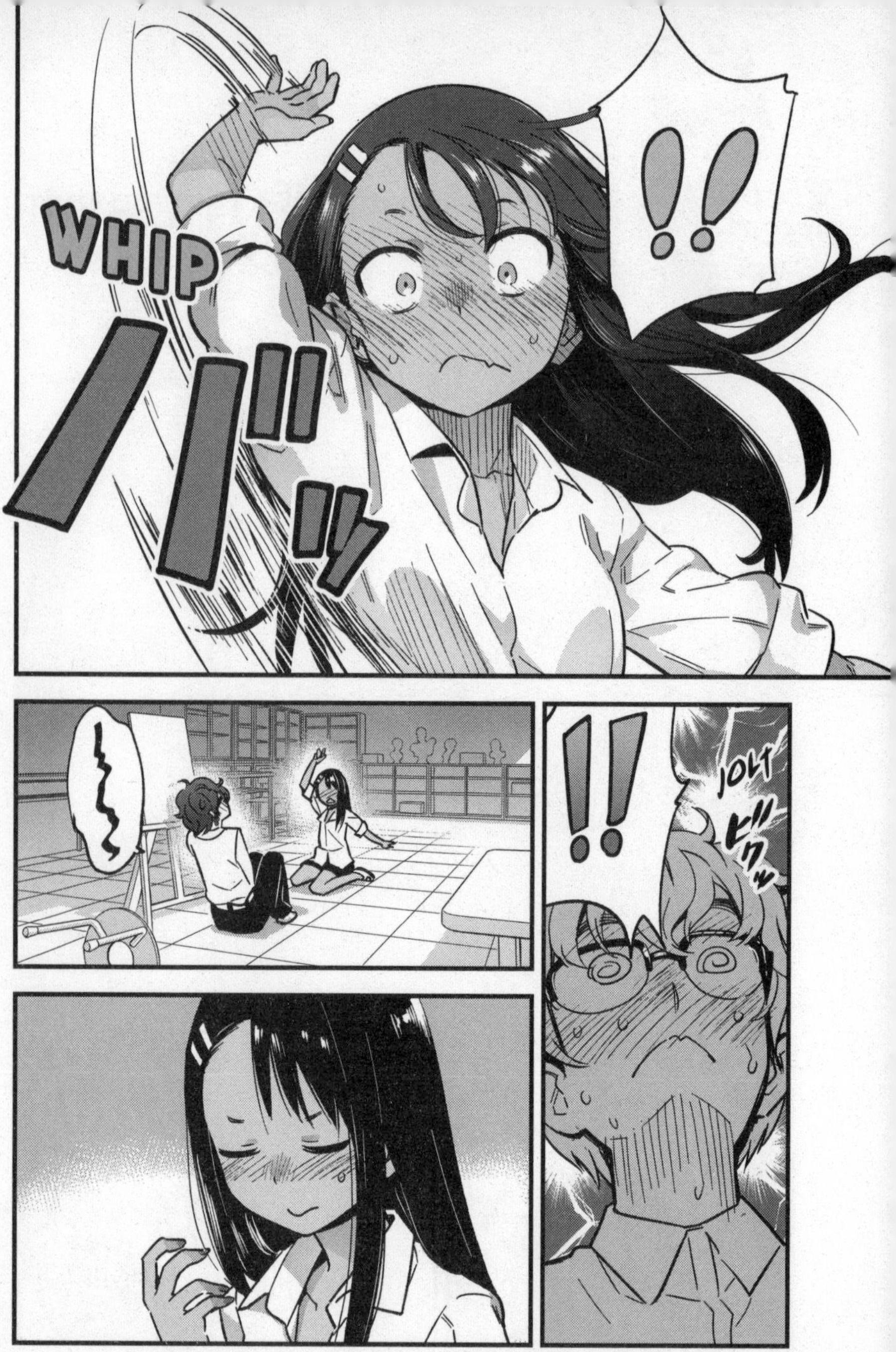
!!
WHIP
バッ
!!
JOLT
ビクッ

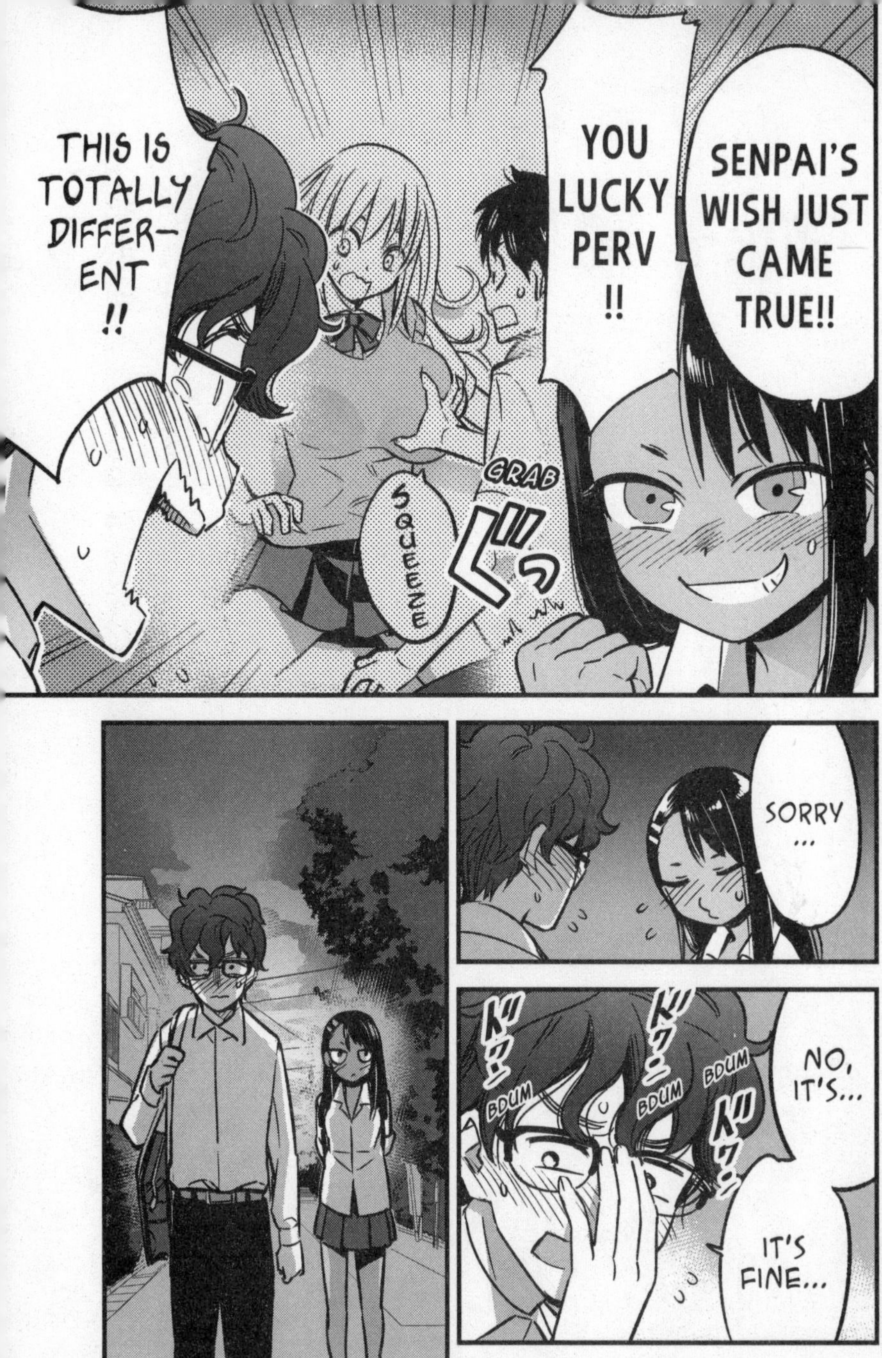
SENPAI'S WISH JUST CAME TRUE!!
YOU LUCKY PERV !!
GRAB
ぐっ
SQUEEZE
THIS IS TOTALLY DIFFER-ENT !!
SORRY ...
NO, IT'S...
BDUM
BDUM
BDUM
BDUM
IT'S FINE...

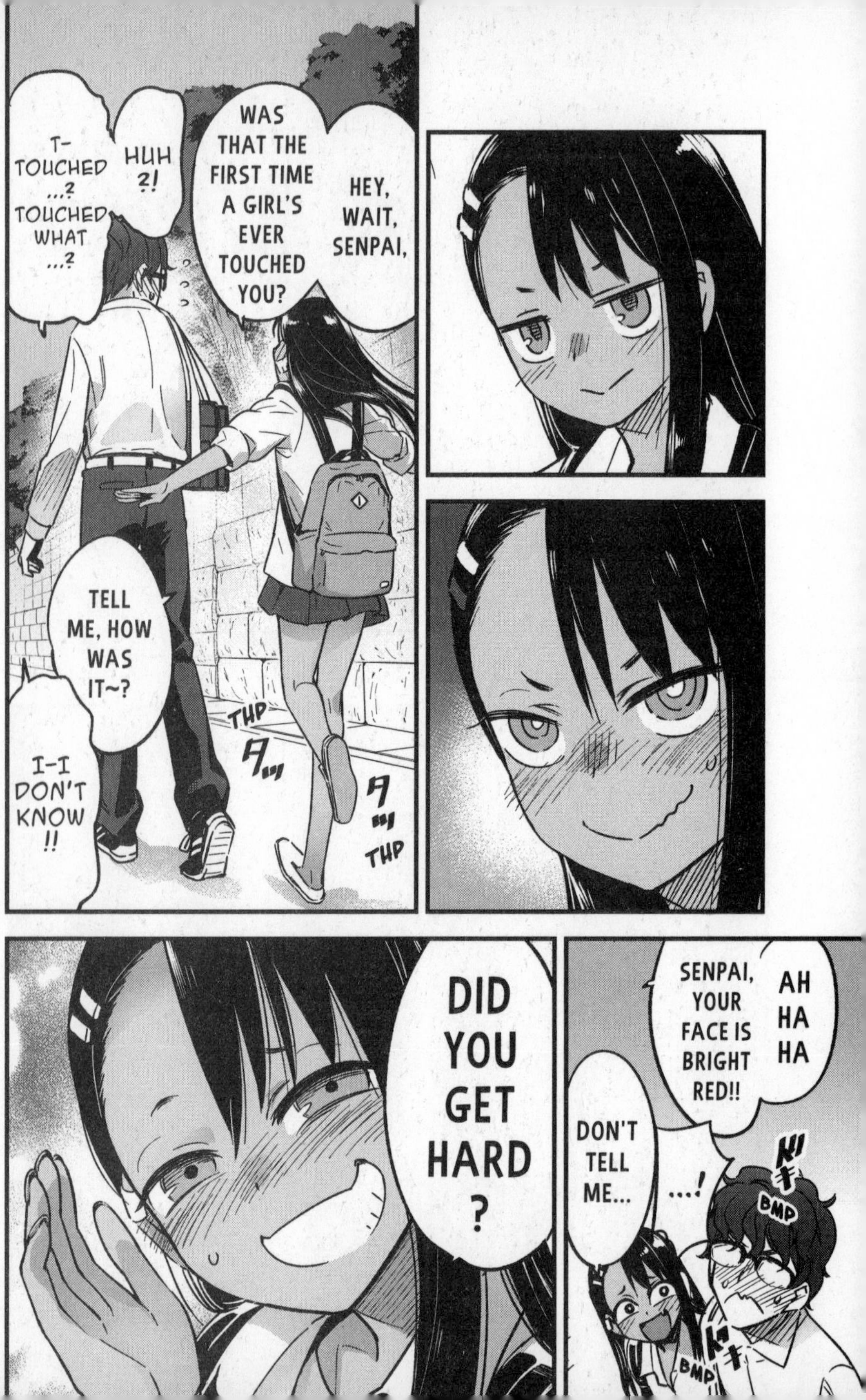
HEY, WAIT, SENPAI,
WAS THAT THE FIRST TIME A GIRL'S EVER TOUCHED YOU?
HUH ?!
T-TOUCHED ...? TOUCHED WHAT ...?
TELL ME, HOW WAS IT~?
THP
タッ
タッ
THP
I-I DON'T KNOW !!
AH HA HA
SENPAI, YOUR FACE IS BRIGHT RED!!
...!
DON'T TELL ME...
BMP
BMP
DID YOU GET HARD ?

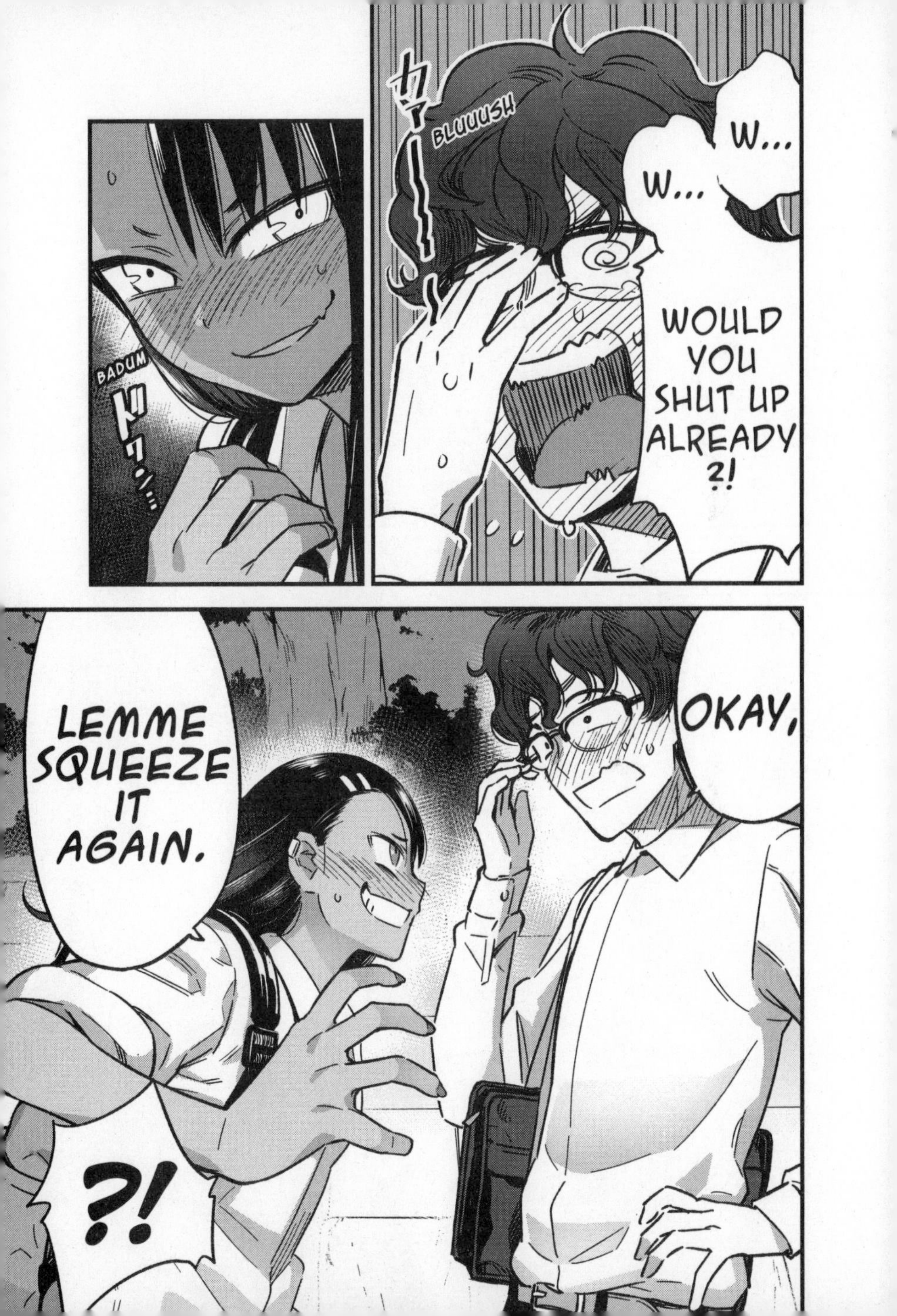
BLUUUSH
W...
W...
WOULD YOU SHUT UP ALREADY ?!
BADUM
OKAY,
LEMME SQUEEZE IT AGAIN.
?!

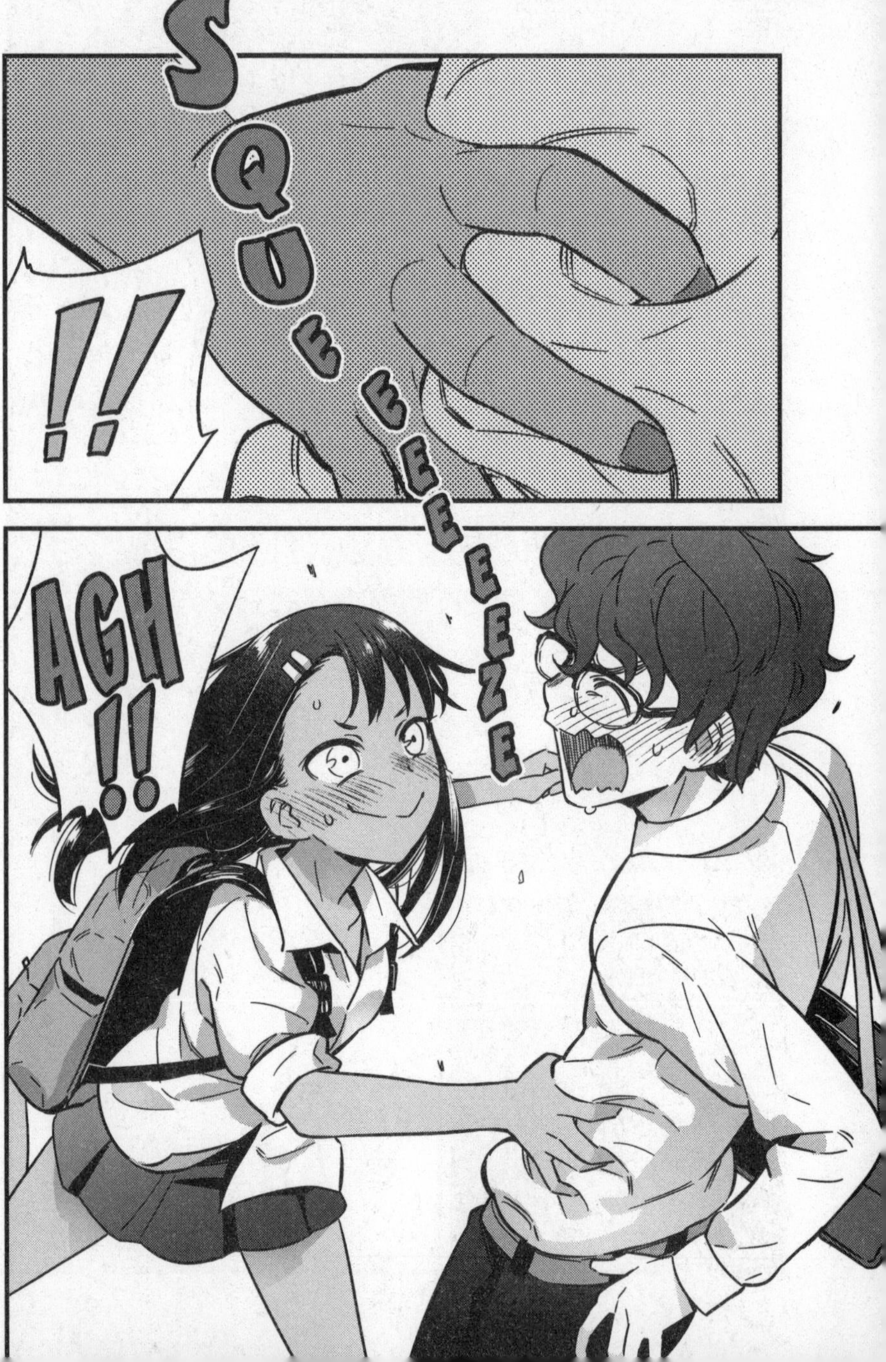
SQUEEEEEEZE
!!
AGH !!

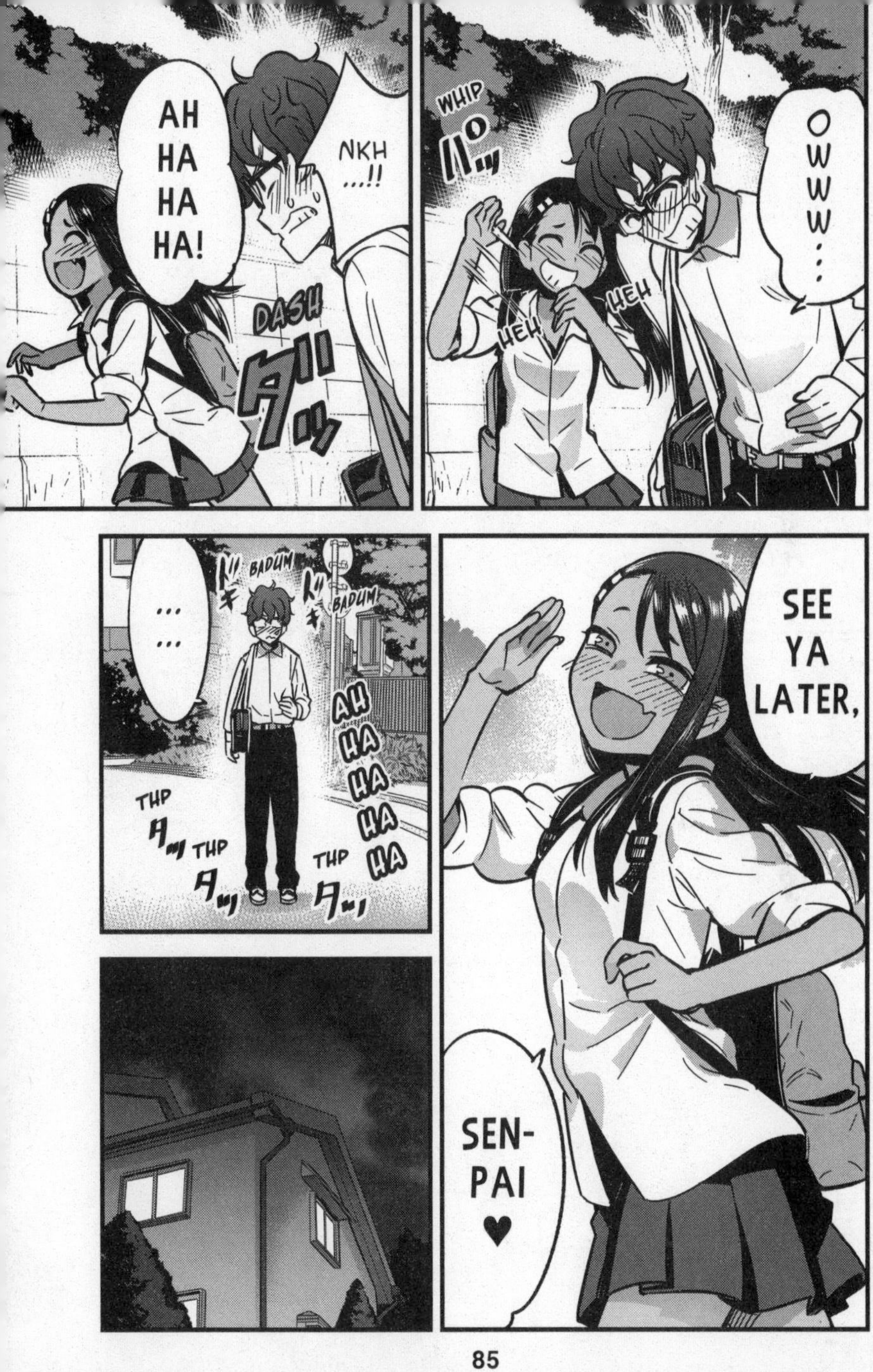
WHIP
OWWW...
HEH
HEH
AH HA HA HA!
NKH ...!!
DASH
SEE YA LATER,
SENPAI ♥
... ...
BADUM
BADUM
AH HA HA HA HA HA
THP
THP
THP

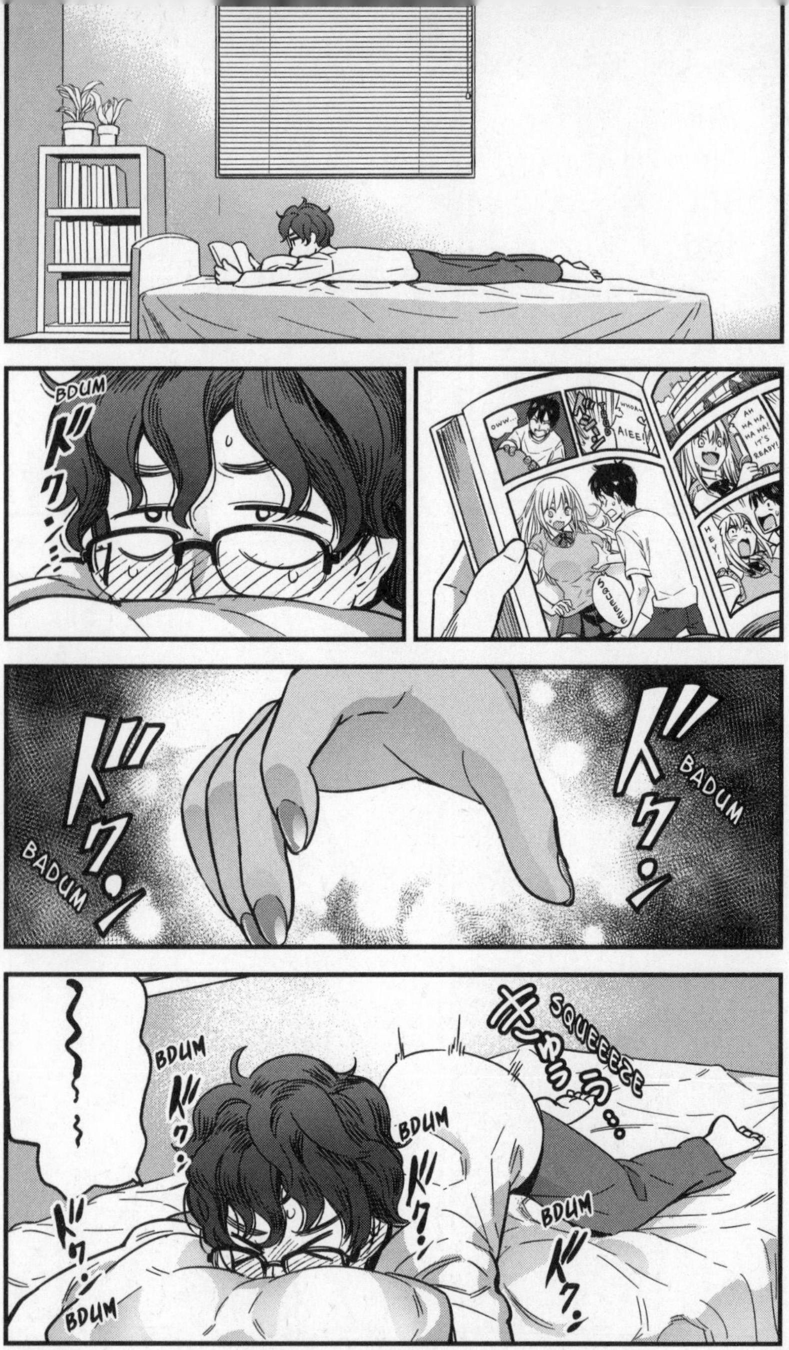

AH HA HA HA HA! IT'S READY!
HEY!
WHOA~
AIEE!
OWW...
SQUEEZE
BDUM
ドクン…
BADUM
ドクン
BADUM
ドクン
SQUEEEZE
ぎゅううう…
〜〜〜〜
BDUM
ドクン
BDUM
ドクン
BDUM
ドクン
BDUM
ドクン

END

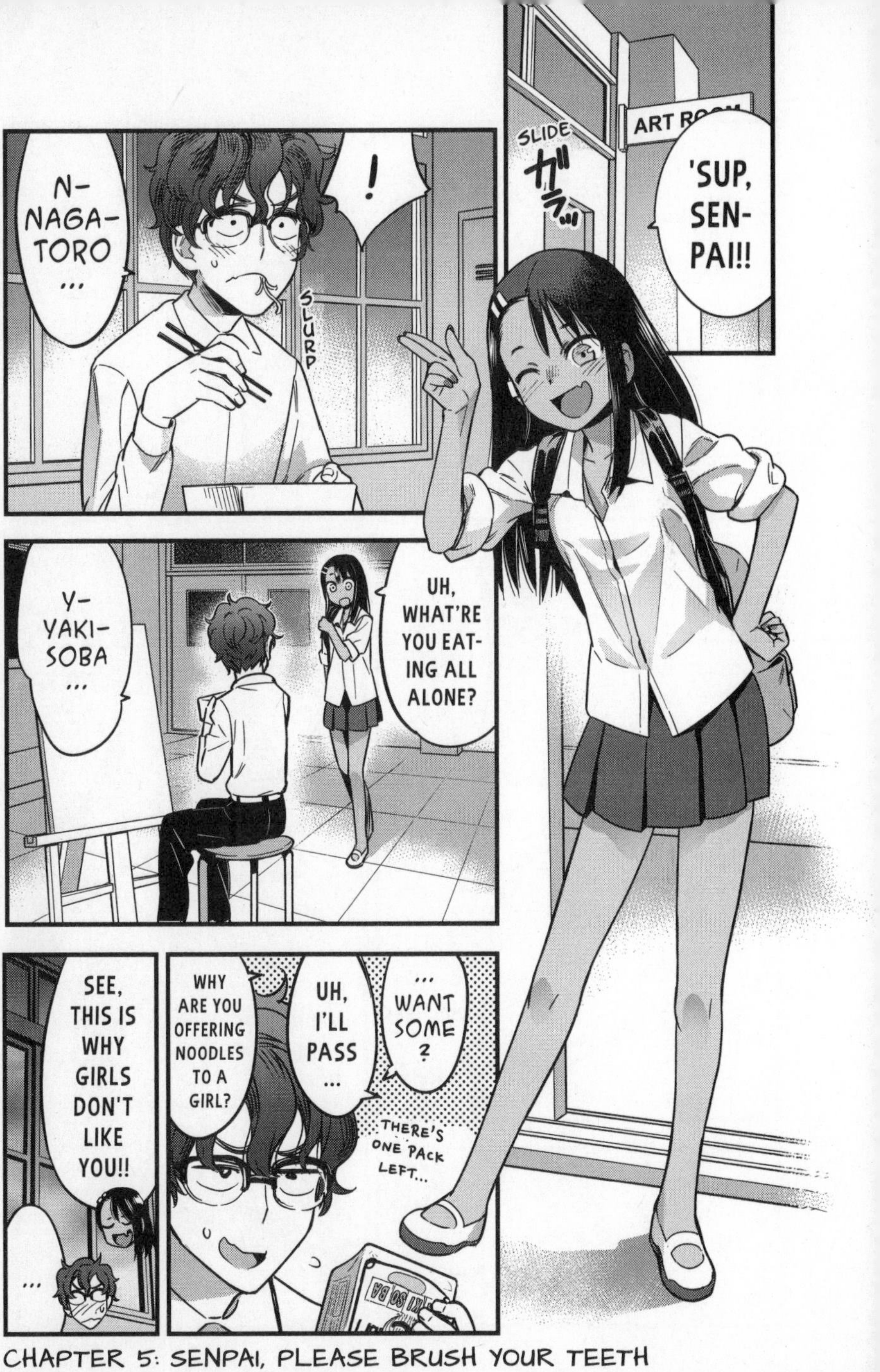
ART ROOM
SLIDE
ガラッ
'SUP, SENPAI!!
!
N-NAGATORO...
SLURP
UH, WHAT'RE YOU EATING ALL ALONE?
Y-YAKISOBA...
... WANT SOME?
UH, I'LL PASS...
THERE'S ONE PACK LEFT...
WHY ARE YOU OFFERING NOODLES TO A GIRL?
SEE, THIS IS WHY GIRLS DON'T LIKE YOU!!
...

CHAPTER 5: SENPAI, PLEASE BRUSH YOUR TEETH

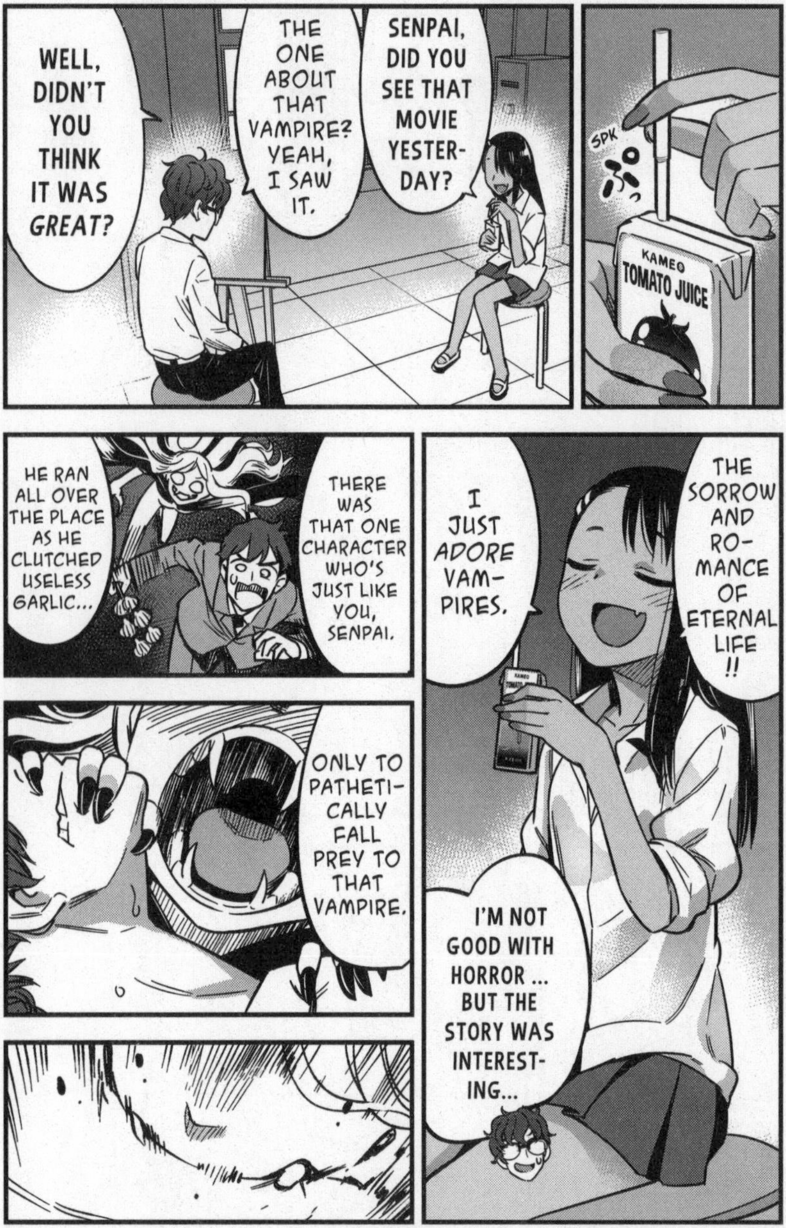
SPK
KAMEO TOMATO JUICE
SENPAI, DID YOU SEE THAT MOVIE YESTERDAY?
THE ONE ABOUT THAT VAMPIRE? YEAH, I SAW IT.
WELL, DIDN'T YOU THINK IT WAS *GREAT*?
THE SORROW AND ROMANCE OF ETERNAL LIFE !!
I JUST *ADORE* VAMPIRES.
I'M NOT GOOD WITH HORROR ... BUT THE STORY WAS INTERESTING...
THERE WAS THAT ONE CHARACTER WHO'S JUST LIKE YOU, SENPAI.
HE RAN ALL OVER THE PLACE AS HE CLUTCHED USELESS GARLIC...
ONLY TO PATHETICALLY FALL PREY TO THAT VAMPIRE.

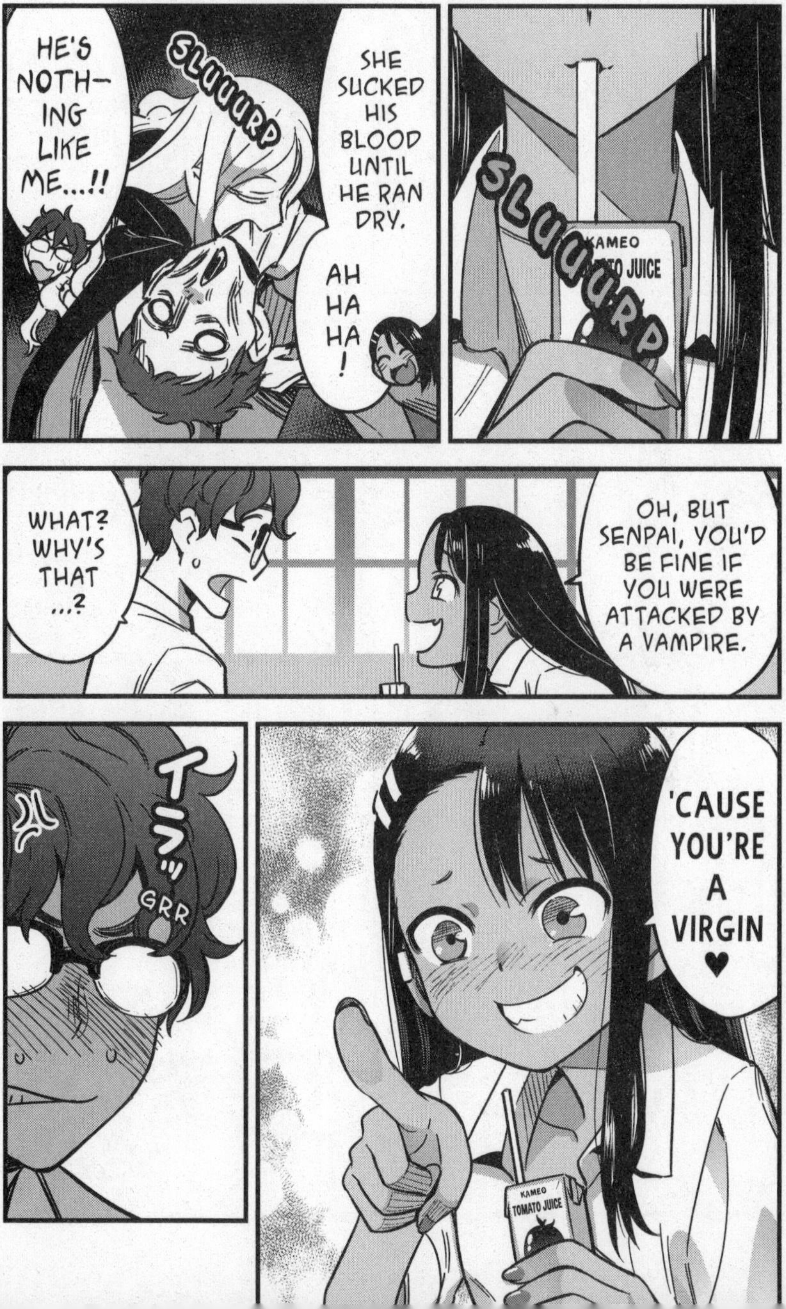
SLUUURP
KAMEO
SHE SUCKED HIS BLOOD UNTIL HE RAN DRY.
SLUUURP
HE'S NOTH-ING LIKE ME...!!
AH HA HA!
OH, BUT SENPAI, YOU'D BE FINE IF YOU WERE ATTACKED BY A VAMPIRE.
WHAT? WHY'S THAT ...?
'CAUSE YOU'RE A VIRGIN ♥
KAMEO TOMATO JUICE
イラッ
GRR

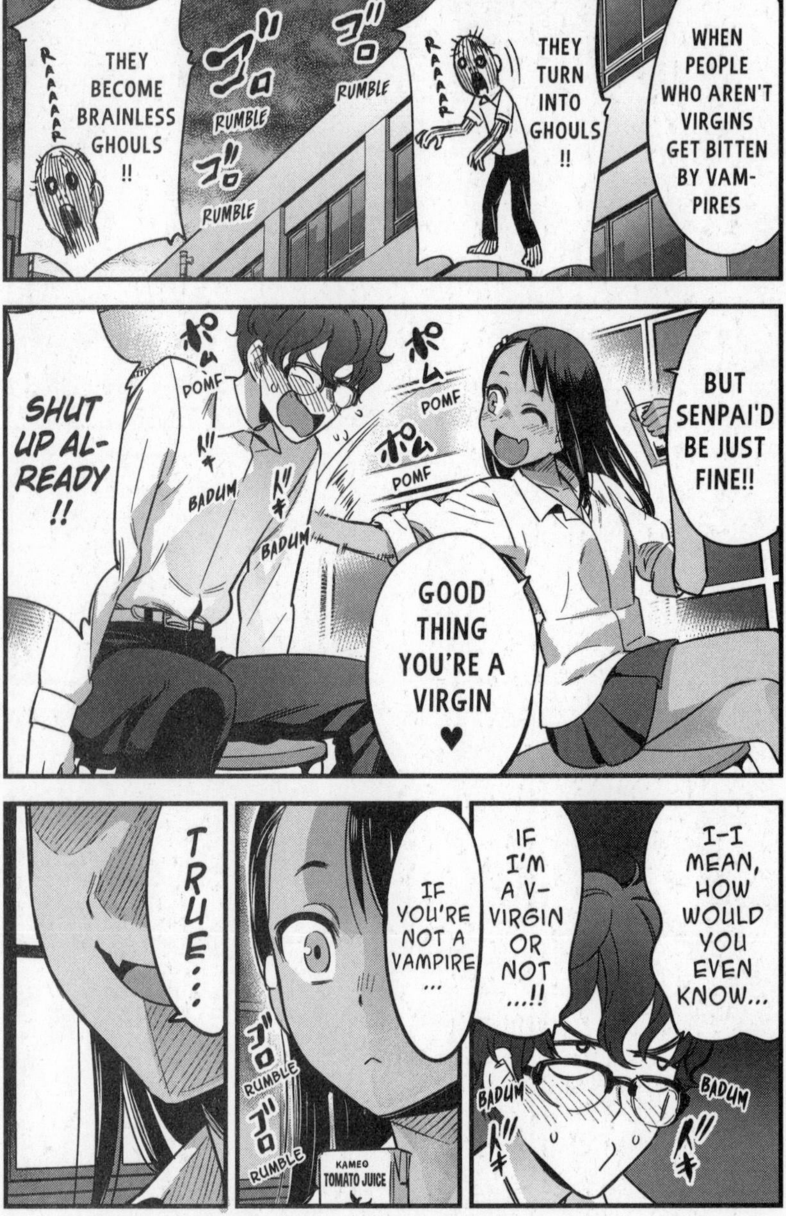
WHEN PEOPLE WHO AREN'T VIRGINS GET BITTEN BY VAMPIRES
THEY TURN INTO GHOULS !!
RAAAAAR
ゴロ RUMBLE
ゴロ RUMBLE
ゴロ RUMBLE
THEY BECOME BRAINLESS GHOULS !!
RAAAAAR
BUT SENPAI'D BE JUST FINE!!
GOOD THING YOU'RE A VIRGIN ♥
ポム POMF
ポム POMF
ポム POMF
ドキ BADUM
ドキ BADUM
SHUT UP AL-READY !!
I-I MEAN, HOW WOULD YOU EVEN KNOW...
IF I'M A V-VIRGIN OR NOT ...!!
ドキ BADUM
ドキ BADUM
IF YOU'RE NOT A VAMPIRE ...
ゴロ RUMBLE
ゴロ RUMBLE
KAMEO TOMATO JUICE
TRUE...

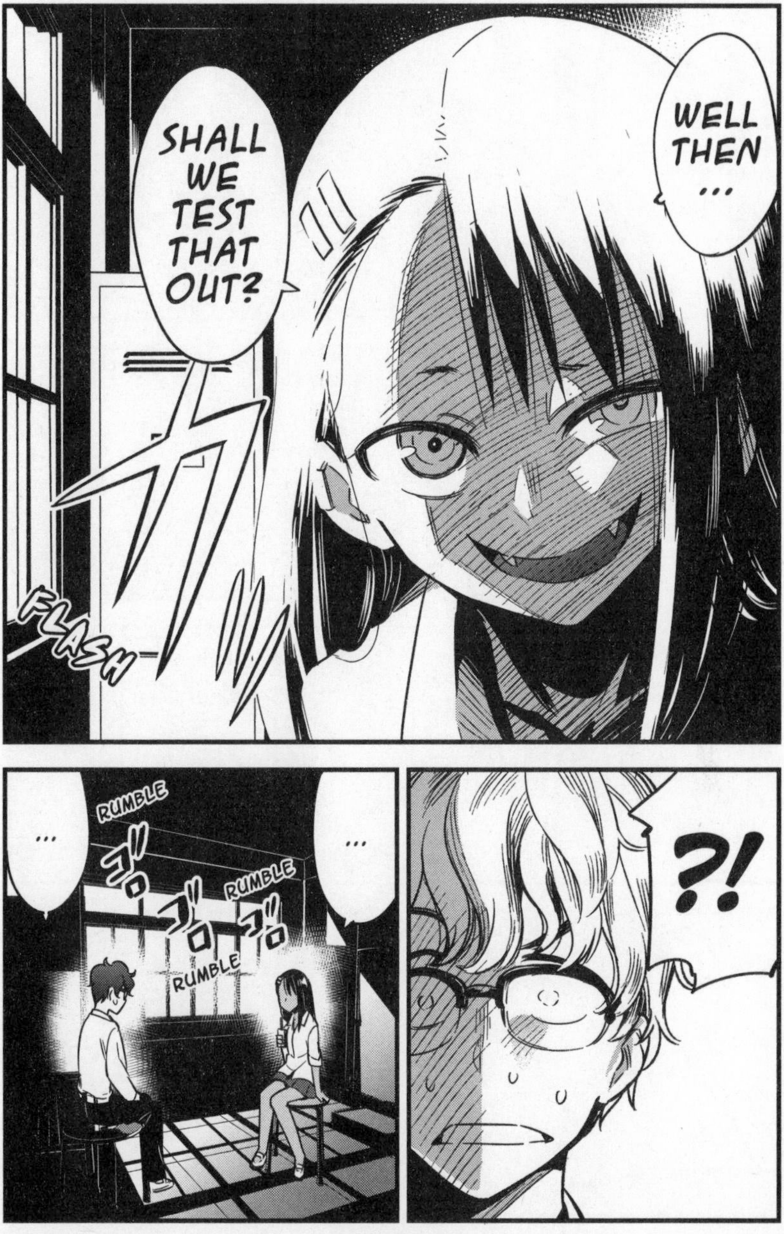
WELL THEN ...
SHALL WE TEST THAT OUT?
FLASH
?!
...
...
RUMBLE
RUMBLE
RUMBLE

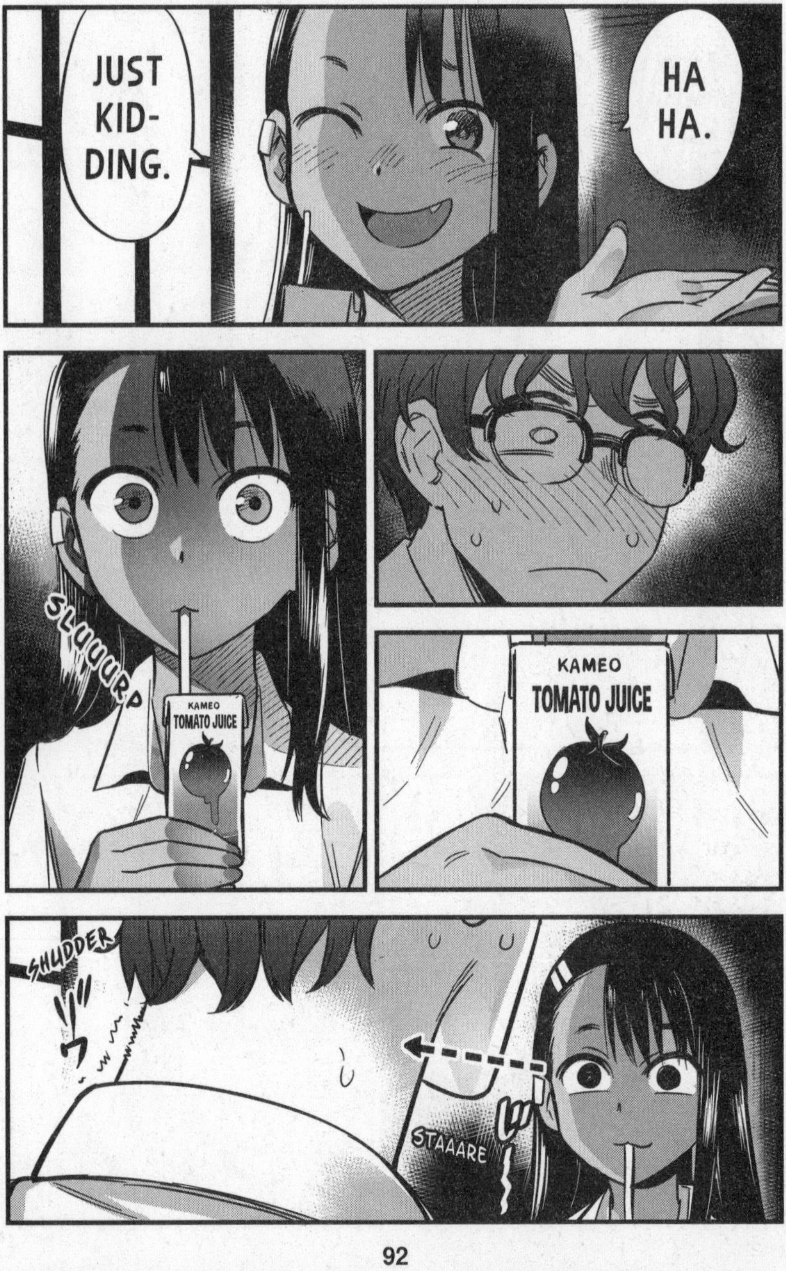
HA HA.
JUST KID-DING.
KAMEO
TOMATO JUICE
SLUUURP
KAMEO
TOMATO JUICE
STAAARE
SHUDDER

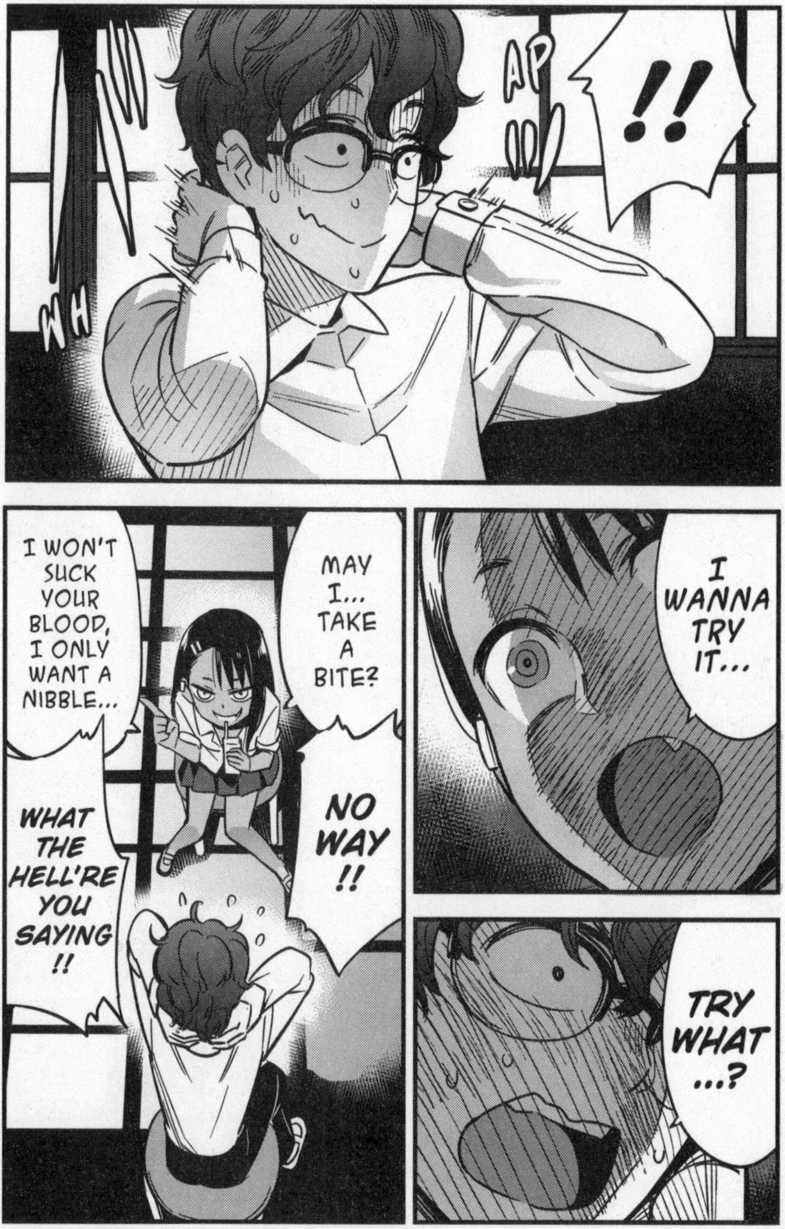
!!
AP
WH
I WANNA TRY IT...
TRY WHAT ...?
MAY I... TAKE A BITE?
I WON'T SUCK YOUR BLOOD, I ONLY WANT A NIBBLE...
NO WAY !!
WHAT THE HELL'RE YOU SAYING !!

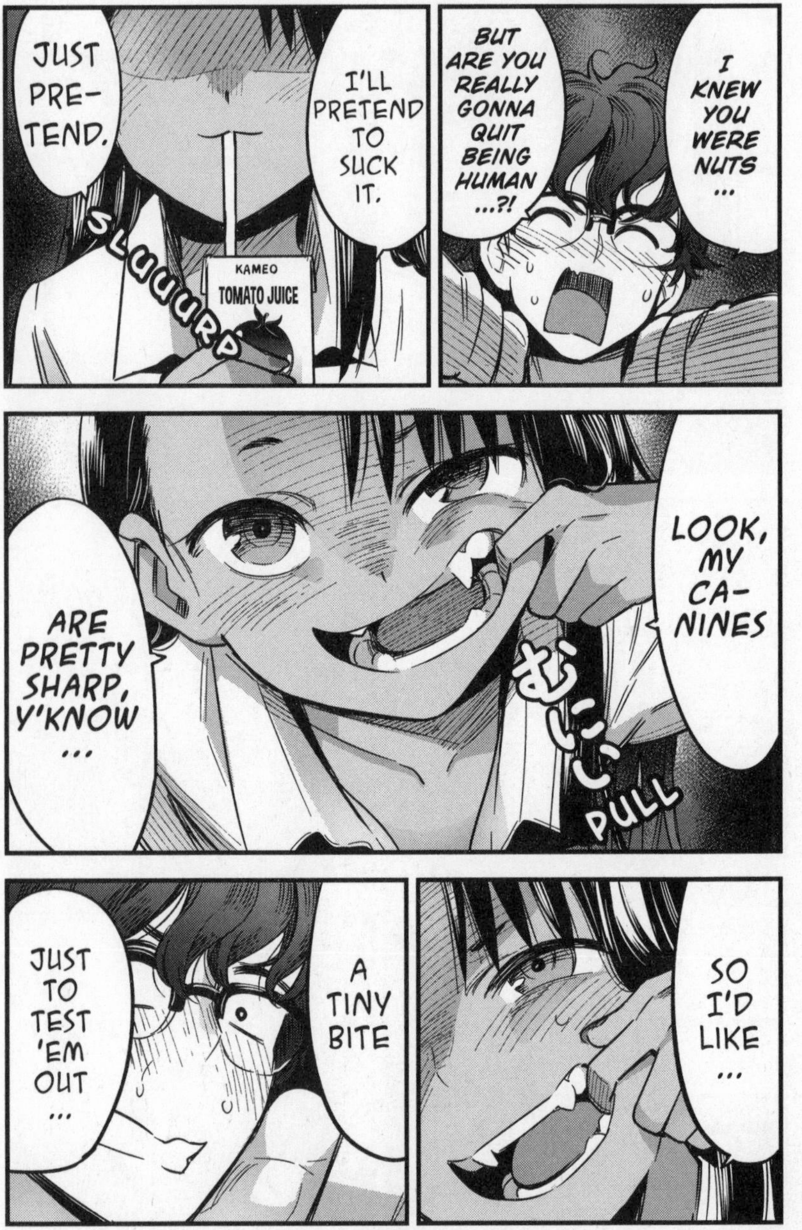
I KNEW YOU WERE NUTS ...
BUT ARE YOU REALLY GONNA QUIT BEING HUMAN ...?!
I'LL PRETEND TO SUCK IT.
JUST PRE-TEND.
SLUUURP
KAMEO
TOMATO JUICE
LOOK, MY CA-NINES
ARE PRETTY SHARP, Y'KNOW ...
むにに
PULL
SO I'D LIKE ...
A TINY BITE
JUST TO TEST 'EM OUT ...

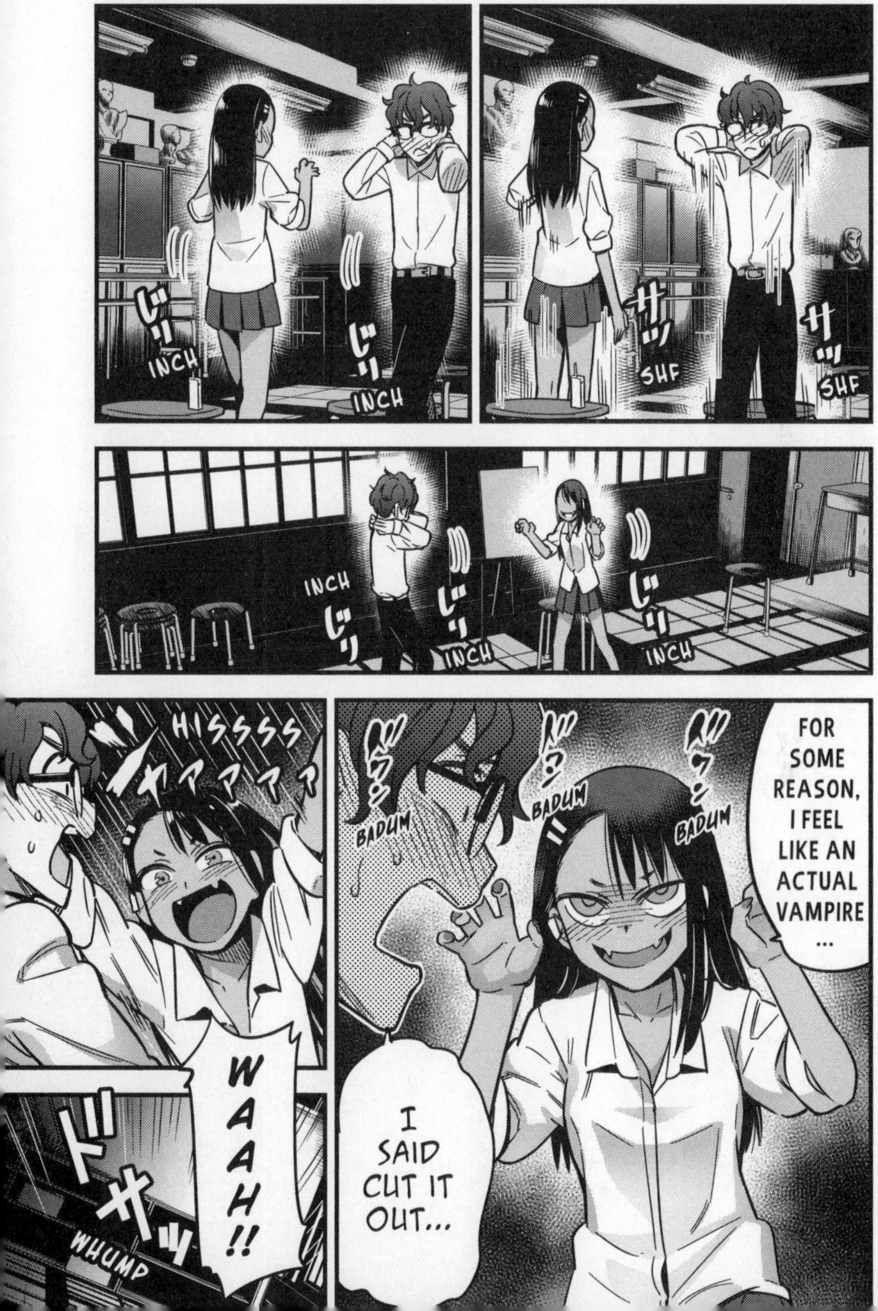
SHF
SHF
INCH
INCH
INCH
INCH
INCH
INCH
BADUM
BADUM
BADUM
FOR SOME REASON, I FEEL LIKE AN ACTUAL VAMPIRE...
I SAID CUT IT OUT...
HISSSSS
WAAAH!!
WHUMP

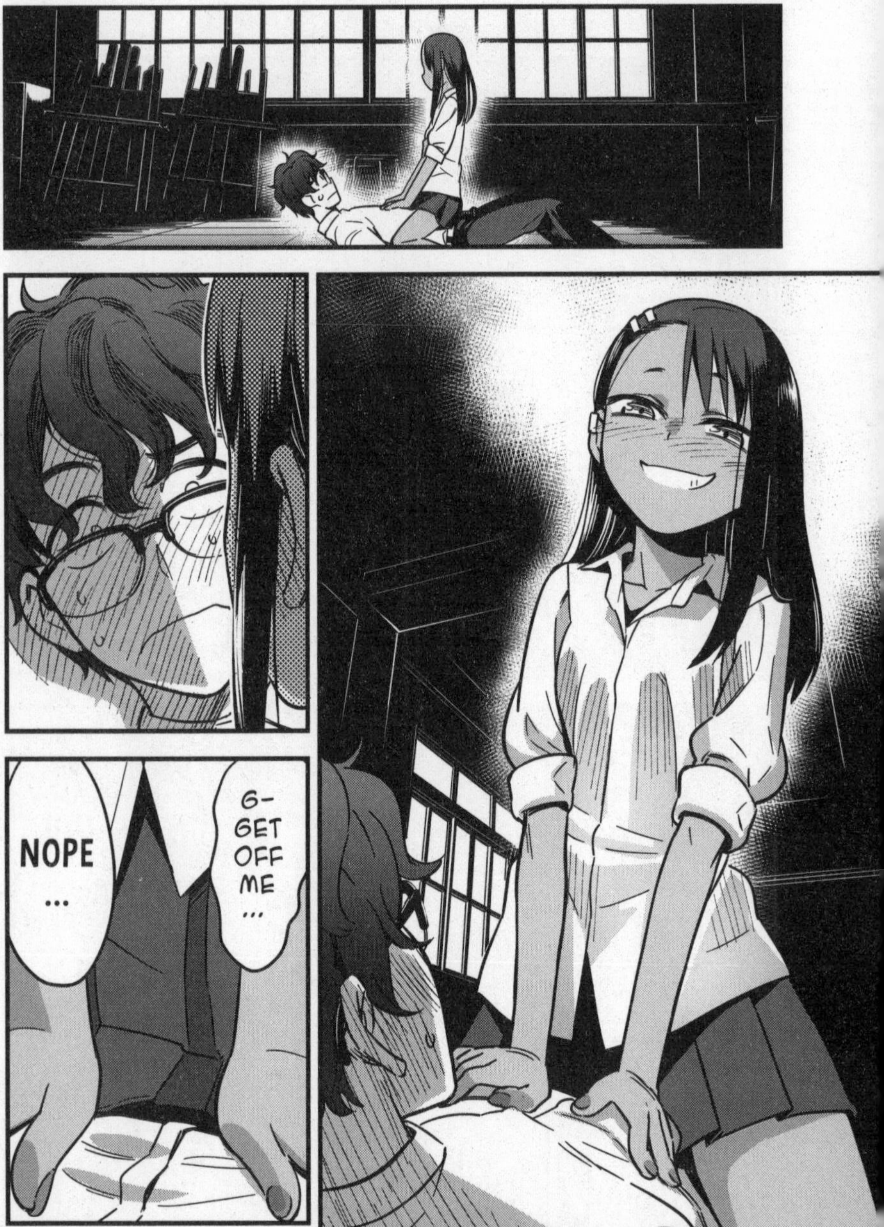
G-GET OFF ME...
NOPE...

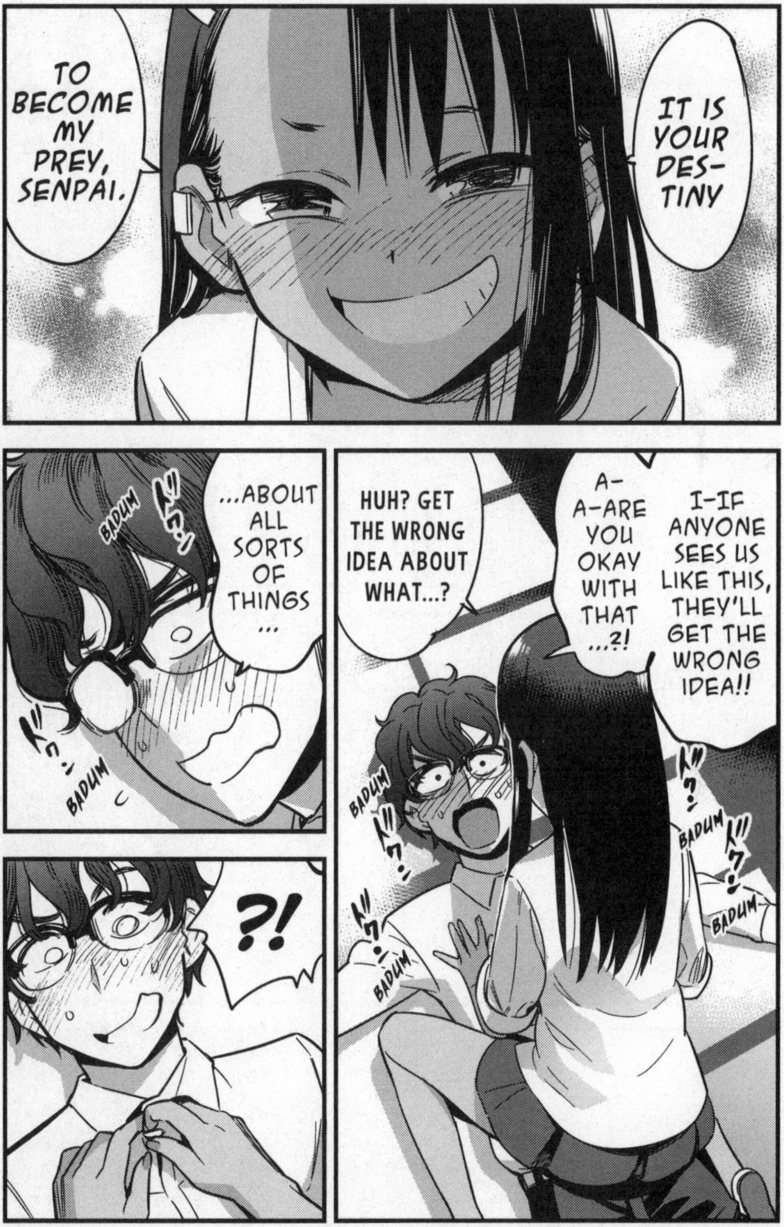
IT IS YOUR DES-TINY
TO BECOME MY PREY, SENPAI.
I-IF ANYONE SEES US LIKE THIS, THEY'LL GET THE WRONG IDEA!!
A-A-ARE YOU OKAY WITH THAT...?!
HUH? GET THE WRONG IDEA ABOUT WHAT...?
BADUM
BADUM
BADUM
BADUM
...ABOUT ALL SORTS OF THINGS...
BADUM
BADUM
?!

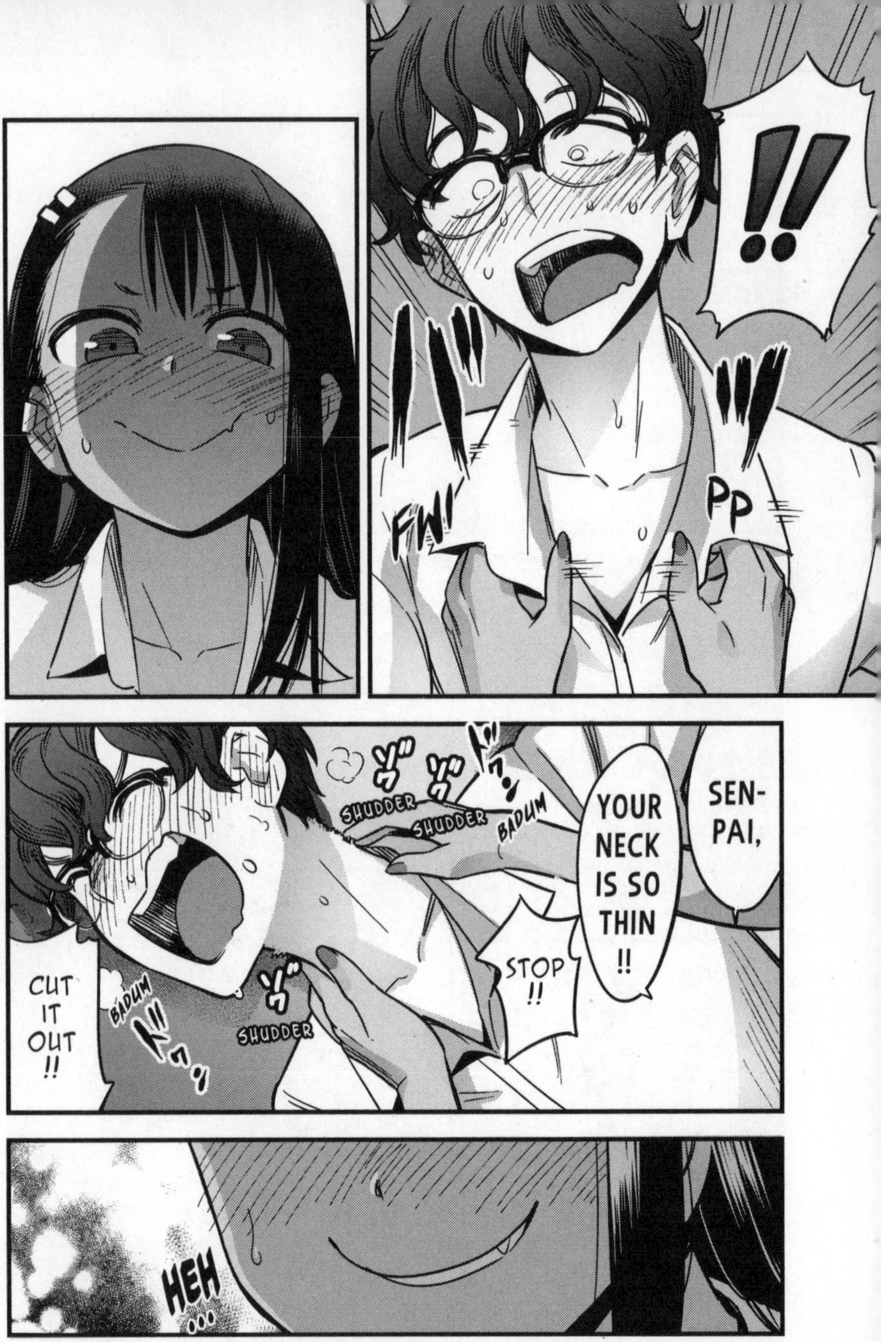
!!
FWIPP
SENPAI,
YOUR NECK IS SO THIN!!
SHUDDER
SHUDDER
BADUM
STOP!!
CUT IT OUT!!
BADUM
SHUDDER
HEH...

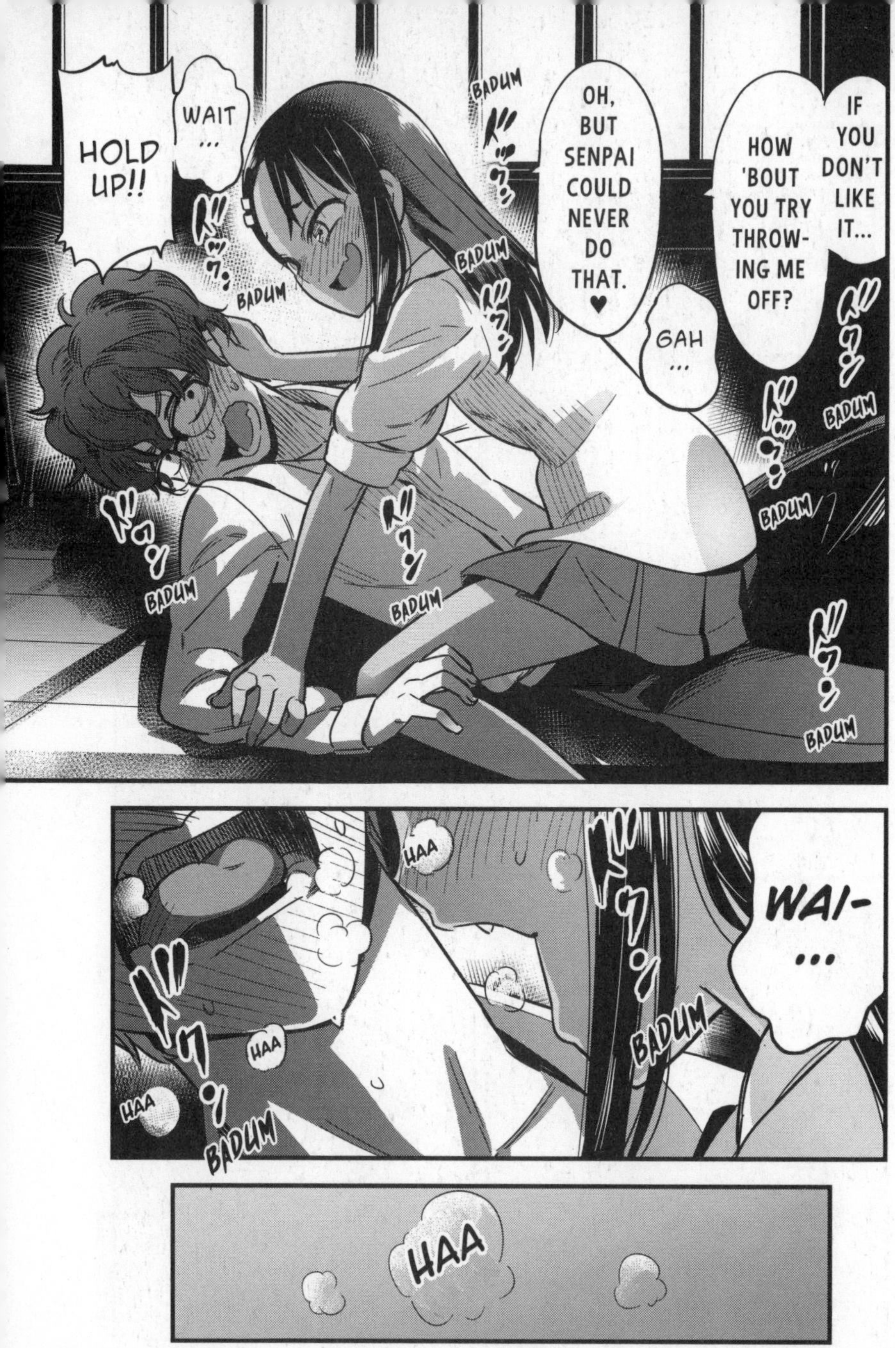
BADUM
IF YOU DON'T LIKE IT...
HOW 'BOUT YOU TRY THROWING ME OFF?
BADUM
OH, BUT SENPAI COULD NEVER DO THAT. ♥
BADUM
GAH...
BADUM
WAIT...
HOLD UP!!
BADUM
BADUM
BADUM
BADUM
BADUM
WAI-...
BADUM
HAA
HAA
HAA
BADUM
HAA

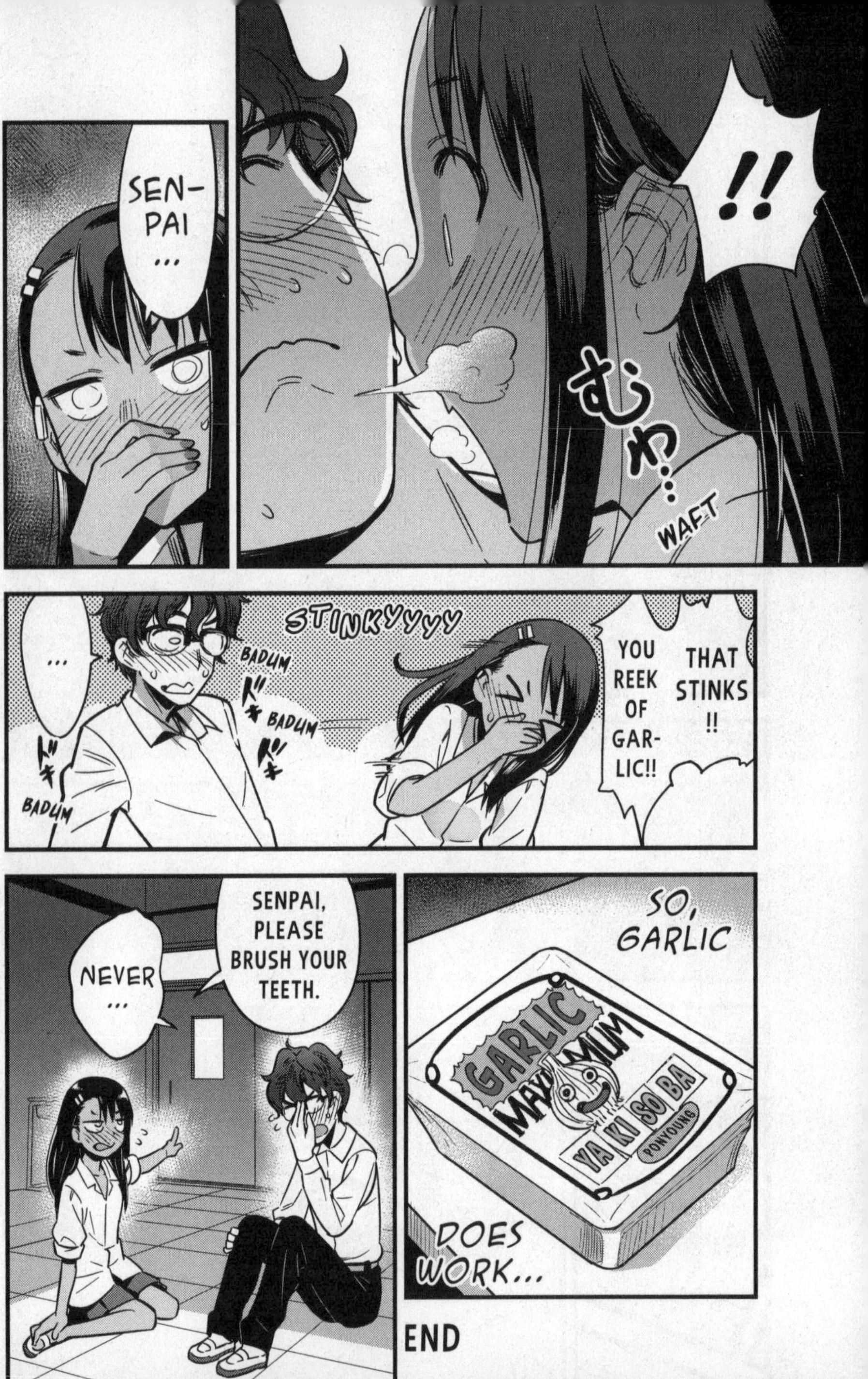
!!
むわ…
WAFT
SEN-PAI ...
THAT STINKS !!
YOU REEK OF GAR-LIC!!
STINKYYYY
BADUM
BADUM
BADUM
...
SO, GARLIC
GARLIC
YA KI SO BA
PONYOUNG
DOES WORK...
SENPAI, PLEASE BRUSH YOUR TEETH.
NEVER ...

END

CHAPTER 6: 'SUP, SENPAI!

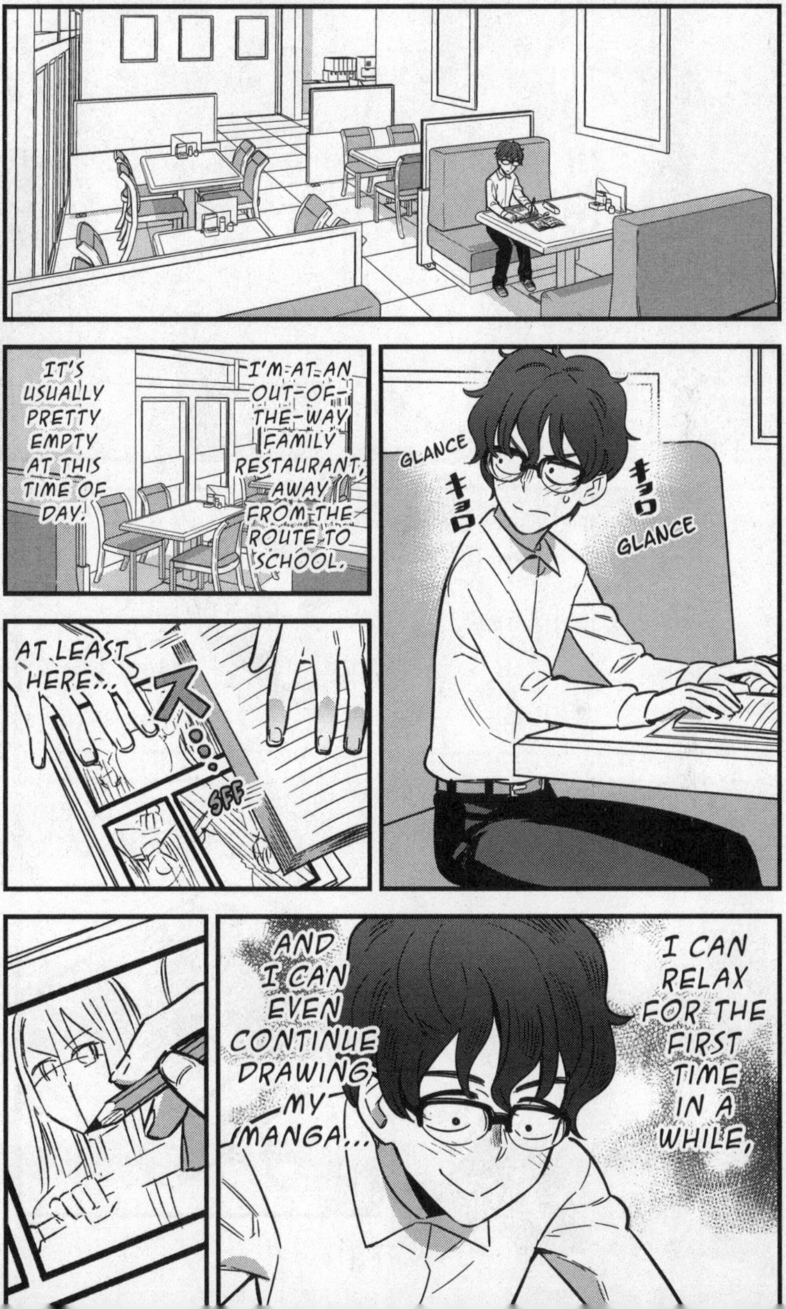
GLANCE
キョロ
キョロ
GLANCE
I'M AT AN OUT-OF-THE-WAY FAMILY RESTAURANT, AWAY FROM THE ROUTE TO SCHOOL.
IT'S USUALLY PRETTY EMPTY AT THIS TIME OF DAY.
AT LEAST HERE...
ス…
SFF
I CAN RELAX FOR THE FIRST TIME IN A WHILE,
AND I CAN EVEN CONTINUE DRAWING MY MANGA...

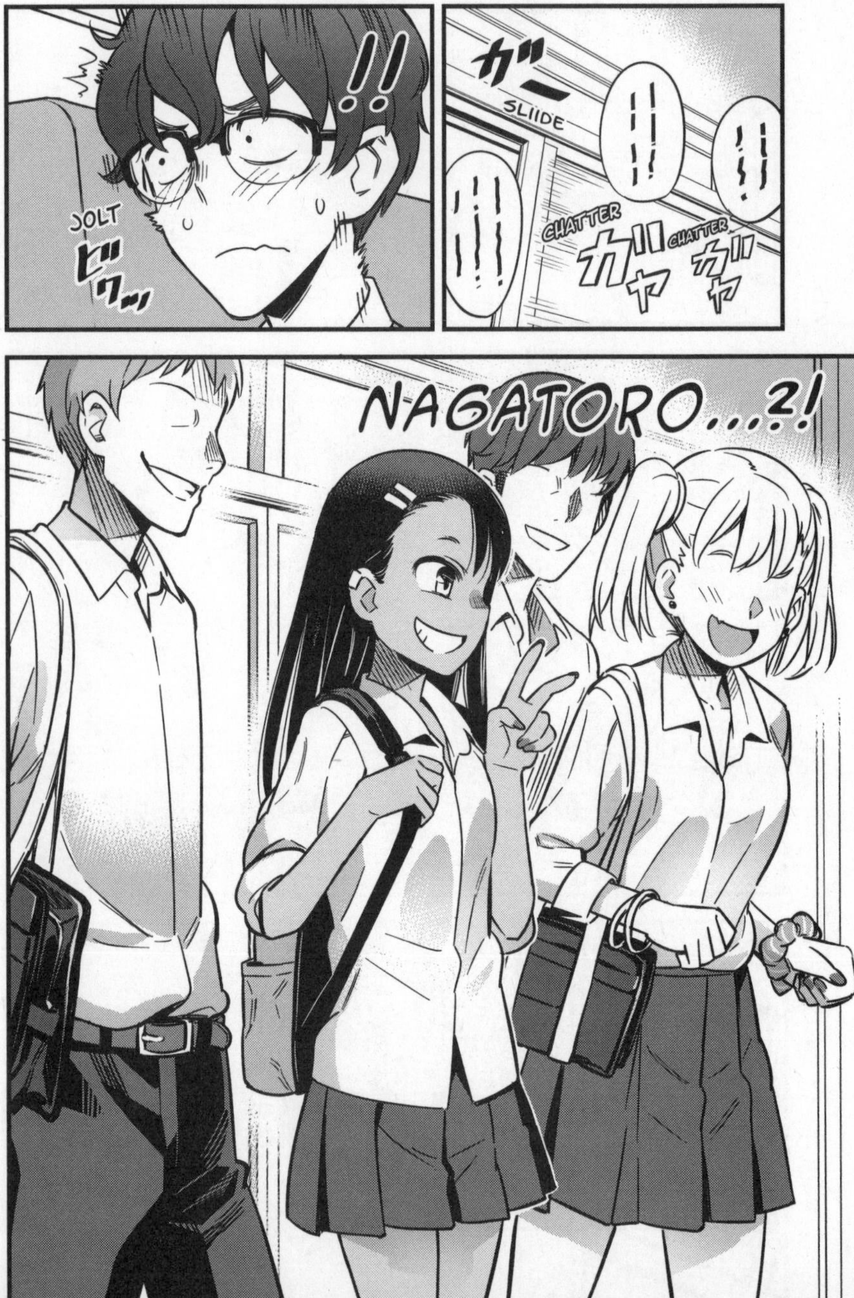
ガー
SLIIDE
!!
!!
!!
CHATTER
CHATTER
!!
JOLT
ビクッ
NAGATORO...?!

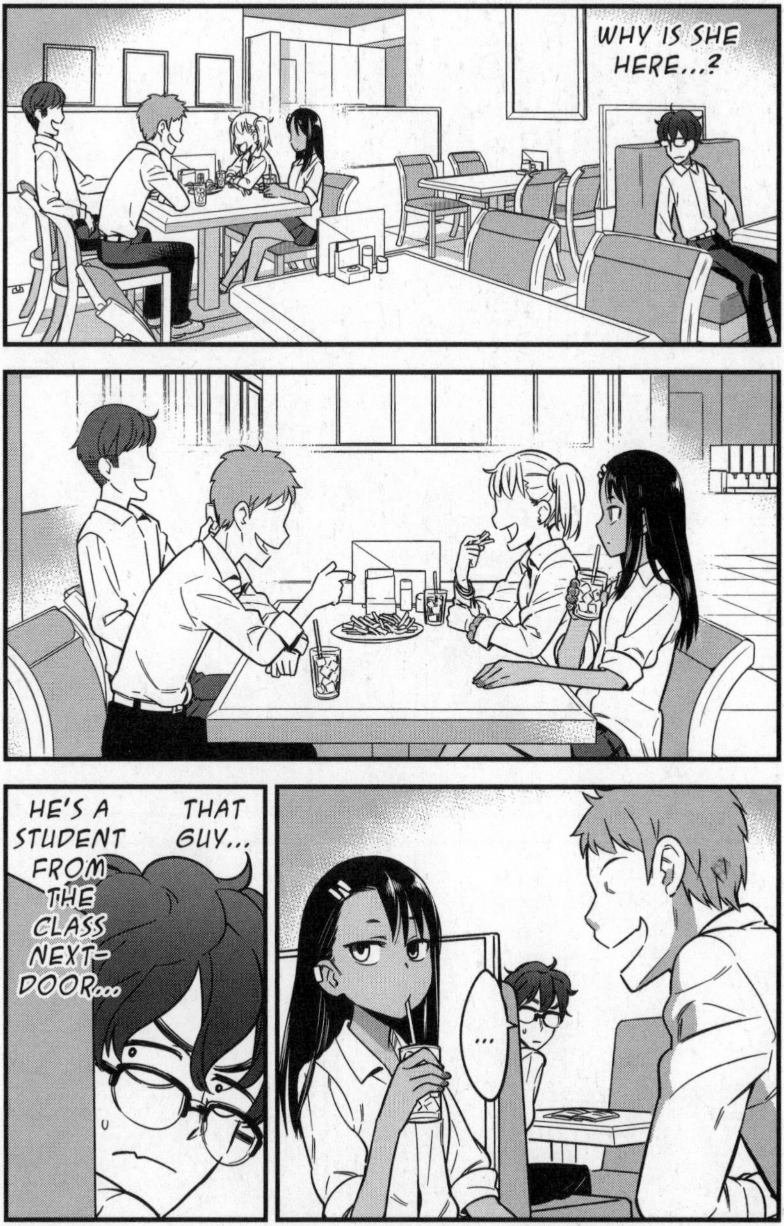
WHY IS SHE HERE...?
...
THAT GUY...
HE'S A STUDENT FROM THE CLASS NEXT-DOOR...

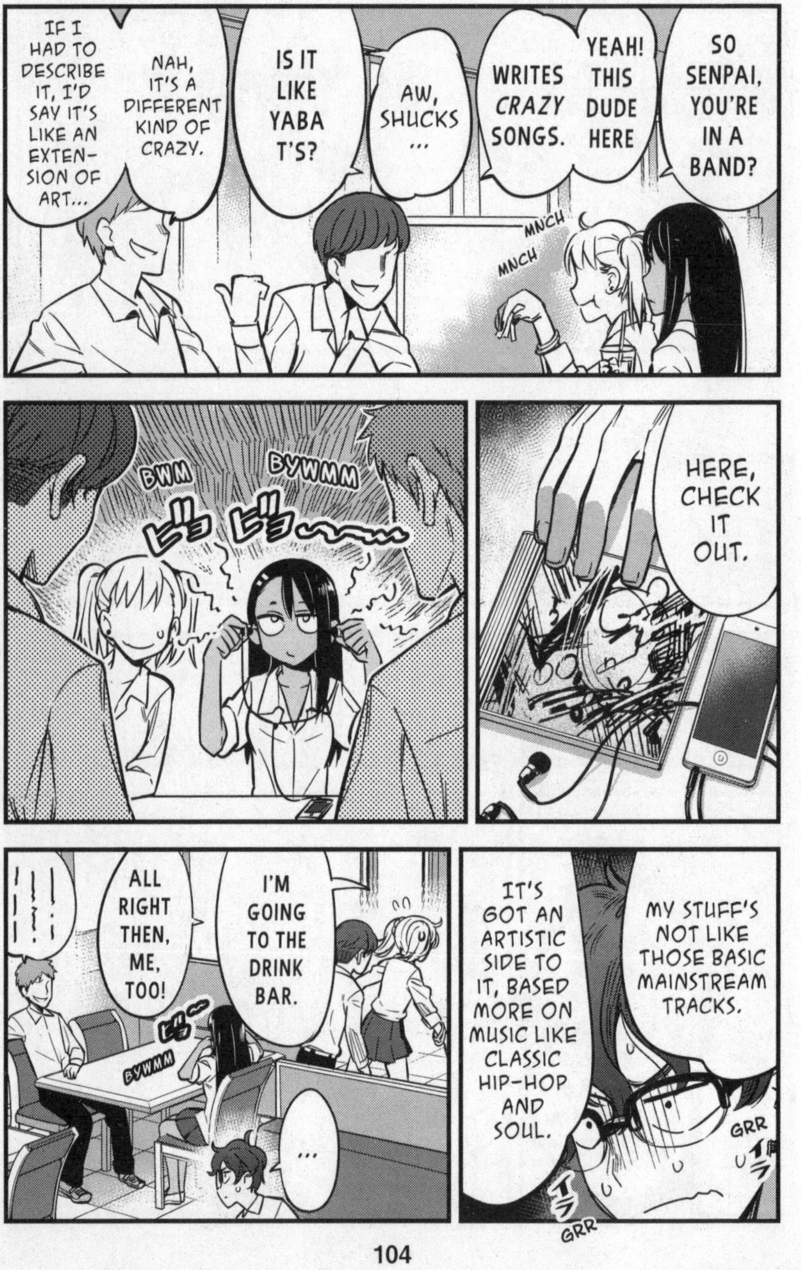
SO SENPAI, YOU'RE IN A BAND?
YEAH! THIS DUDE HERE
WRITES *CRAZY* SONGS.
AW, SHUCKS ...
IS IT LIKE YABA T'S?
NAH, IT'S A DIFFERENT KIND OF CRAZY.
IF I HAD TO DESCRIBE IT, I'D SAY IT'S LIKE AN EXTENSION OF ART...
MNCH
MNCH
HERE, CHECK IT OUT.
BYWMM
BWM
MY STUFF'S NOT LIKE THOSE BASIC MAINSTREAM TRACKS.
IT'S GOT AN ARTISTIC SIDE TO IT, BASED MORE ON MUSIC LIKE CLASSIC HIP-HOP AND SOUL.
GRR
GRR
I'M GOING TO THE DRINK BAR.
ALL RIGHT THEN, ME, TOO!
...
BYWMM

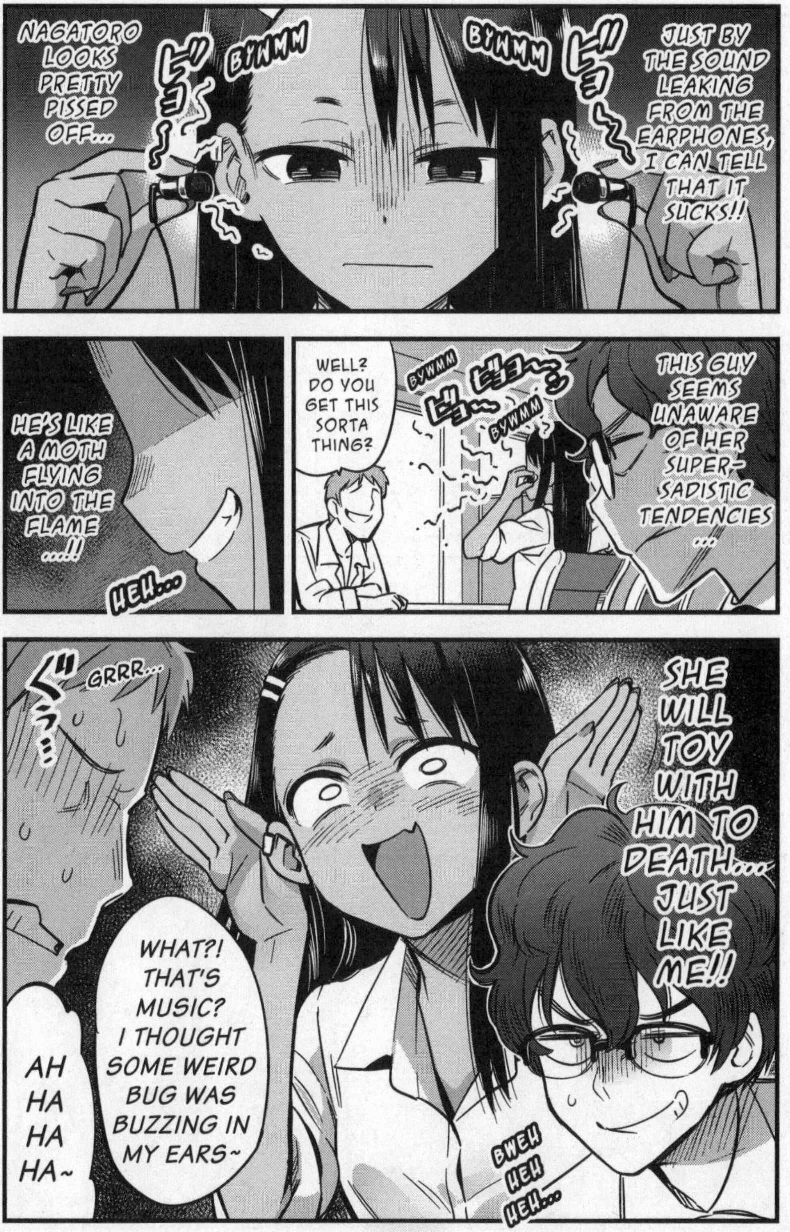
JUST BY THE SOUND LEAKING FROM THE EARPHONES, I CAN TELL THAT IT SUCKS!!
BYWMM
BYWMM
NAGATORO LOOKS PRETTY PISSED OFF...
THIS GUY SEEMS UNAWARE OF HER SUPER-SADISTIC TENDENCIES...
BYWMM
BYWMM
WELL? DO YOU GET THIS SORTA THING?
HE'S LIKE A MOTH FLYING INTO THE FLAME...!!
HEH...
SHE WILL TOY WITH HIM TO DEATH... JUST LIKE ME!!
GRRR...
BWEH HEH HEH...
WHAT?! THAT'S MUSIC? I THOUGHT SOME WEIRD BUG WAS BUZZING IN MY EARS~
AH HA HA HA~

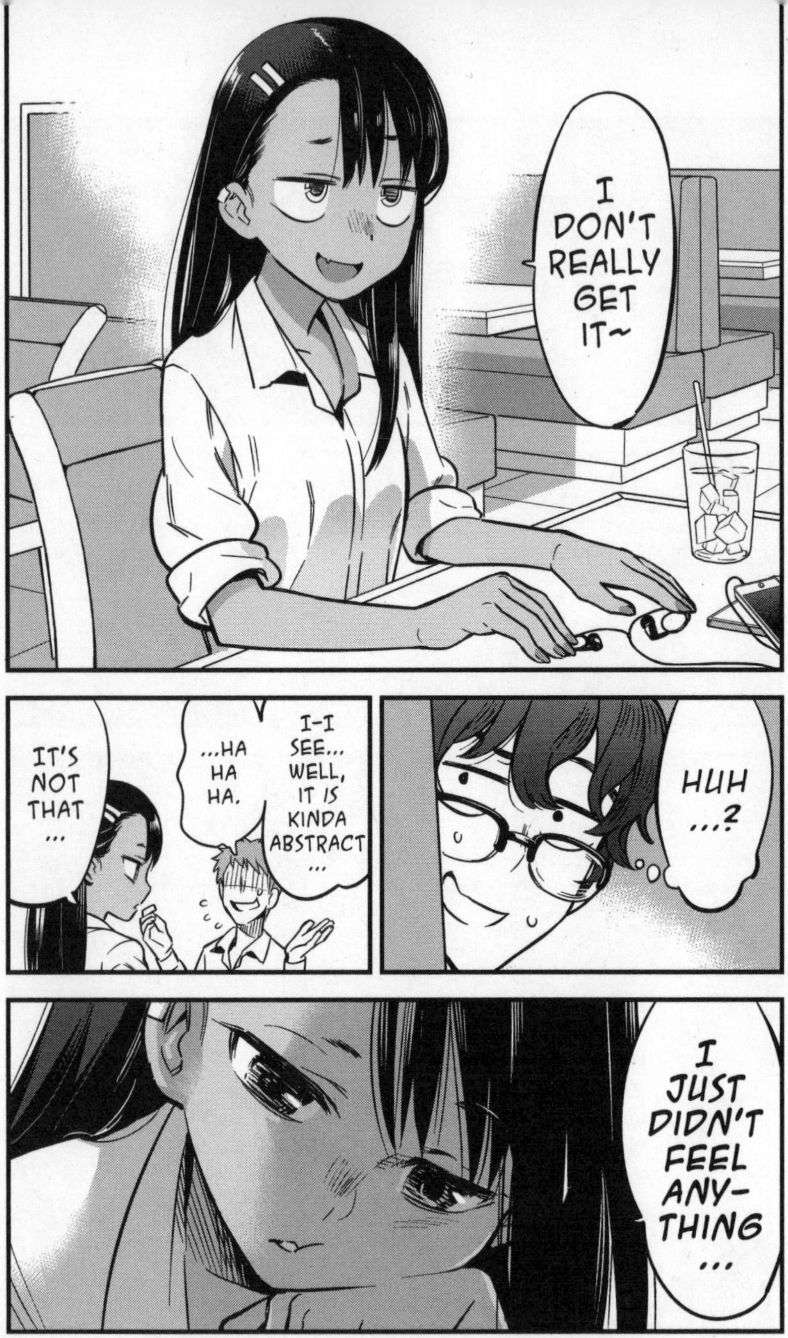
I DON'T REALLY GET IT~
HUH ...?
I-I SEE... WELL, IT IS KINDA ABSTRACT ...
...HA HA HA.
IT'S NOT THAT ...
I JUST DIDN'T FEEL ANY-THING ...

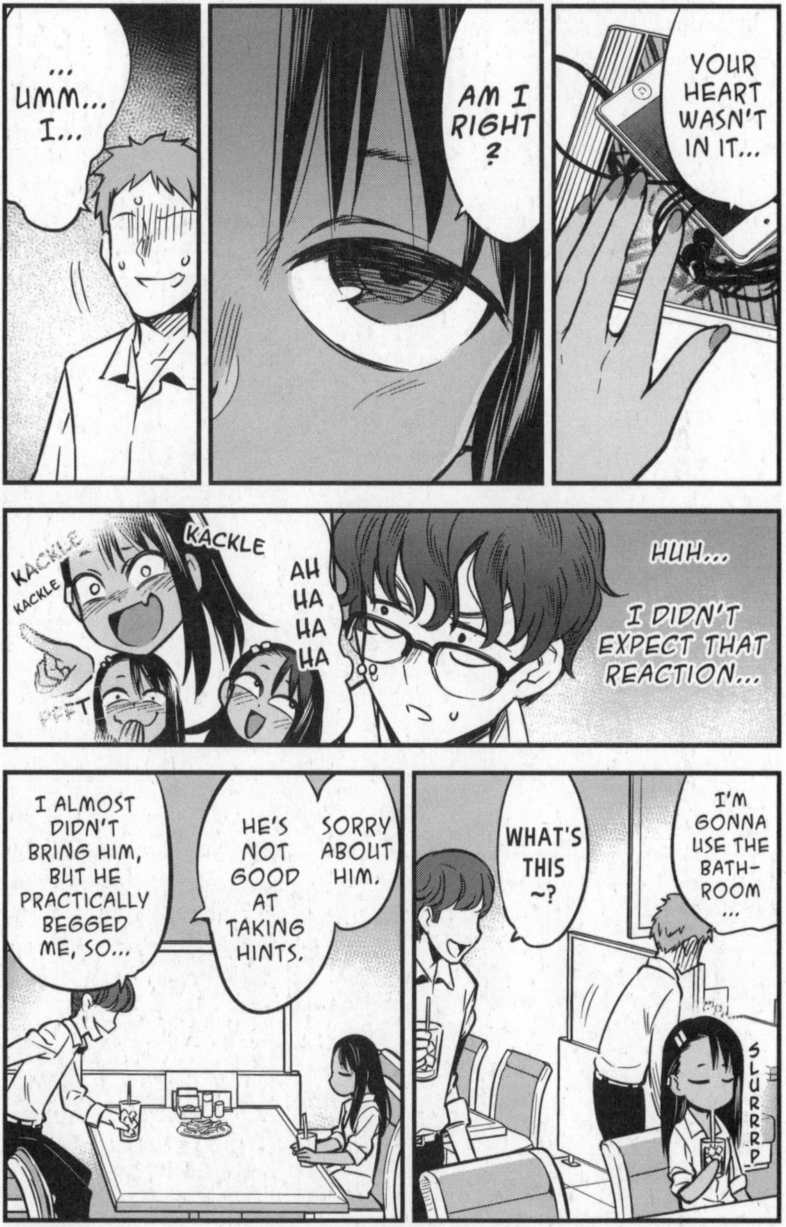
YOUR HEART WASN'T IN IT...
AM I RIGHT?
... UMM... I...
HUH...
I DIDN'T EXPECT THAT REACTION...
KACKLE
AH HA HA HA
KACKLE
KACKLE
PFFT
I'M GONNA USE THE BATH-ROOM...
WHAT'S THIS ~?
SLURRRP
SORRY ABOUT HIM.
HE'S NOT GOOD AT TAKING HINTS.
I ALMOST DIDN'T BRING HIM, BUT HE PRACTICALLY BEGGED ME, SO...

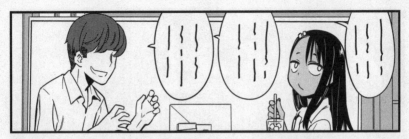

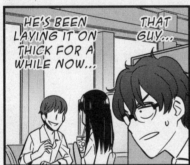

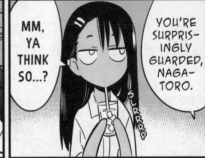

YOU'RE SURPRISINGLY GUARDED, NAGATORO.
MM, YA THINK SO...?
SLRRRP
THAT GUY...
HE'S BEEN LAYING IT ON THICK FOR A WHILE NOW...
IT'S FINE, YOU CAN LET DOWN YOUR GUARD A LITTLE.
I WENT TO AN ALL-BOYS' MIDDLE SCHOOL,
SO I'M NOT USED TO DEALING WITH GIRLS AND STUFF AT ALL~
...
イラッ
GRR
わさ
WRIGGLE
I'VE NEVER EVEN SQUEEZED A BOOB BEFORE!
FOR REAL, FOR REAL!
WRIGGLE
わさ

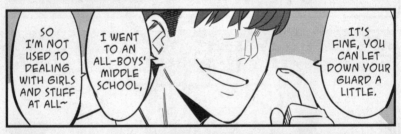

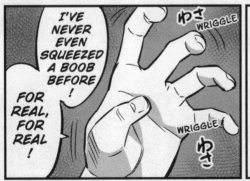

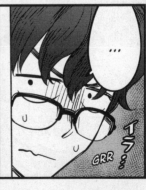

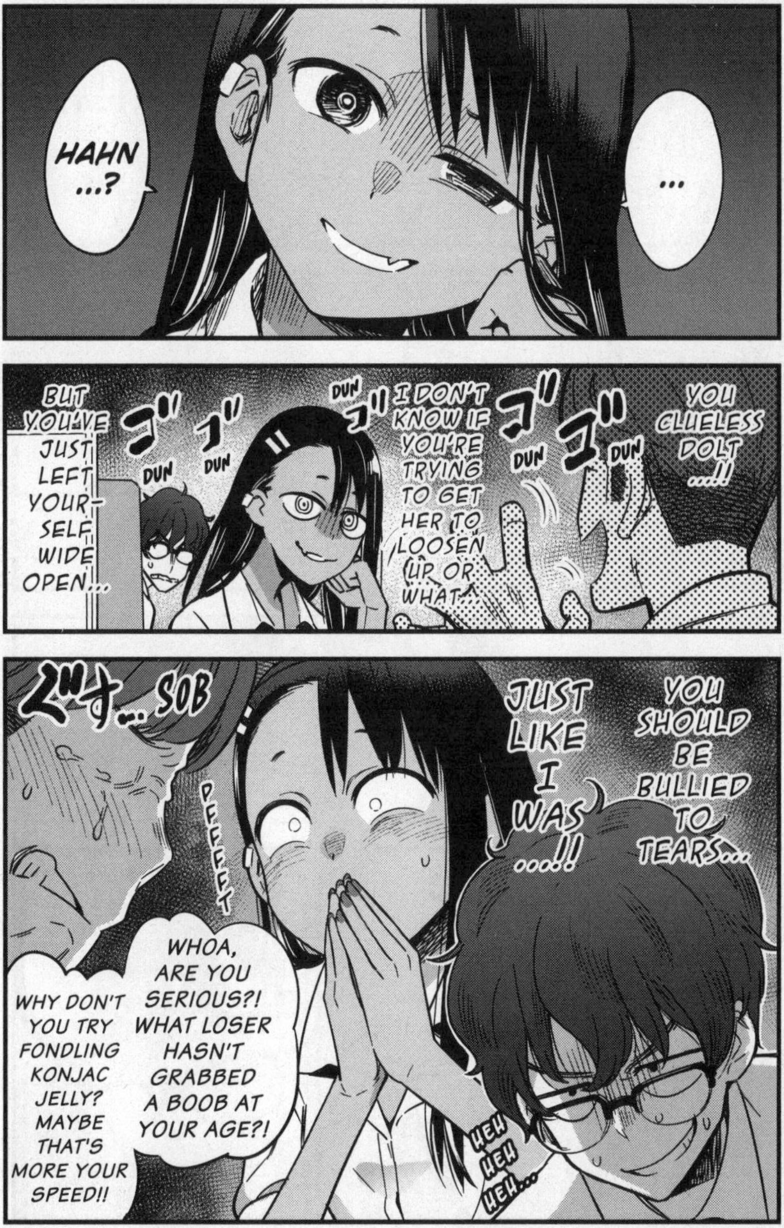
...
HAHN ...?
YOU CLUELESS DOLT ...!!
DUN
DUN
I DON'T KNOW IF YOU'RE TRYING TO GET HER TO LOOSEN UP OR WHAT...
DUN
DUN
DUN
BUT YOU'VE JUST LEFT YOURSELF WIDE OPEN...
YOU SHOULD BE BULLIED TO TEARS...
JUST LIKE I WAS...!!
SOB
PFFFFFT
WHOA, ARE YOU SERIOUS?! WHAT LOSER HASN'T GRABBED A BOOB AT YOUR AGE?!
WHY DON'T YOU TRY FONDLING KONJAC JELLY? MAYBE THAT'S MORE YOUR SPEED!!
HEH HEH HEH...

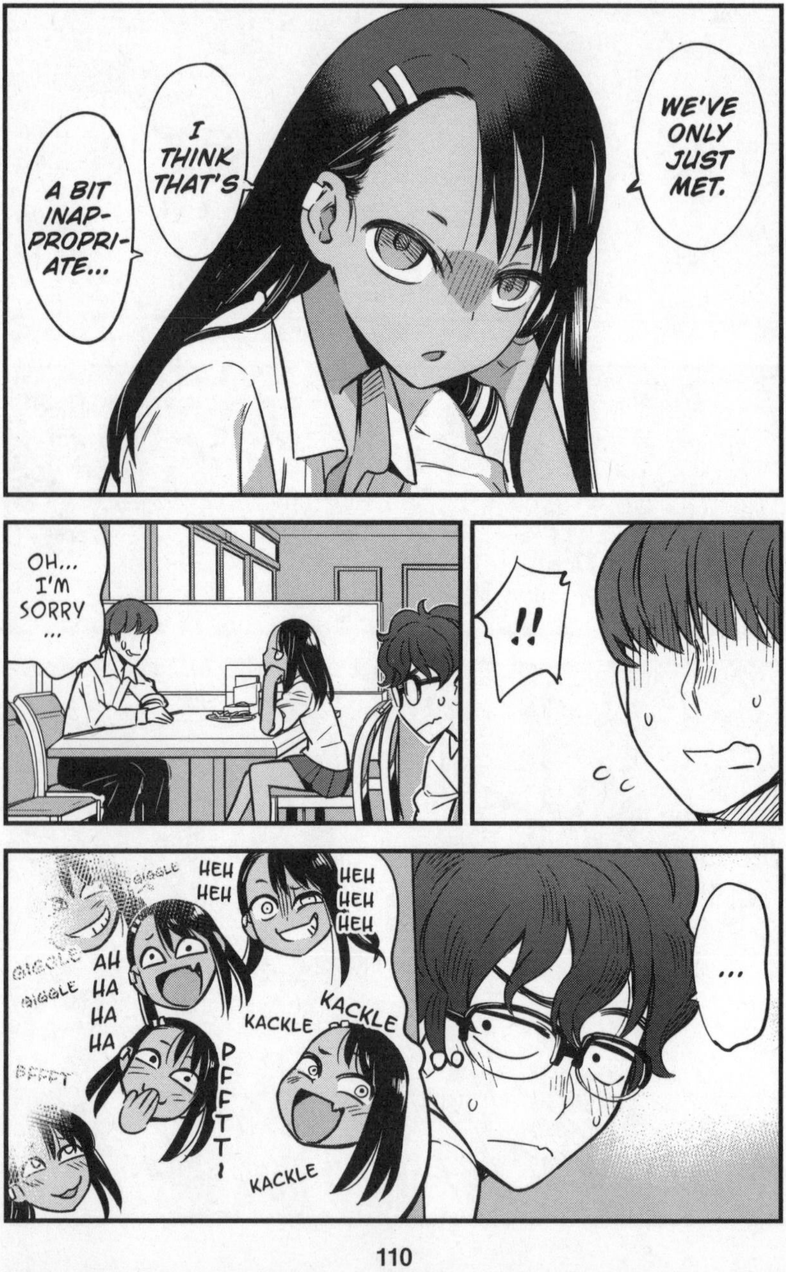
WE'VE ONLY JUST MET.
I THINK THAT'S
A BIT INAP-PROPRI-ATE...
!!
OH... I'M SORRY ...
...
HEH HEH HEH
HEH HEH
GIGGLE
GIGGLE
GIGGLE
AH HA HA HA
KACKLE
KACKLE
PFFTT
BFFFT
KACKLE

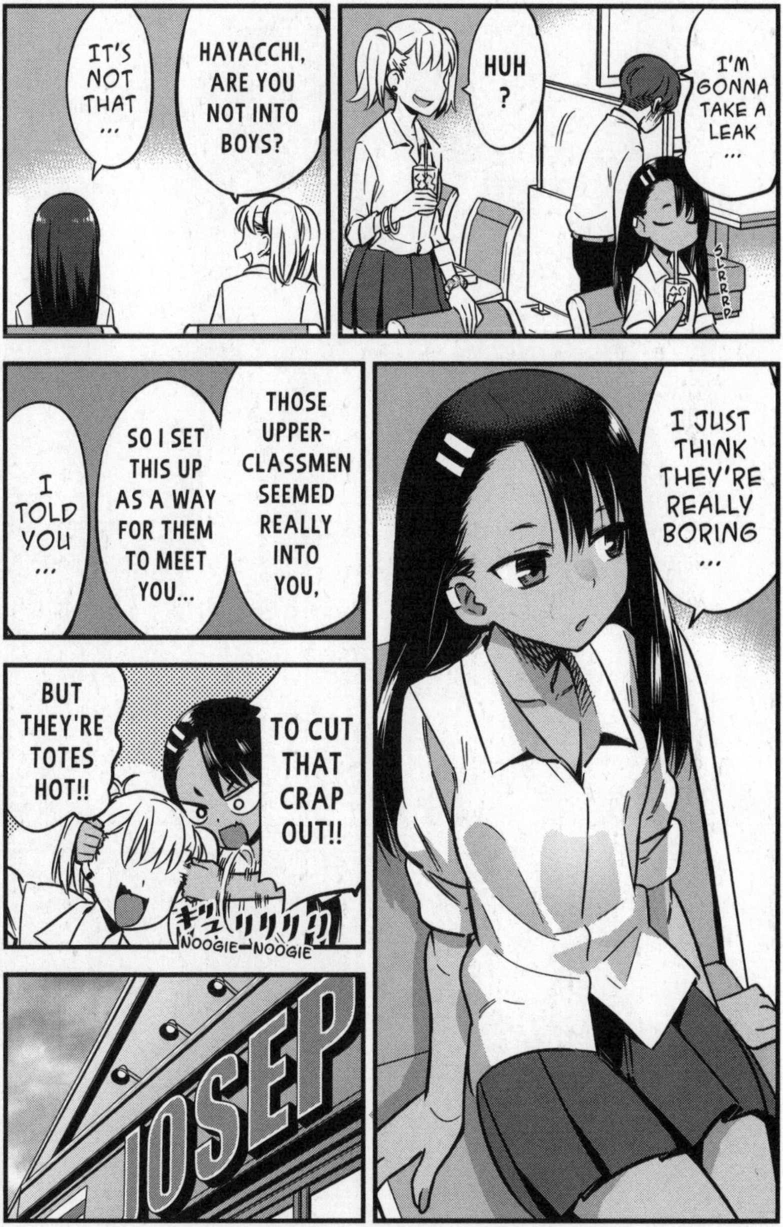
I'M GONNA TAKE A LEAK ...
HUH ?
SLRRRP
HAYACCHI, ARE YOU NOT INTO BOYS?
IT'S NOT THAT ...
I JUST THINK THEY'RE REALLY BORING ...
THOSE UPPER-CLASSMEN SEEMED REALLY INTO YOU,
SO I SET THIS UP AS A WAY FOR THEM TO MEET YOU...
I TOLD YOU ...
TO CUT THAT CRAP OUT!!
BUT THEY'RE TOTES HOT!!
NOOGIE NOOGIE
JOSEP

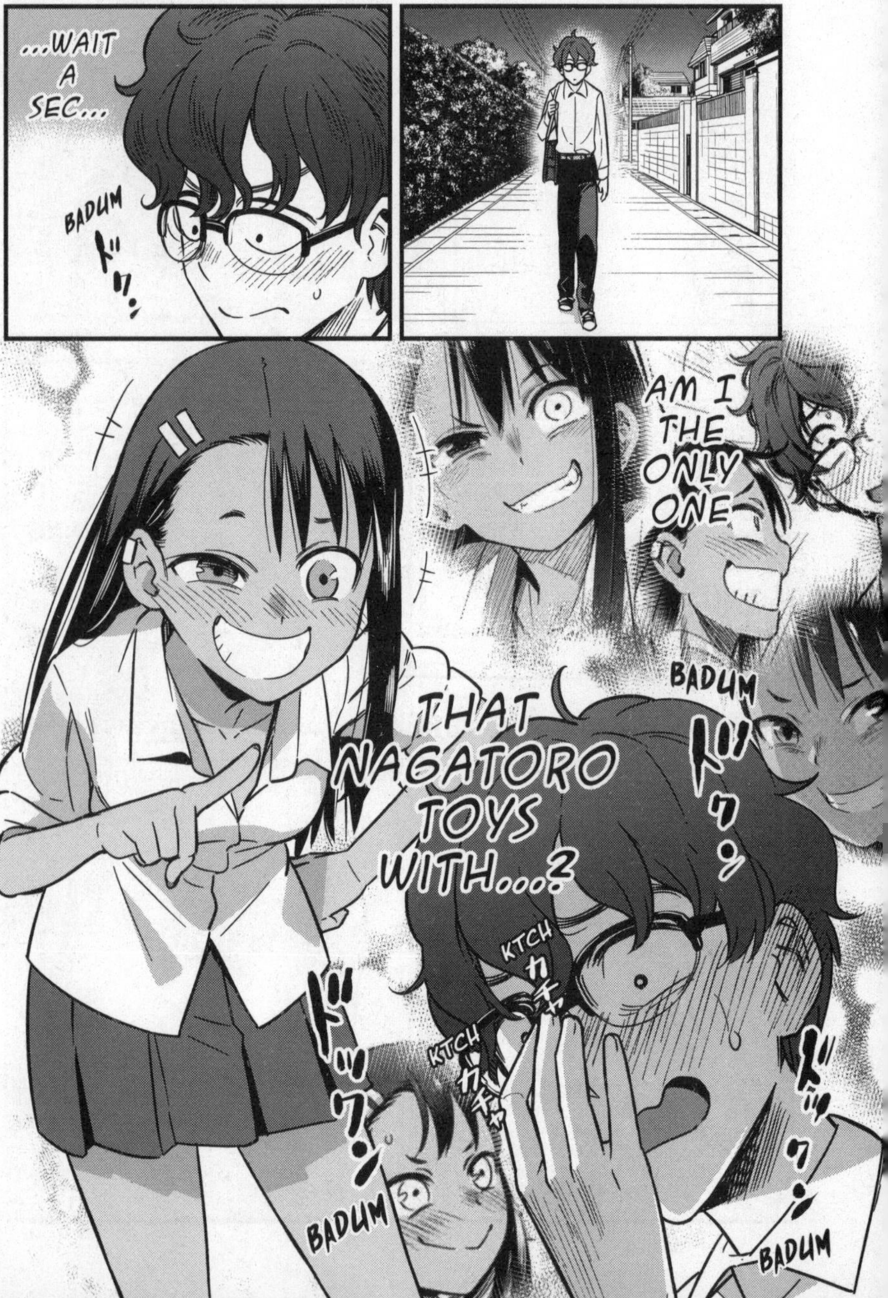
...WAIT A SEC...
BADUM
AM I THE ONLY ONE
THAT NAGATORO TOYS WITH...?
BADUM
KTCH
カチャ
KTCH
カチャ
BADUM
BADUM

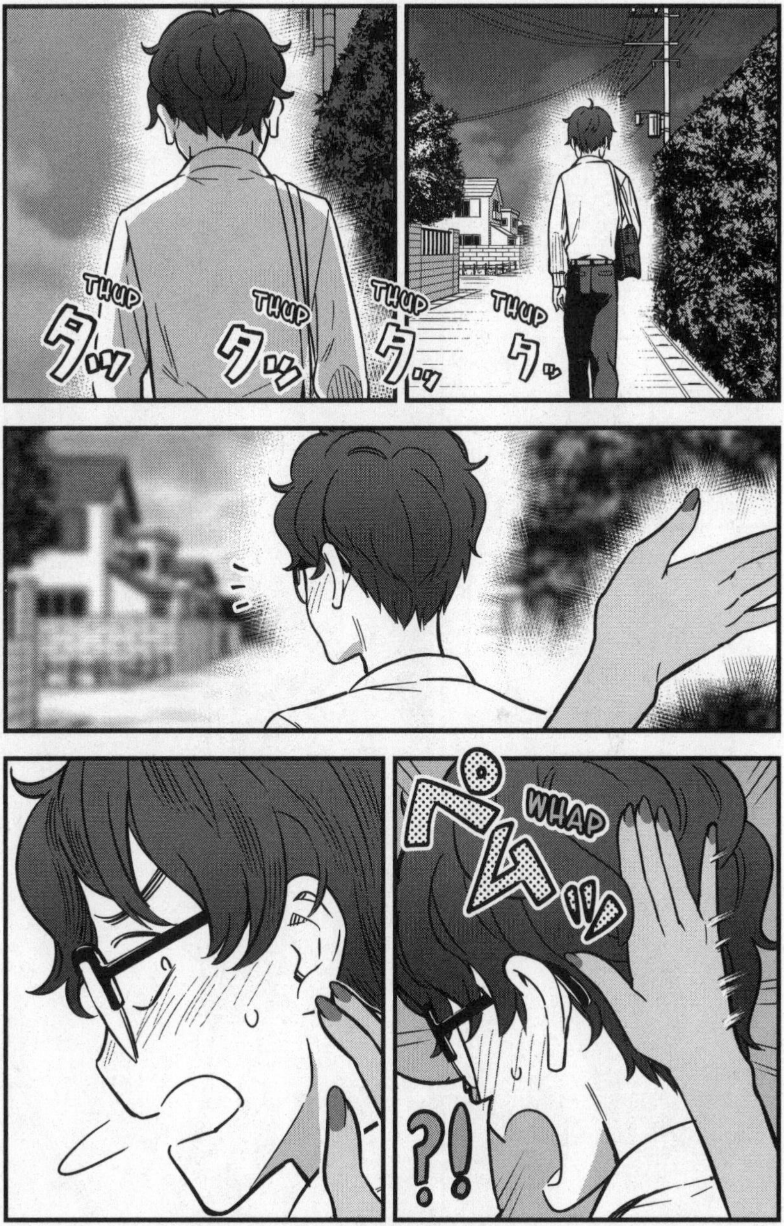

THUP
タッ
THUP
タッ
THUP
タッ
THUP
タッ
ペムッ
WHAP
?!

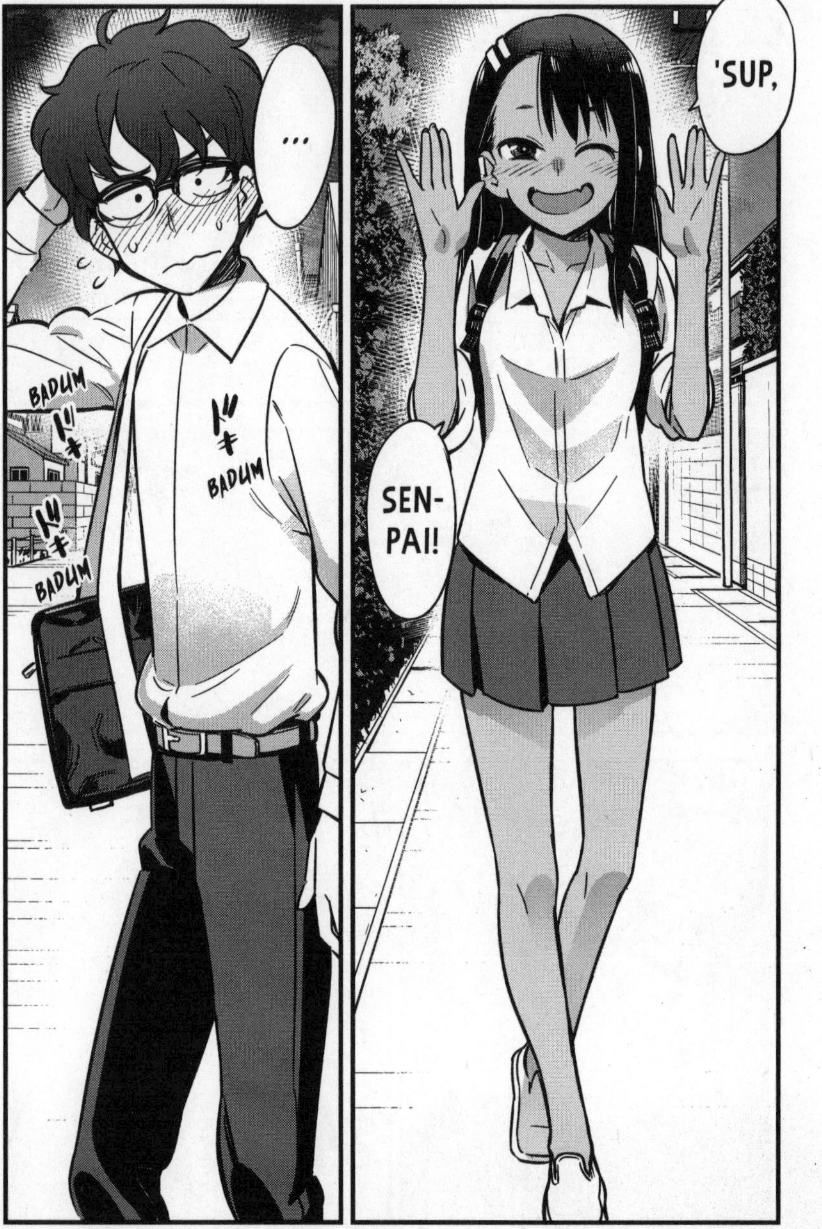
'SUP,
SEN-PAI!
...
ドキ
BADUM
BADUM
ドキ
ドキ
BADUM

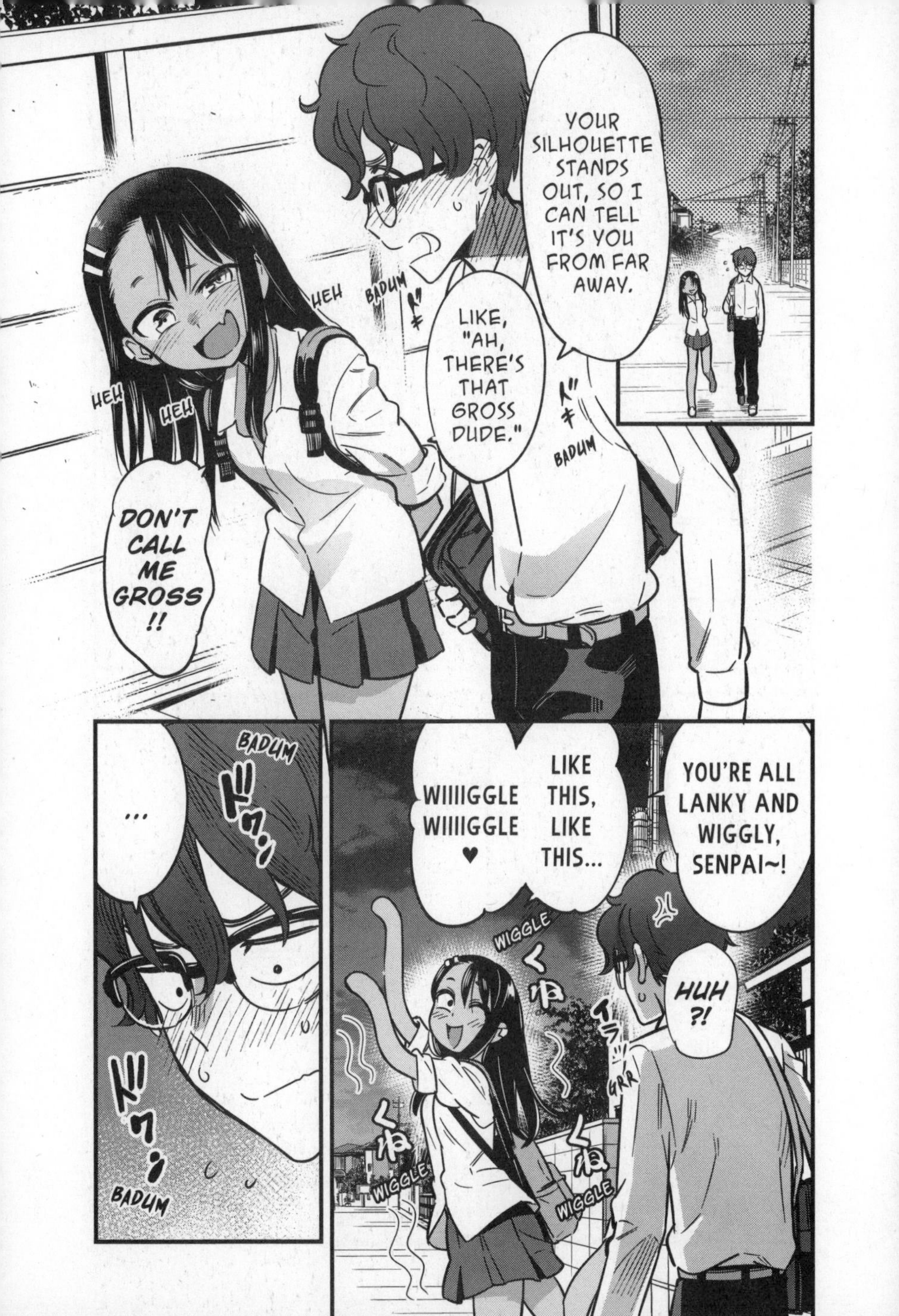
YOUR SILHOUETTE STANDS OUT, SO I CAN TELL IT'S YOU FROM FAR AWAY.
LIKE, "AH, THERE'S THAT GROSS DUDE."
BADUM
BADUM
HEH
HEH
HEH
DON'T CALL ME GROSS!!
YOU'RE ALL LANKY AND WIGGLY, SENPAI~!
LIKE THIS, LIKE THIS...
WIIIGGLE WIIIGGLE ♥
WIGGLE
HUH?!
GRR
WIGGLE
WIGGLE
BADUM
...
BADUM

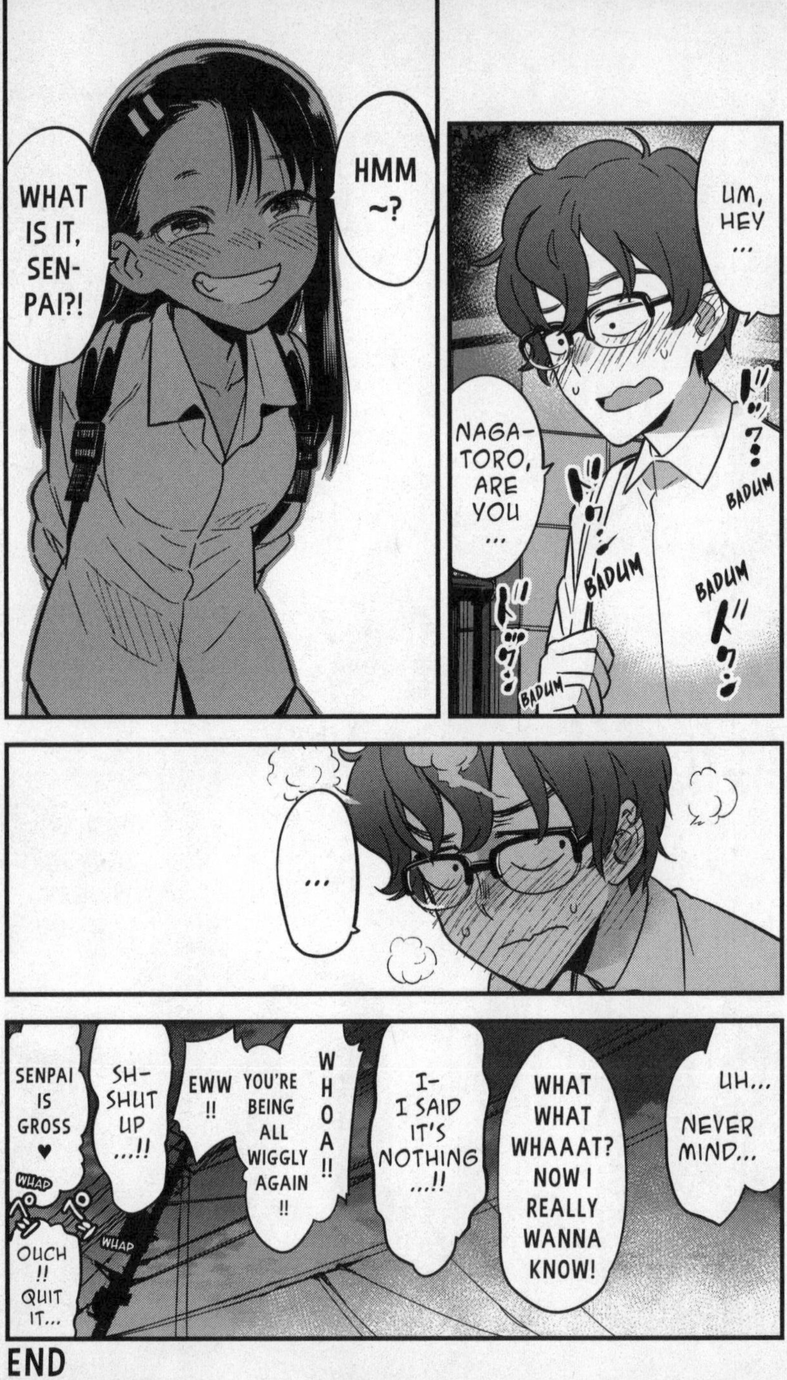
UM, HEY ...
NAGA-TORO, ARE YOU ...
BADUM
BADUM
BADUM
BADUM
HMM ~?
WHAT IS IT, SEN-PAI?!
...
UH... NEVER MIND...
WHAT WHAT WHAAAT? NOW I REALLY WANNA KNOW!
I- I SAID IT'S NOTHING ...!!
WHOA!!
YOU'RE BEING ALL WIGGLY AGAIN !!
EWW !!
SH- SHUT UP ...!!
SENPAI IS GROSS ♥
WHAP
WHAP
OUCH !! QUIT IT...

END

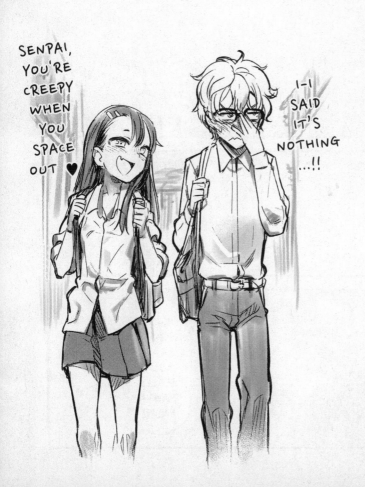

I-I SAID IT'S NOTHING ...!!
SENPAI, YOU'RE CREEPY WHEN YOU SPACE OUT ♥

DON'T TOY WITH ME, MISS NAGATORO

CHAPTER 7: SENPAI, YOU'RE STILL SOAPY...

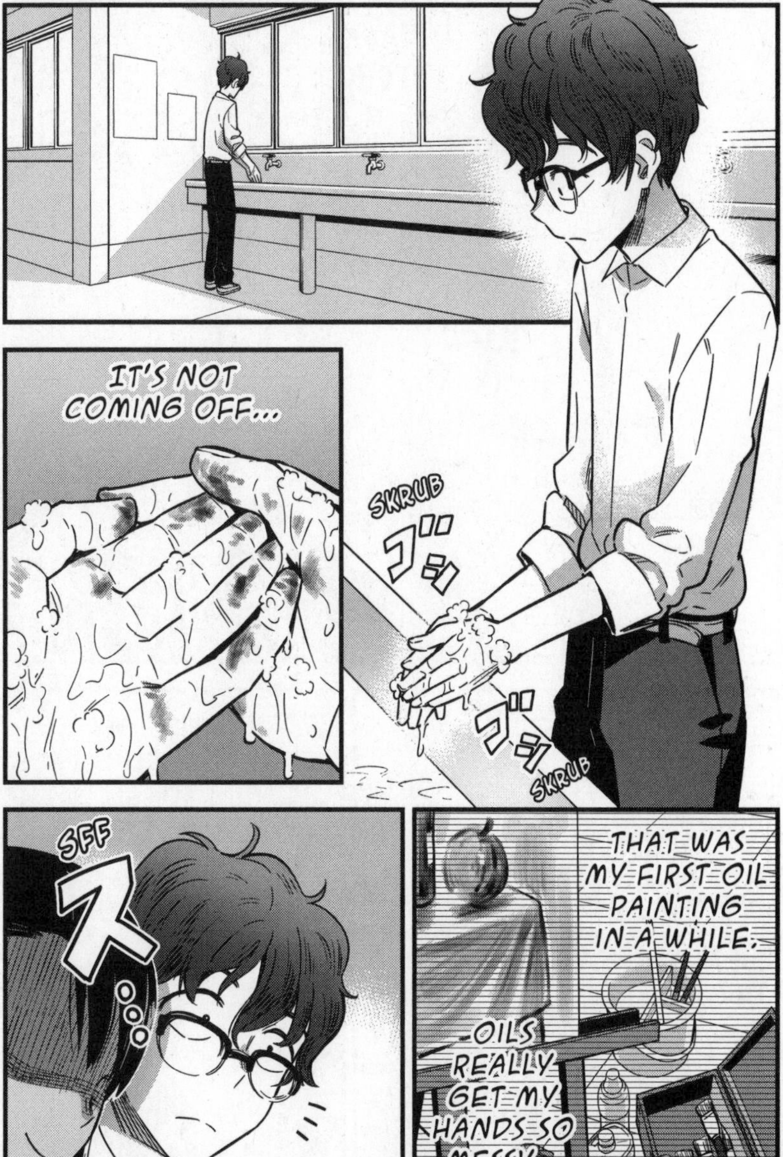
SKRUB
ゴシ
ゴシ
SKRUB
IT'S NOT COMING OFF...
THAT WAS MY FIRST OIL PAINTING IN A WHILE.
OILS REALLY GET MY HANDS SO MESSY...
SFF
ス

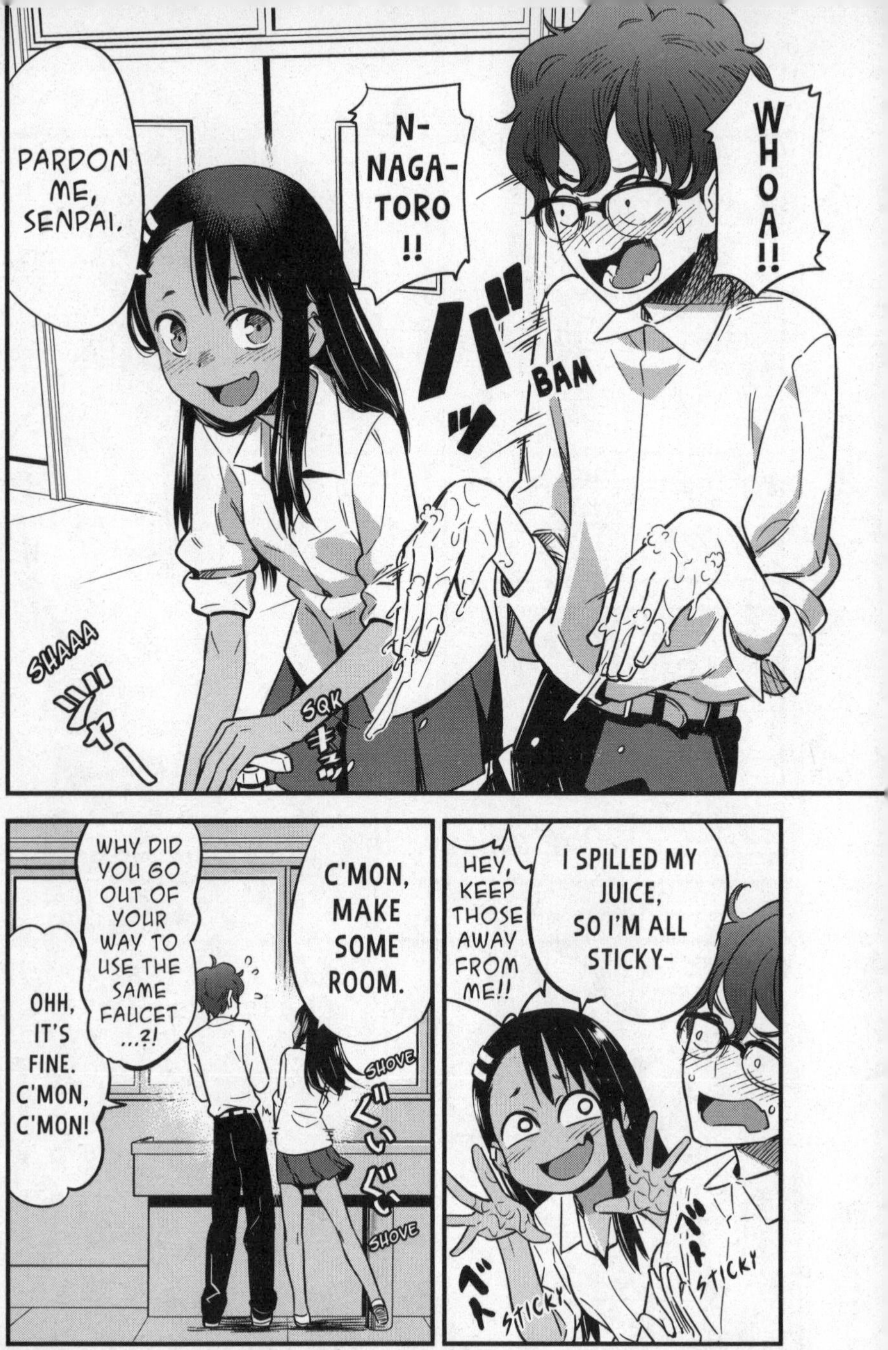
WHOA!!
N-NAGATORO!!
BAM
PARDON ME, SENPAI.
SHAAA
SQK
I SPILLED MY JUICE, SO I'M ALL STICKY-
HEY, KEEP THOSE AWAY FROM ME!!
STICKY
STICKY
C'MON, MAKE SOME ROOM.
WHY DID YOU GO OUT OF YOUR WAY TO USE THE SAME FAUCET ...?!
OHH, IT'S FINE. C'MON, C'MON!
SHOVE
SHOVE

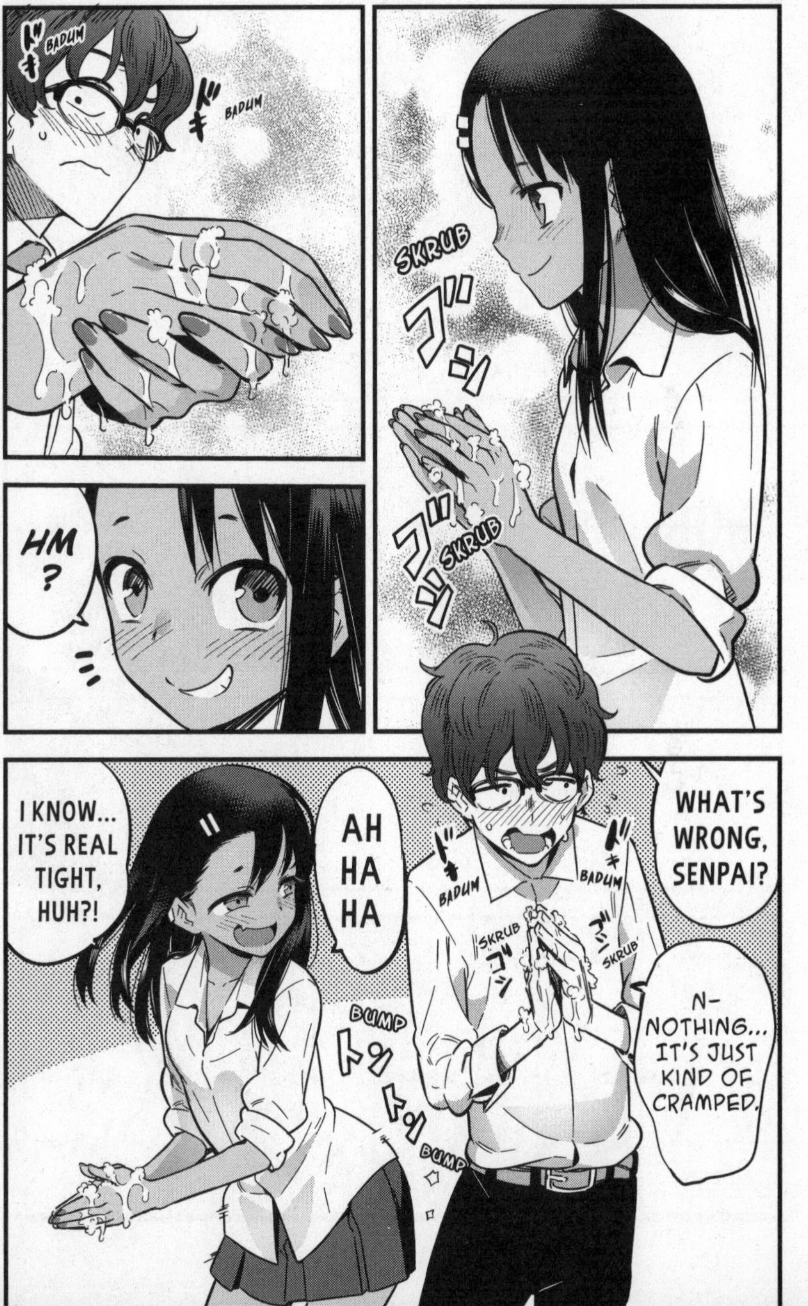
SKRUB
SKRUB
BADUM
BADUM
HM?
WHAT'S WRONG, SENPAI?
N-NOTHING... IT'S JUST KIND OF CRAMPED.
BADUM
BADUM
SKRUB
SKRUB
AH HA HA
I KNOW... IT'S REAL TIGHT, HUH?!
BUMP
BUMP

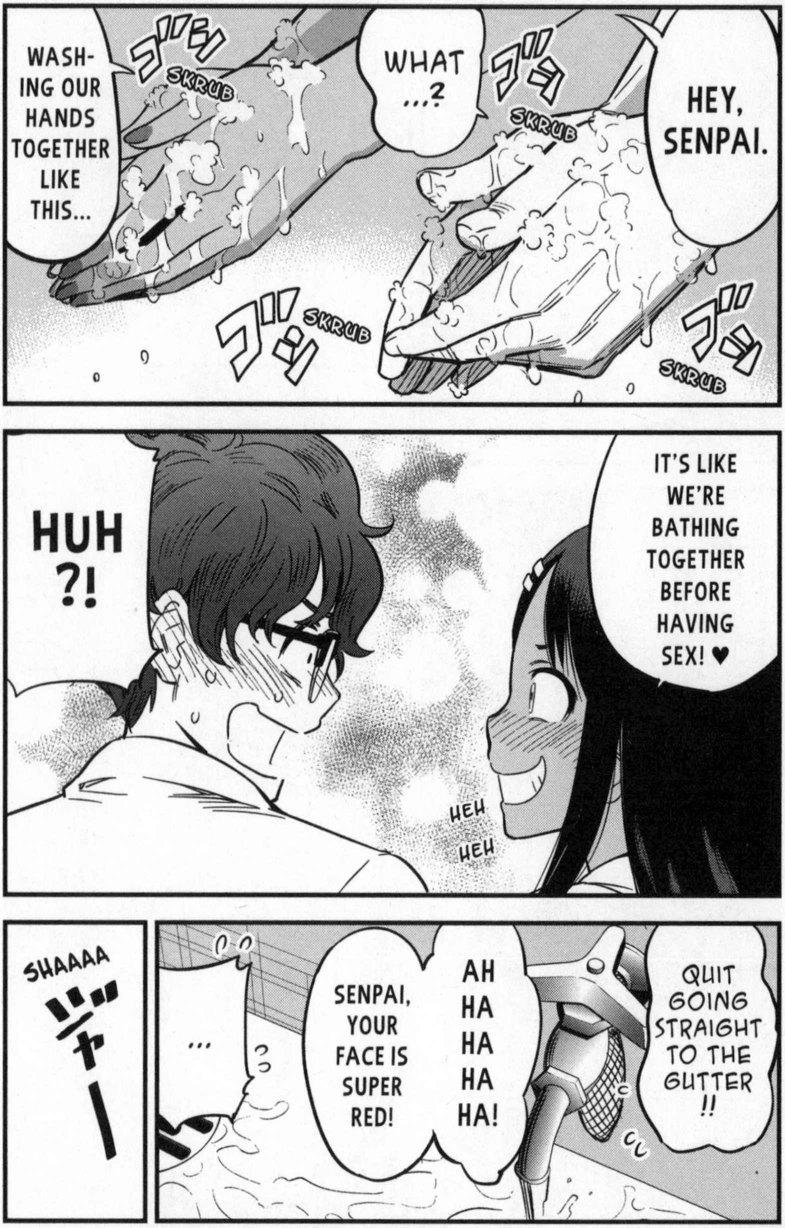
HEY, SENPAI.
WHAT ...?
SKRUB
SKRUB
WASHING OUR HANDS TOGETHER LIKE THIS...
SKRUB
SKRUB
IT'S LIKE WE'RE BATHING TOGETHER BEFORE HAVING SEX! ♥
HEH HEH
HUH ?!
QUIT GOING STRAIGHT TO THE GUTTER !!
AH HA HA HA HA HA!
SENPAI, YOUR FACE IS SUPER RED!
...
SHAAAA

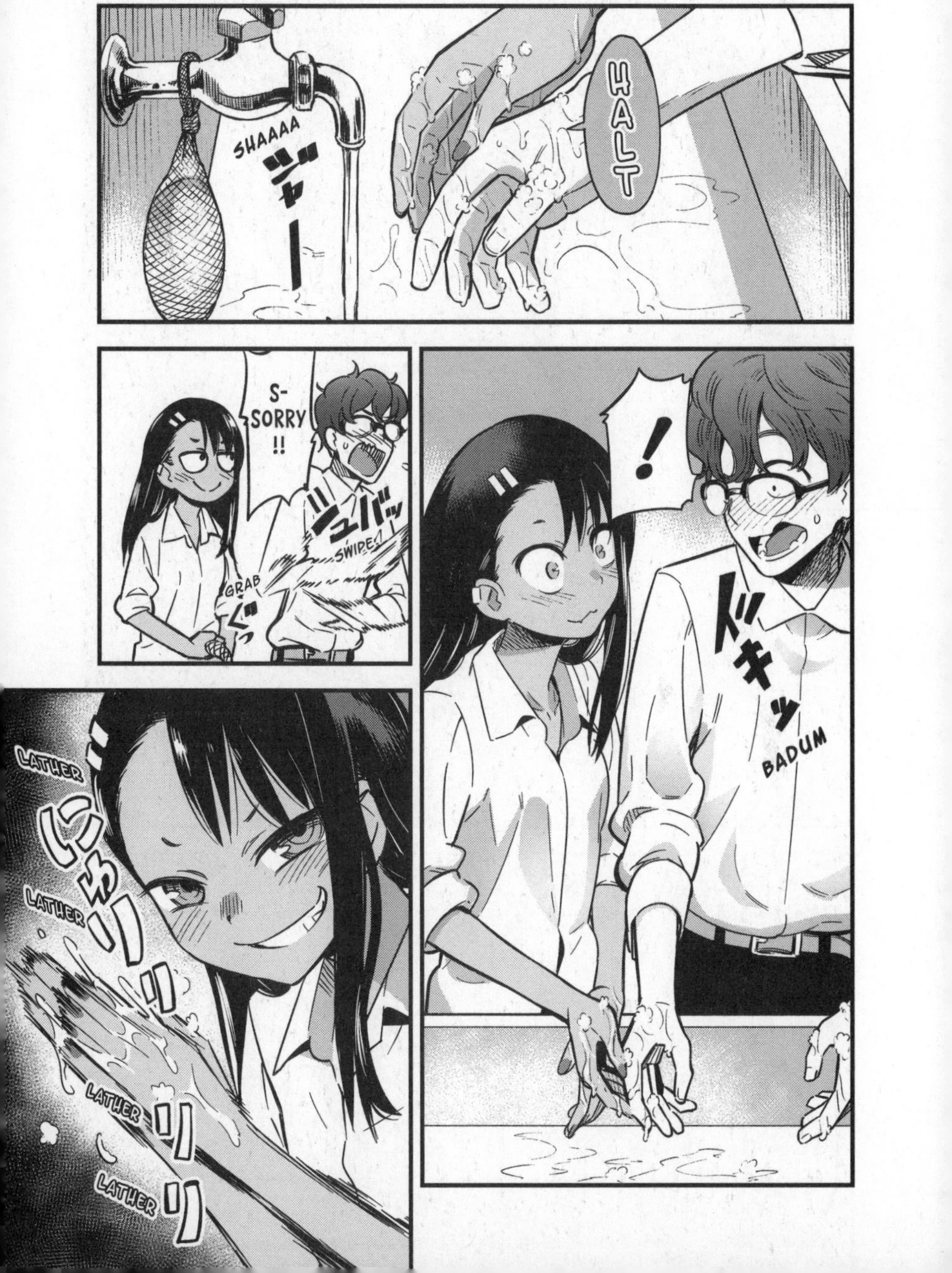
HALT
SHAAAA
ジャー
!
ドキッ
BADUM
S-SORRY!!
ジュバッ
SWIPE
GRAB
ぐっ
LATHER
LATHER
LATHER
LATHER

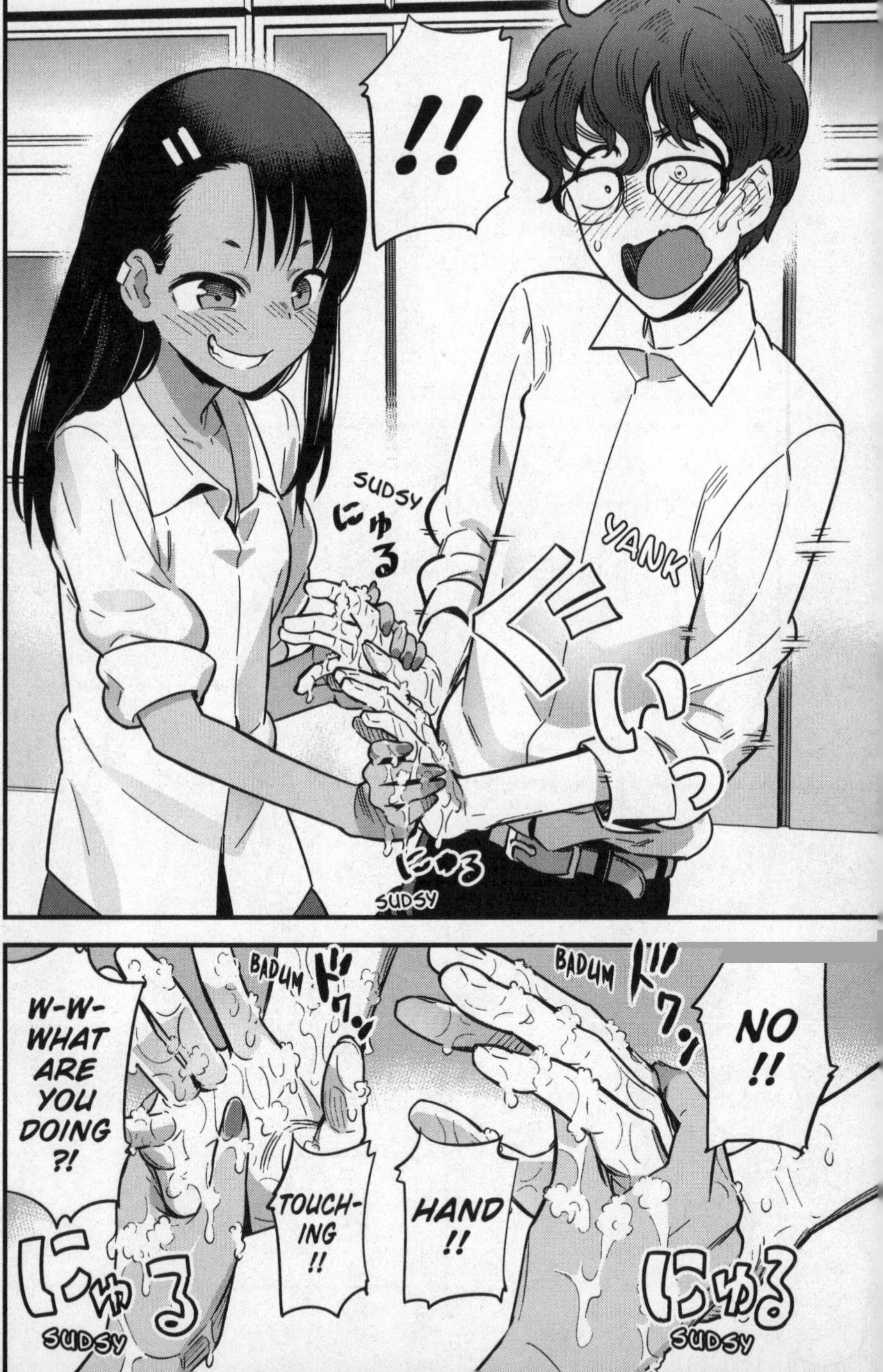
!!
YANK
ぐいっ
SUDSY
にゅる
にゅる
SUDSY
NO !!
BADUM
ドクッ
HAND !!
TOUCHING !!
BADUM
ドクッ
W-W-WHAT ARE YOU DOING ?!
にゅる
SUDSY
にゅる
SUDSY

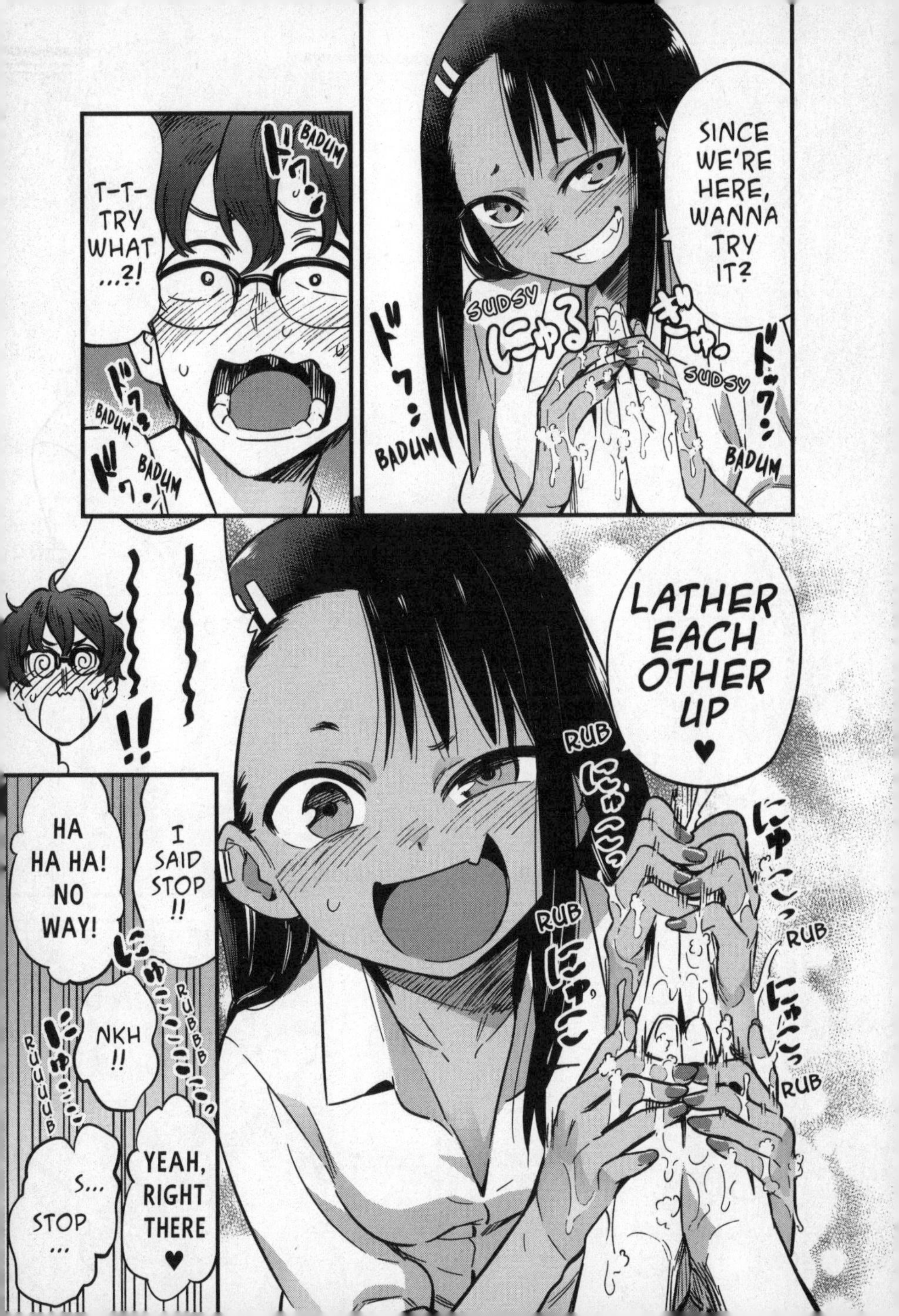
SINCE WE'RE HERE, WANNA TRY IT?
SUDSY
にゅる
SUDSY
BADUM
BADUM
BADUM
T-T-TRY WHAT ...?!
BADUM
BADUM
LATHER EACH OTHER UP ♥
RUB
RUB
RUB
RUB
!!
I SAID STOP !!
HA HA HA! NO WAY!
RUBBB
NKH !!
RUUUUB
YEAH, RIGHT THERE ♥
S... STOP ...

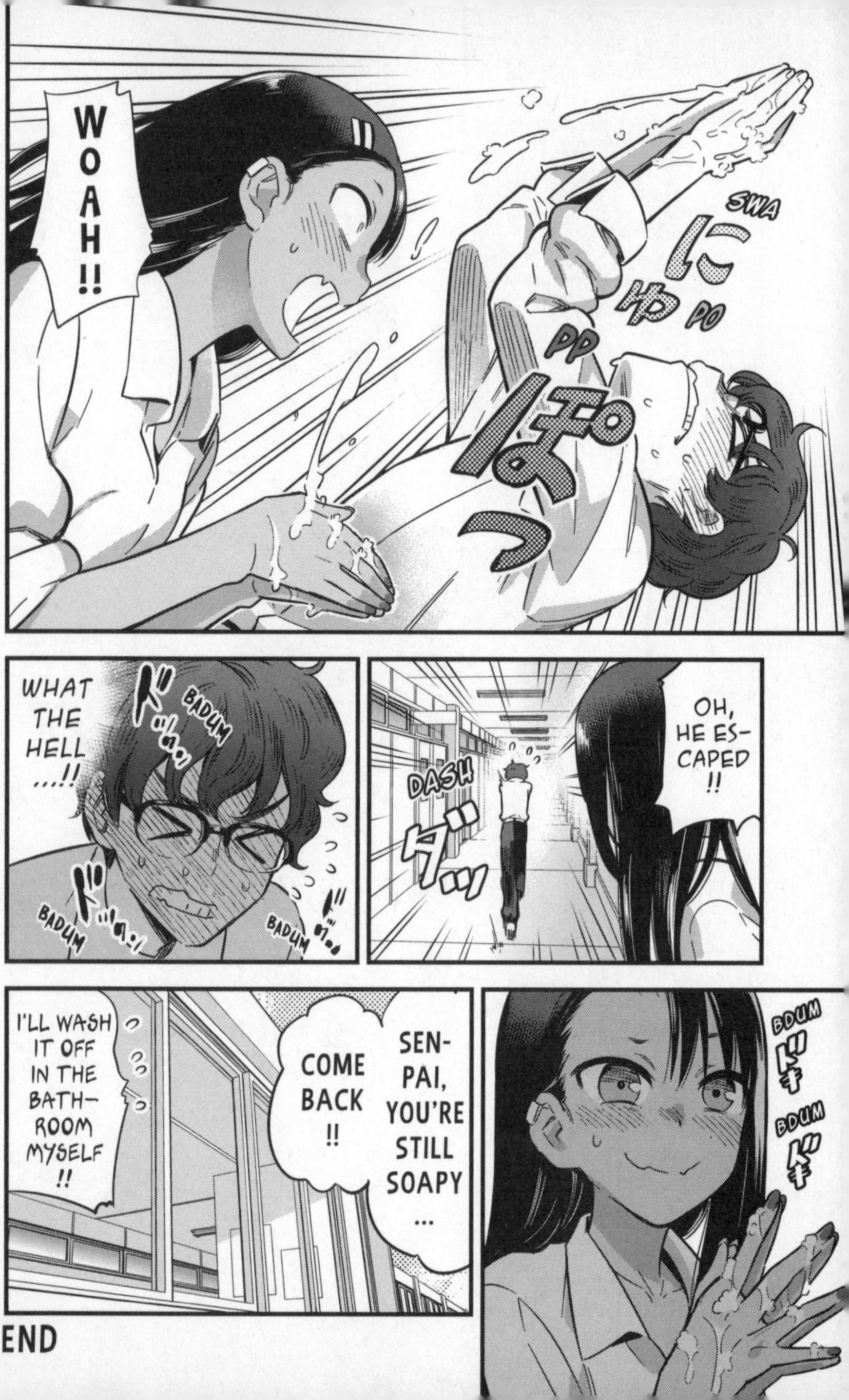
SWA
にゅ
PO
PP
ぽっ
WOAH!!
OH, HE ES-CAPED!!
DASH
ダッ
BADUM
WHAT THE HELL...!!
BADUM
BADUM
BDUM
ドキ
BDUM
ドキ
SEN-PAI, YOU'RE STILL SOAPY...
COME BACK!!
I'LL WASH IT OFF IN THE BATH-ROOM MYSELF!!

END

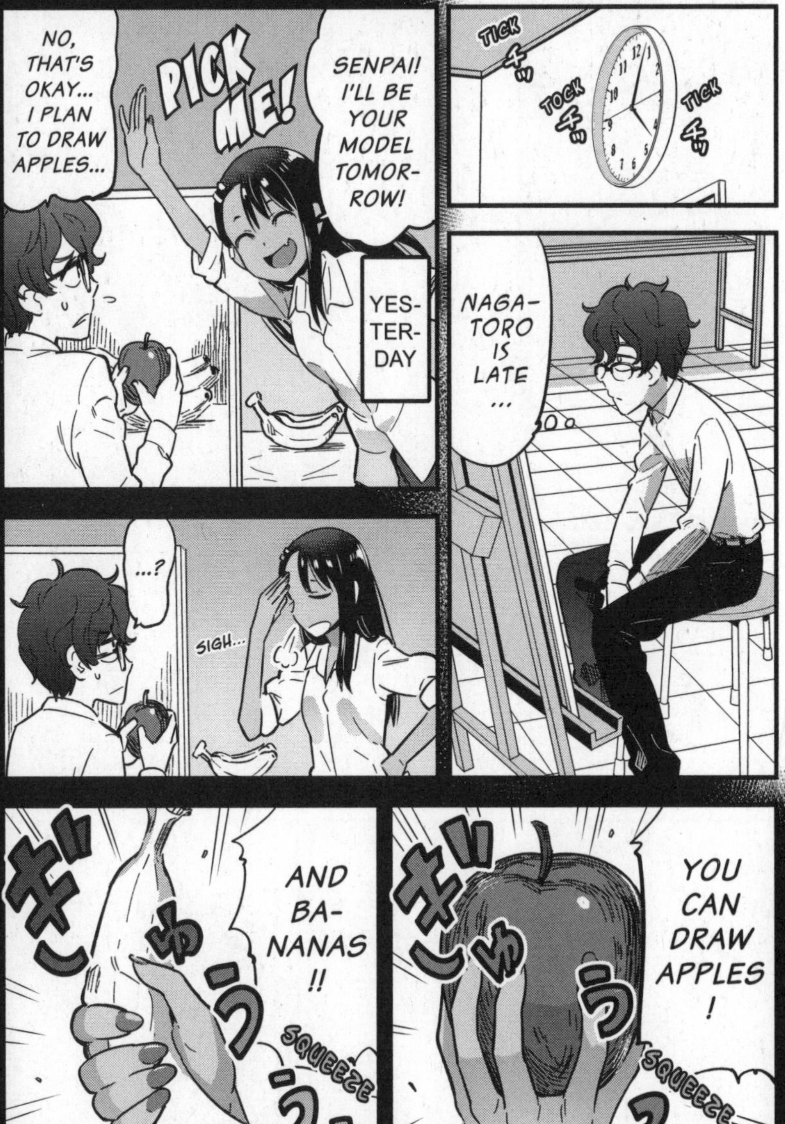
TICK
TOCK
TICK
NAGATORO IS LATE ...
YESTERDAY
SENPAI! I'LL BE YOUR MODEL TOMORROW!
PICK ME!
NO, THAT'S OKAY... I PLAN TO DRAW APPLES...
SIGH...
...?
YOU CAN DRAW APPLES!
SQUEEZE
AND BANANAS!!
SQUEEZE

CHAPTER 8: SENPAI NEEDS A LITTLE MORE...

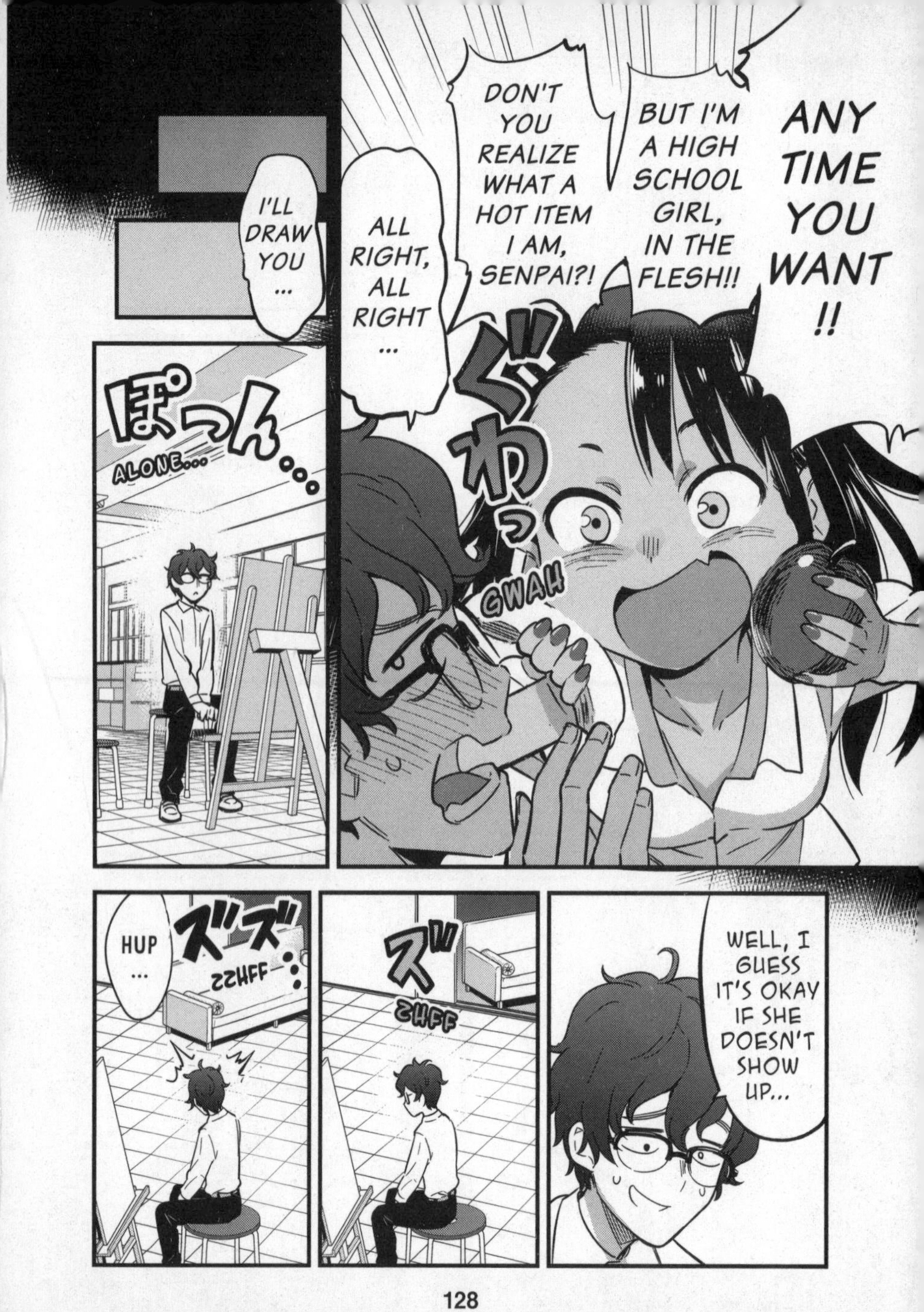
ANY TIME YOU WANT!!
BUT I'M A HIGH SCHOOL GIRL, IN THE FLESH!!
DON'T YOU REALIZE WHAT A HOT ITEM I AM, SENPAI?!
ぐわっ
GWAH
ALL RIGHT, ALL RIGHT...
I'LL DRAW YOU...
ぽつん…
ALONE...
WELL, I GUESS IT'S OKAY IF SHE DOESN'T SHOW UP...
ズ
ZHFF
HUP...
ズズ…
ZZHFF

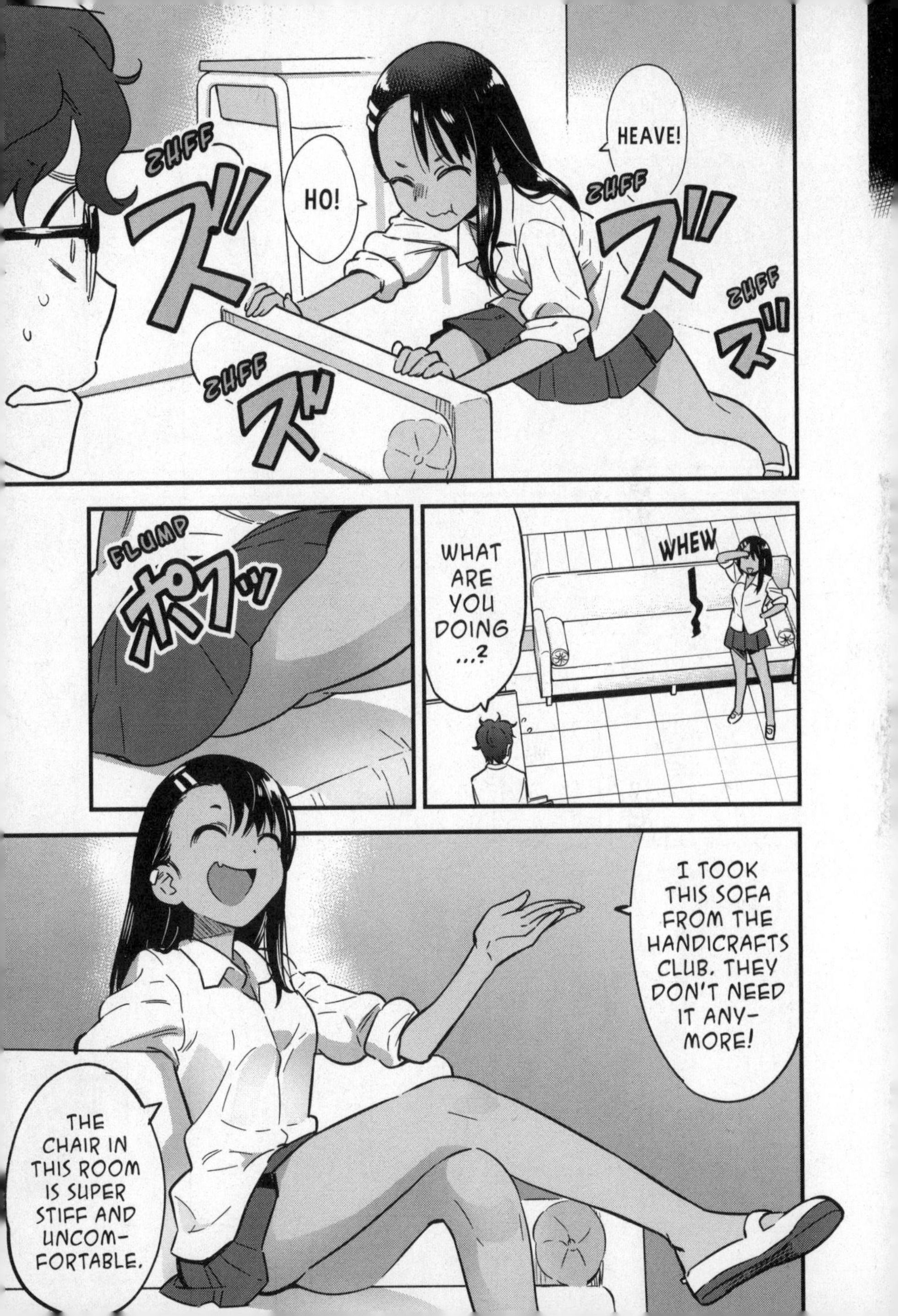
HEAVE!
ZHFF
ズズ
ZHFF
ズ
HO!
ZHFF
ズズ
ZHFF
ズ
WHAT ARE YOU DOING ...?
WHEW
FLUMP
ポフッ
I TOOK THIS SOFA FROM THE HANDICRAFTS CLUB. THEY DON'T NEED IT ANY-MORE!
THE CHAIR IN THIS ROOM IS SUPER STIFF AND UNCOM-FORTABLE.

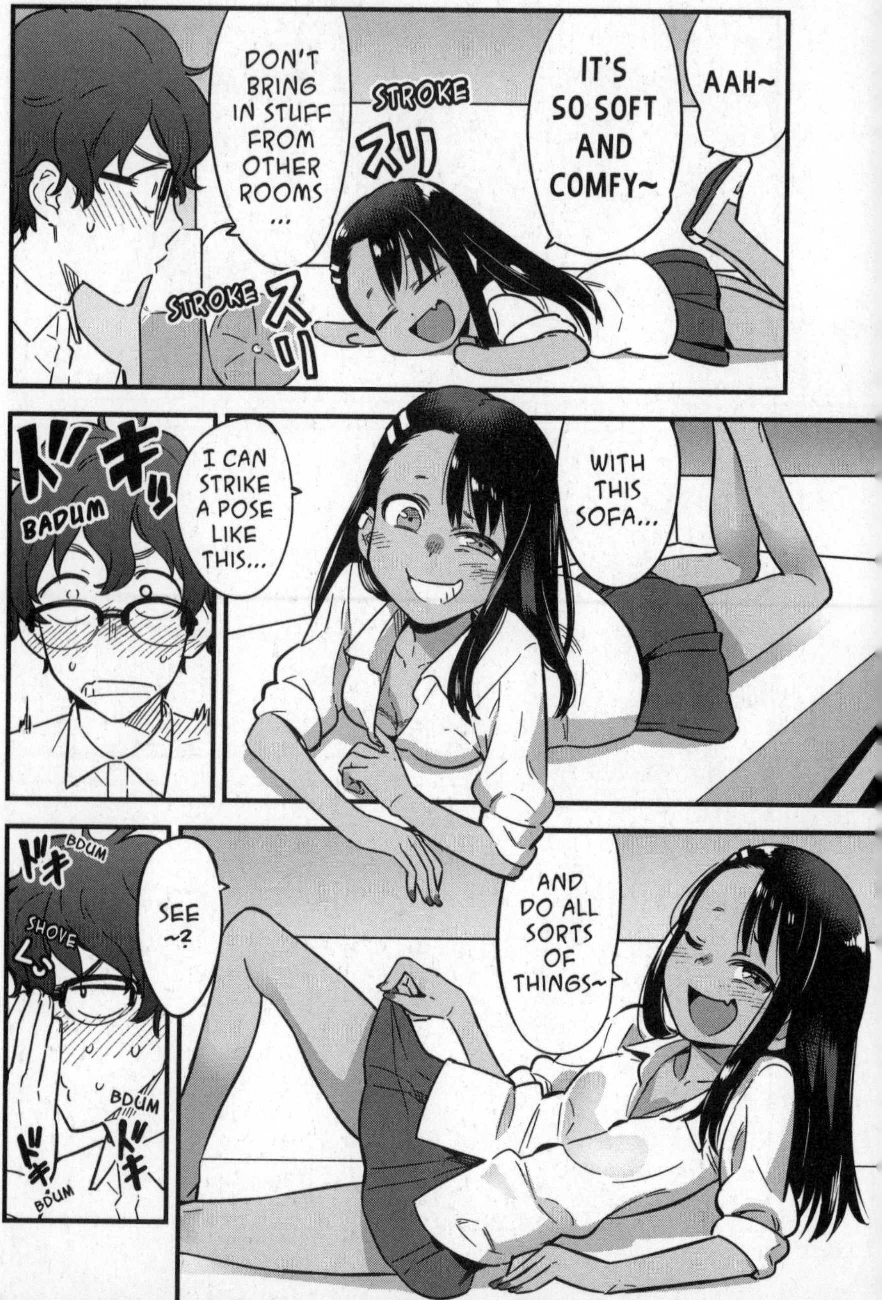
AAH~
IT'S SO SOFT AND COMFY~
STROKE
スリ
DON'T BRING IN STUFF FROM OTHER ROOMS ...
STROKE
スリ
WITH THIS SOFA...
I CAN STRIKE A POSE LIKE THIS...
ドキッ
BADUM
AND DO ALL SORTS OF THINGS~
SEE ~?
ドキ
BDUM
SHOVE
BDUM
ドキドキ
BDUM

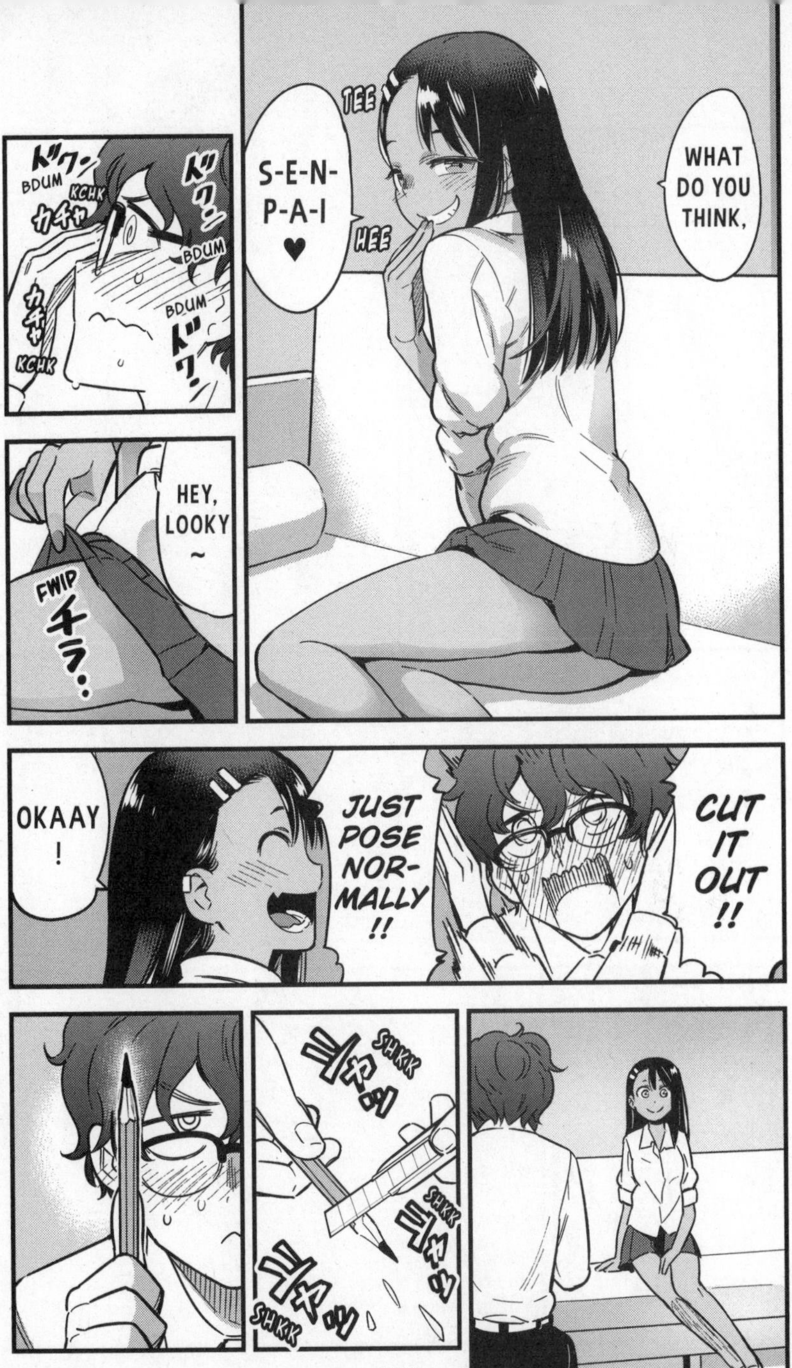
WHAT DO YOU THINK,
TEE
HEE
S-E-N-P-A-I ♥
BDUM
BDUM
BDUM
KCHK
KCHK
HEY, LOOKY ~
FWIP
CUT IT OUT !!
JUST POSE NOR-MALLY !!
OKAAY !
SHKK
SHKK
SHKK

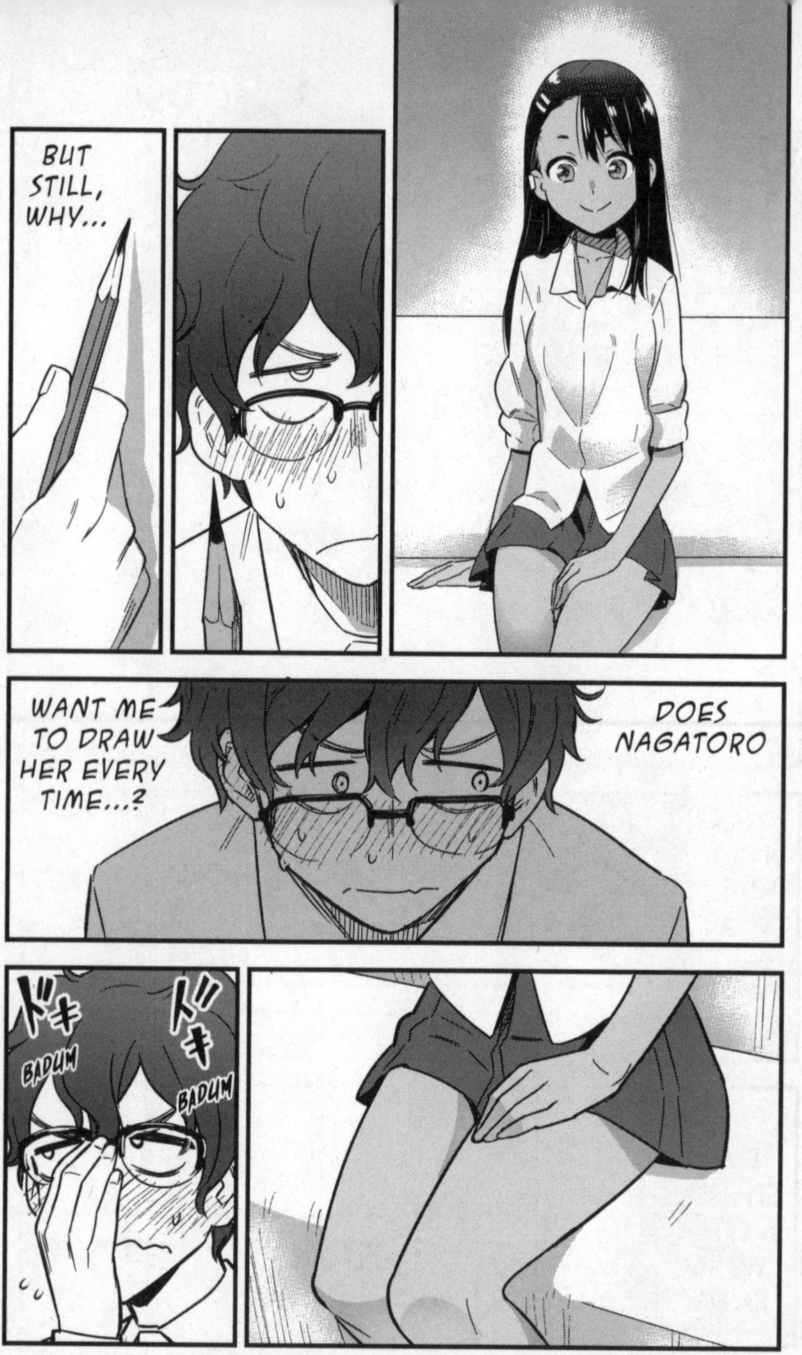
BUT STILL, WHY...
DOES NAGATORO
WANT ME TO DRAW HER EVERY TIME...?
ドキ
BADUM
ドキ
BADUM

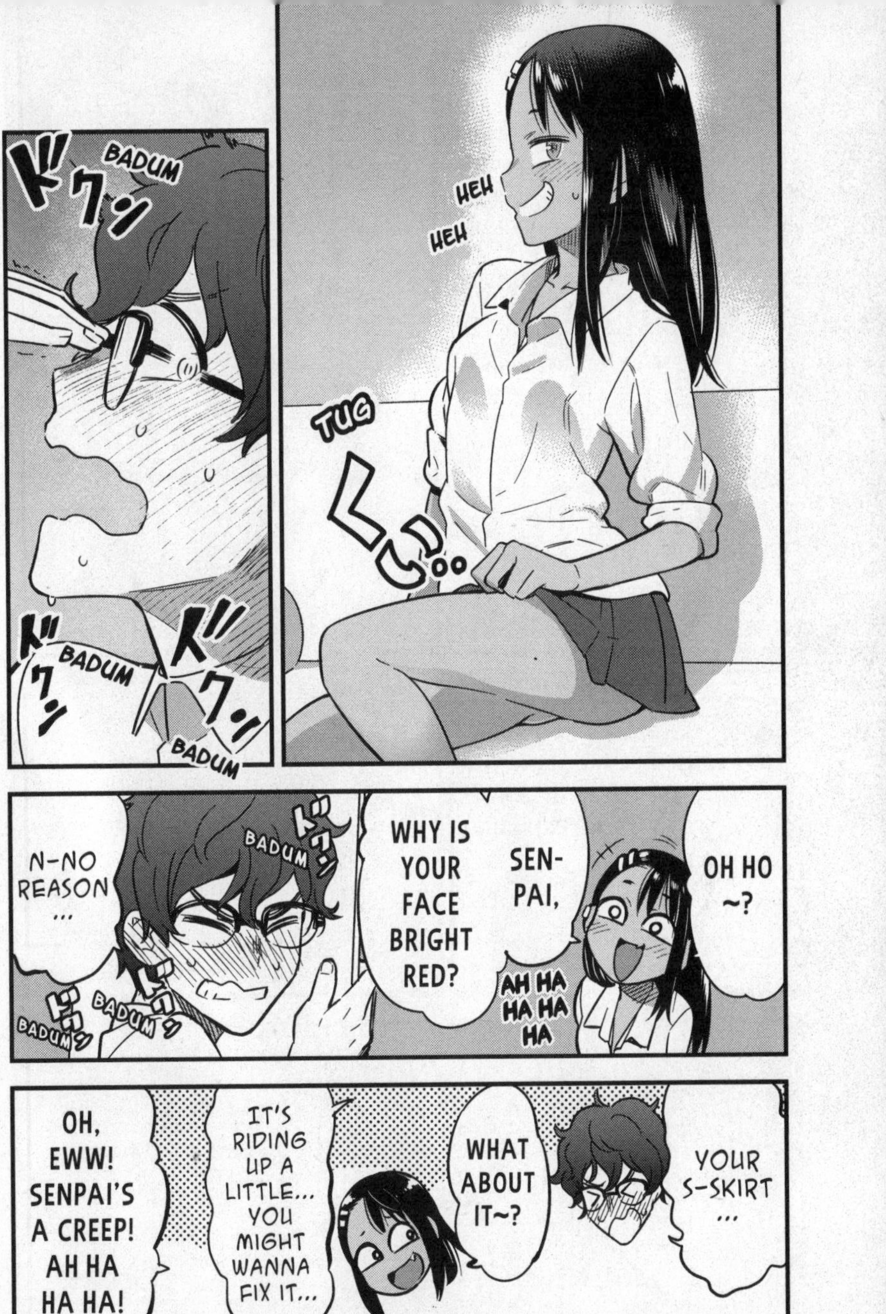
HEH
HEH
TUG
BADUM
BADUM
BADUM
BADUM
OH HO ~?
SEN-PAI,
WHY IS YOUR FACE BRIGHT RED?
AH HA HA HA HA HA
BADUM
N-NO REASON ...
BADUM
BADUM
YOUR S-SKIRT ...
WHAT ABOUT IT~?
IT'S RIDING UP A LITTLE... YOU MIGHT WANNA FIX IT...
OH, EWW! SENPAI'S A CREEP! AH HA HA HA!

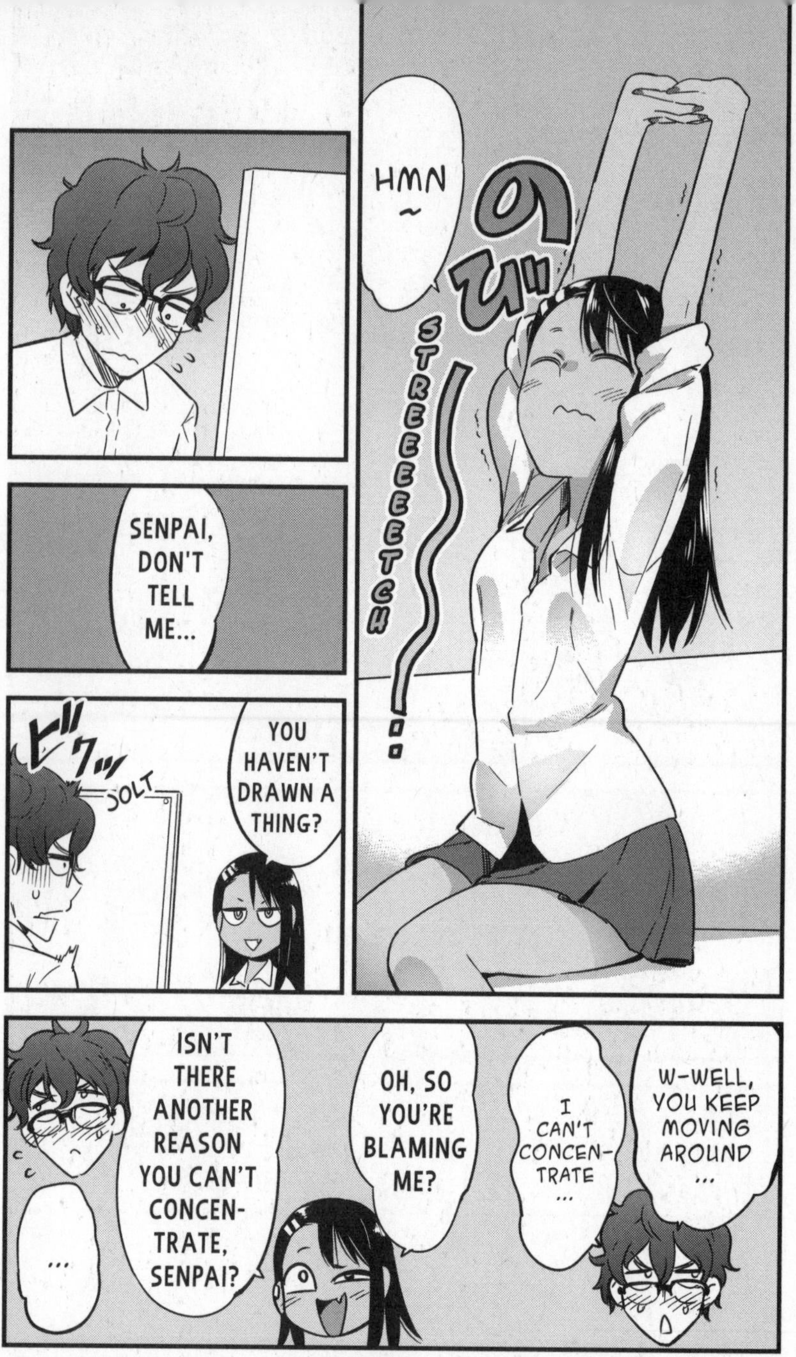
HMN ~
のび
STREEEEEETCH...!
SENPAI, DON'T TELL ME...
ビクッ
JOLT
YOU HAVEN'T DRAWN A THING?
W-WELL, YOU KEEP MOVING AROUND...
I CAN'T CONCENTRATE...
OH, SO YOU'RE BLAMING ME?
ISN'T THERE ANOTHER REASON YOU CAN'T CONCENTRATE, SENPAI?
...

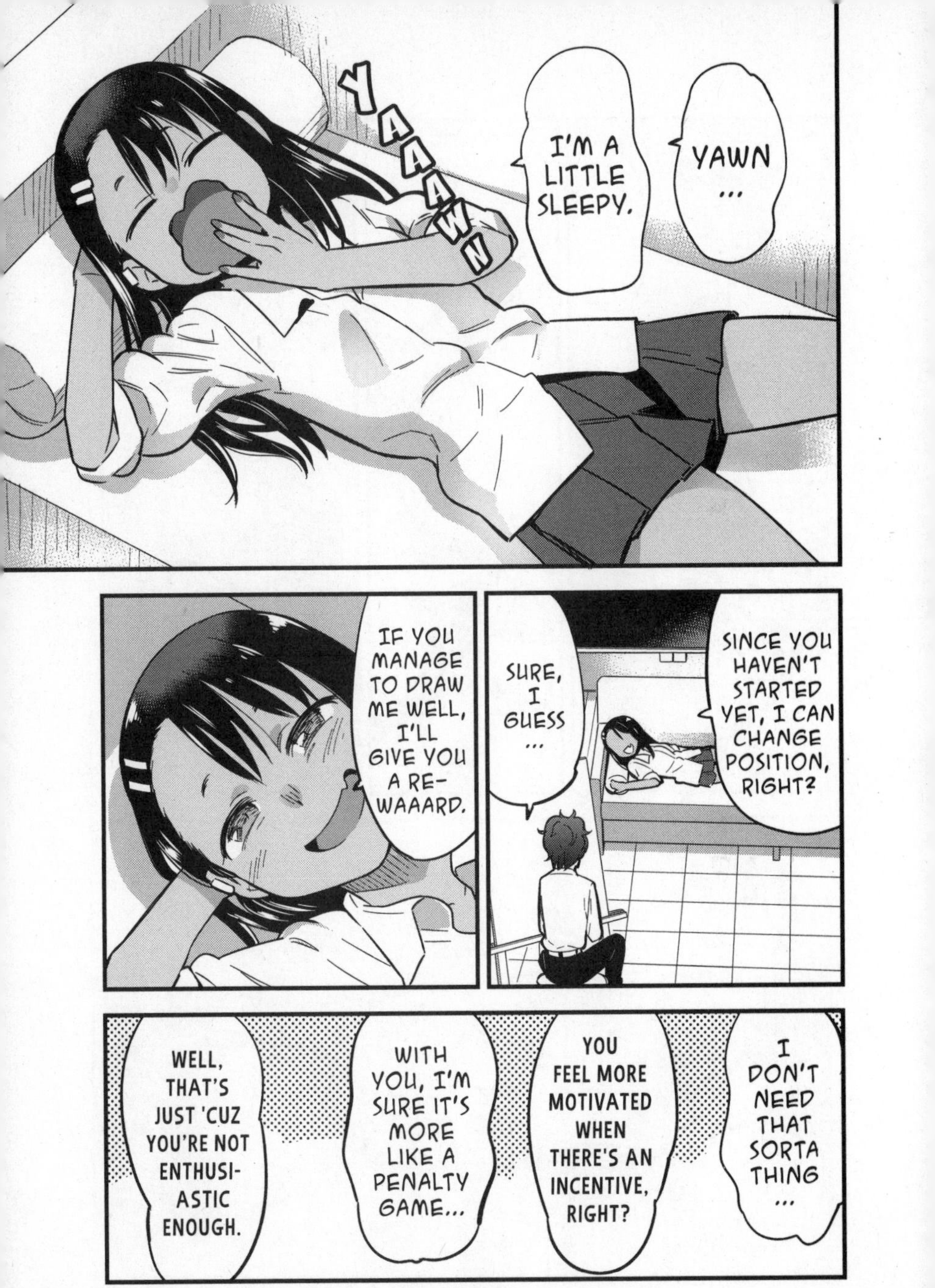
YAWN ...
YAAAAWN
I'M A LITTLE SLEEPY.
SINCE YOU HAVEN'T STARTED YET, I CAN CHANGE POSITION, RIGHT?
SURE, I GUESS ...
IF YOU MANAGE TO DRAW ME WELL, I'LL GIVE YOU A RE-WAAARD.
I DON'T NEED THAT SORTA THING ...
YOU FEEL MORE MOTIVATED WHEN THERE'S AN INCENTIVE, RIGHT?
WITH YOU, I'M SURE IT'S MORE LIKE A PENALTY GAME...
WELL, THAT'S JUST 'CUZ YOU'RE NOT ENTHUSI-ASTIC ENOUGH.

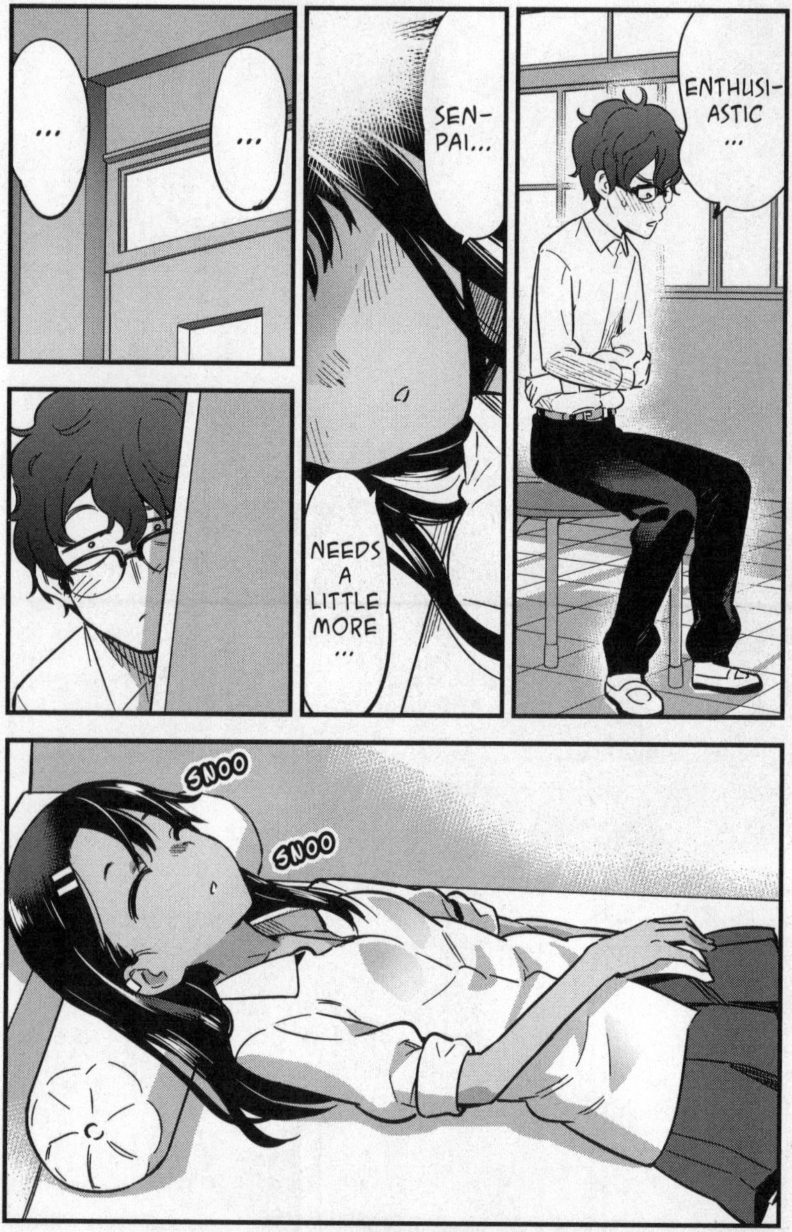
ENTHUSI-ASTIC ...
SEN-PAI...
NEEDS A LITTLE MORE ...
...
...
SNOO
SNOO

IS SHE ASLEEP ...?

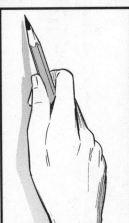

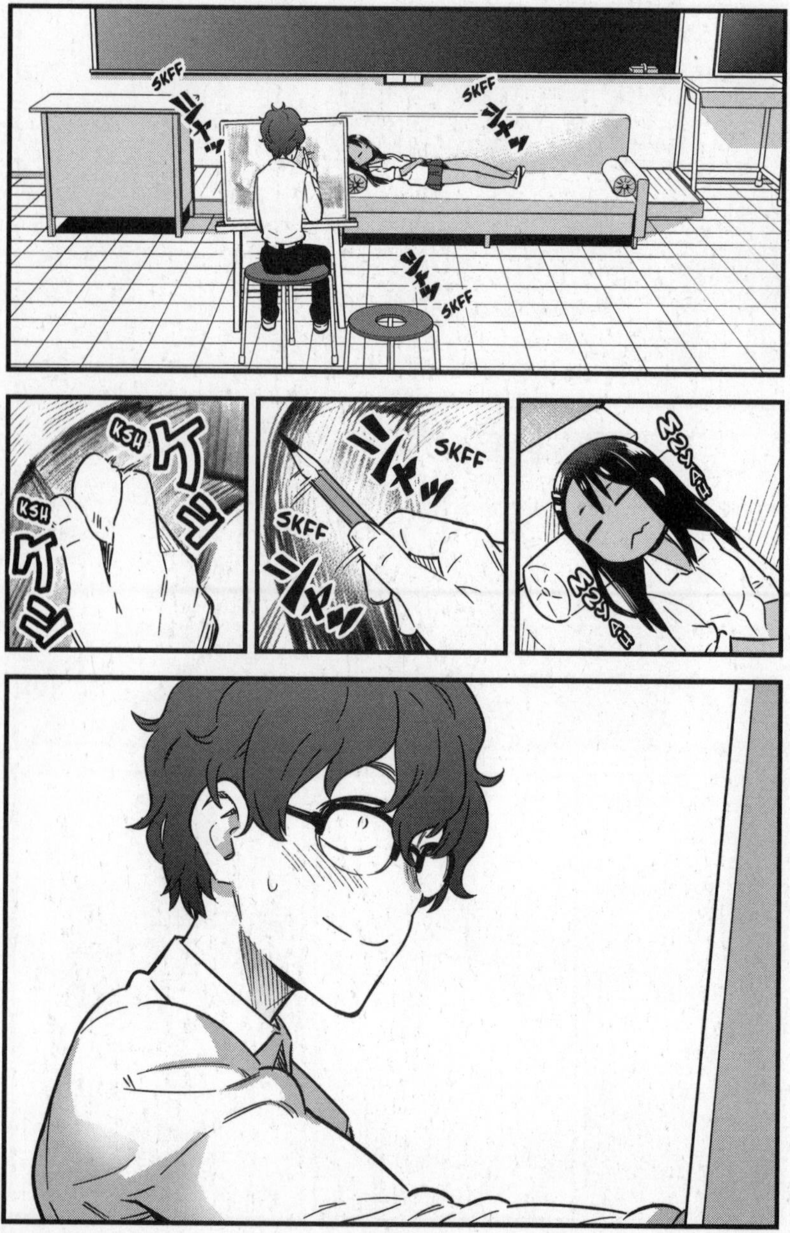
SKFF
SKFF
SKFF
SKFF
SKFF
KSH
KSH

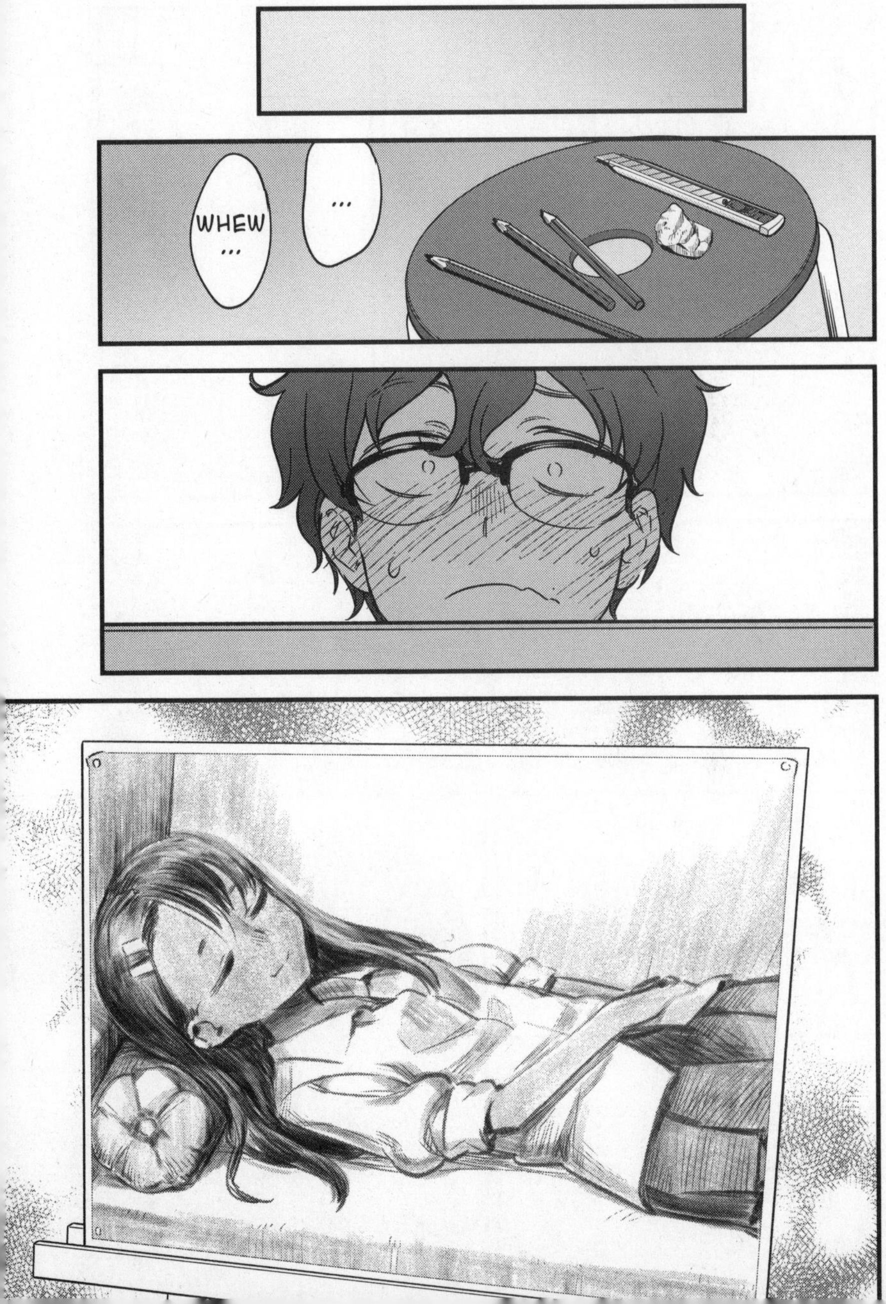
...
WHEW ...

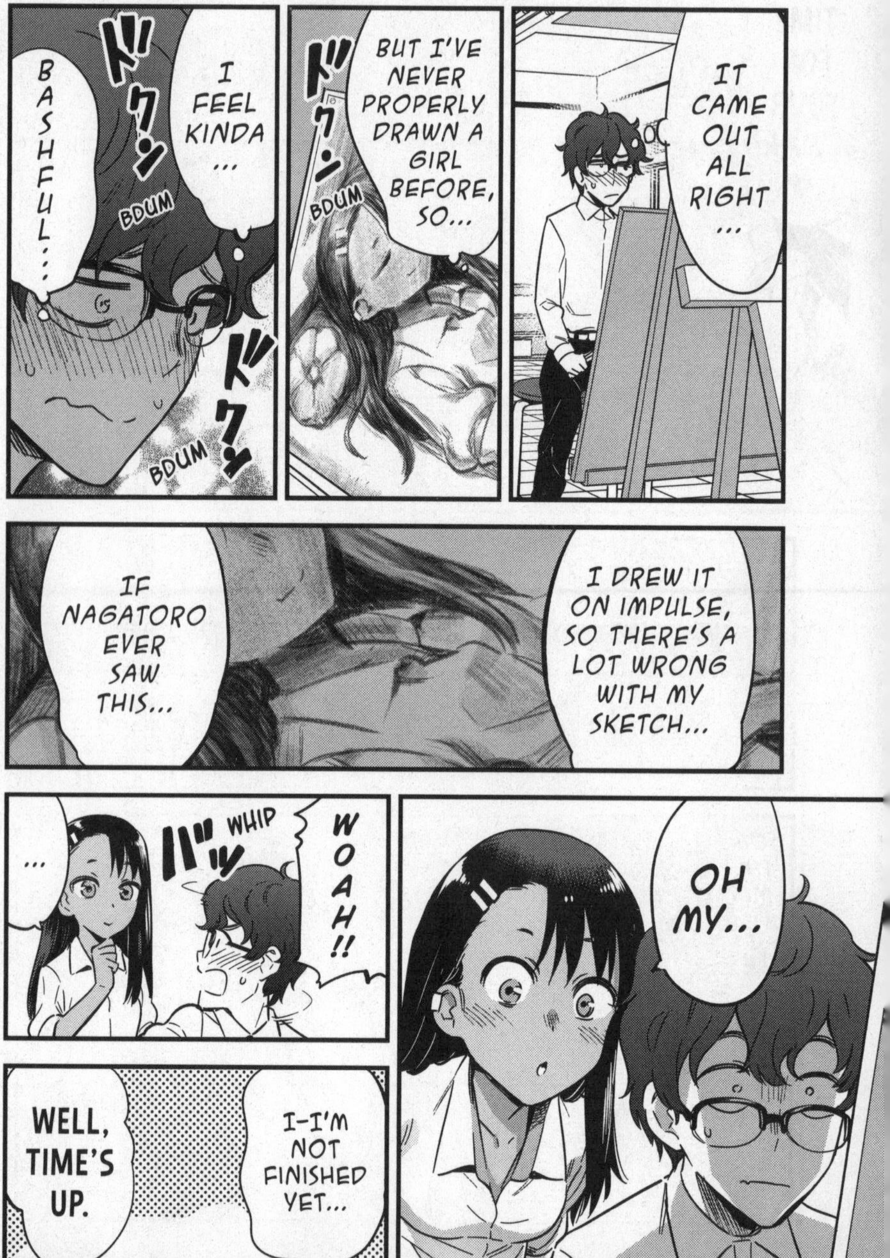
IT CAME OUT ALL RIGHT...
BUT I'VE NEVER PROPERLY DRAWN A GIRL BEFORE, SO...
BDUM
I FEEL KINDA...
BASHFUL...
BDUM
BDUM
I DREW IT ON IMPULSE, SO THERE'S A LOT WRONG WITH MY SKETCH...
IF NAGATORO EVER SAW THIS...
OH MY...
WOAH!!
WHIP
...
I-I'M NOT FINISHED YET...
WELL, TIME'S UP.

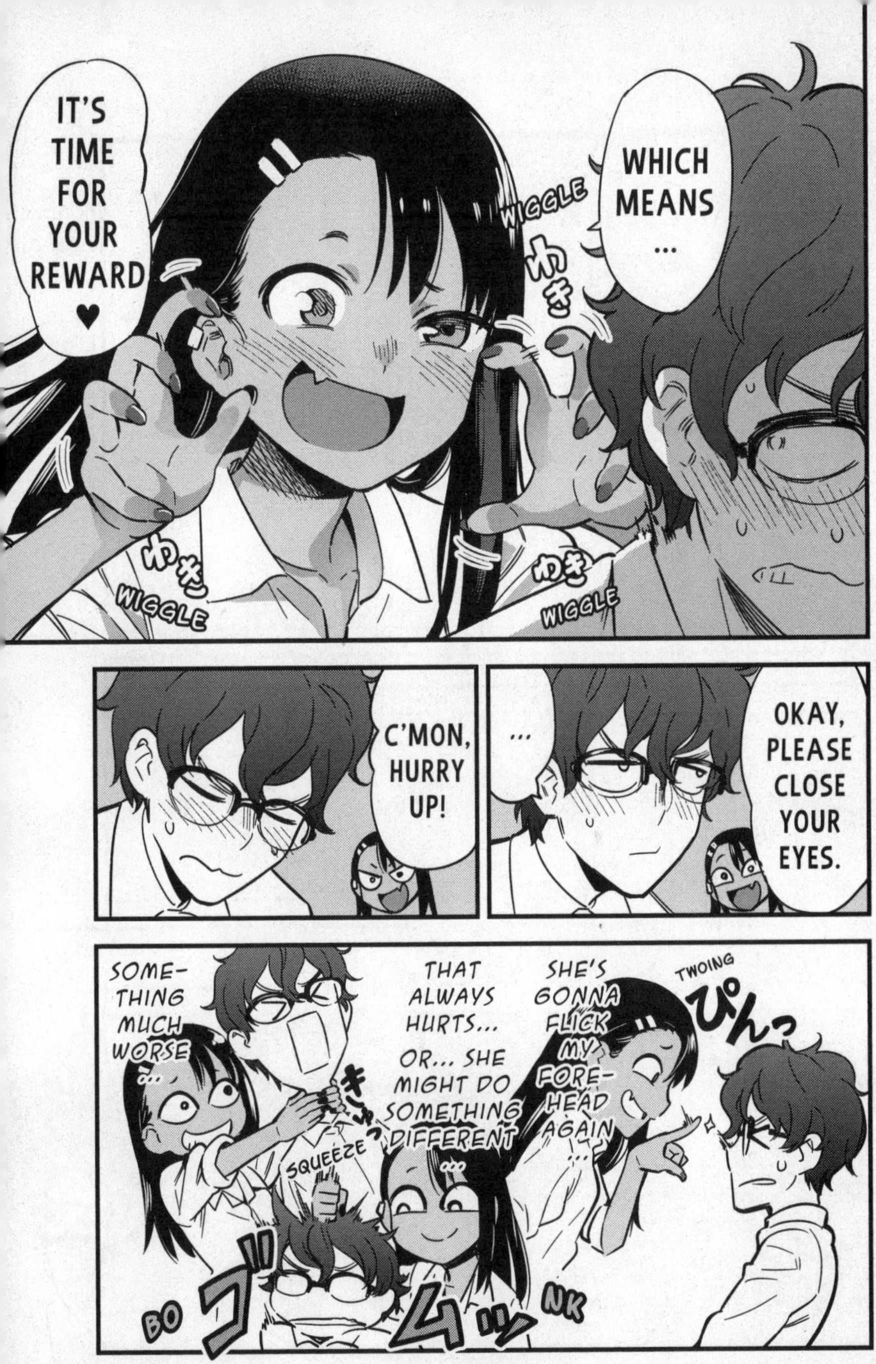
WHICH MEANS ...
WIGGLE
わき
IT'S TIME FOR YOUR REWARD ♥
わき
WIGGLE
わき
WIGGLE
OKAY, PLEASE CLOSE YOUR EYES.
...
C'MON, HURRY UP!
TWOING
ぴんっ
SHE'S GONNA FLICK MY FOREHEAD AGAIN ...
THAT ALWAYS HURTS...
OR... SHE MIGHT DO SOMETHING DIFFERENT ...
SOME-THING MUCH WORSE ...
きゅっ
SQUEEZE
BO ゴムッ NK

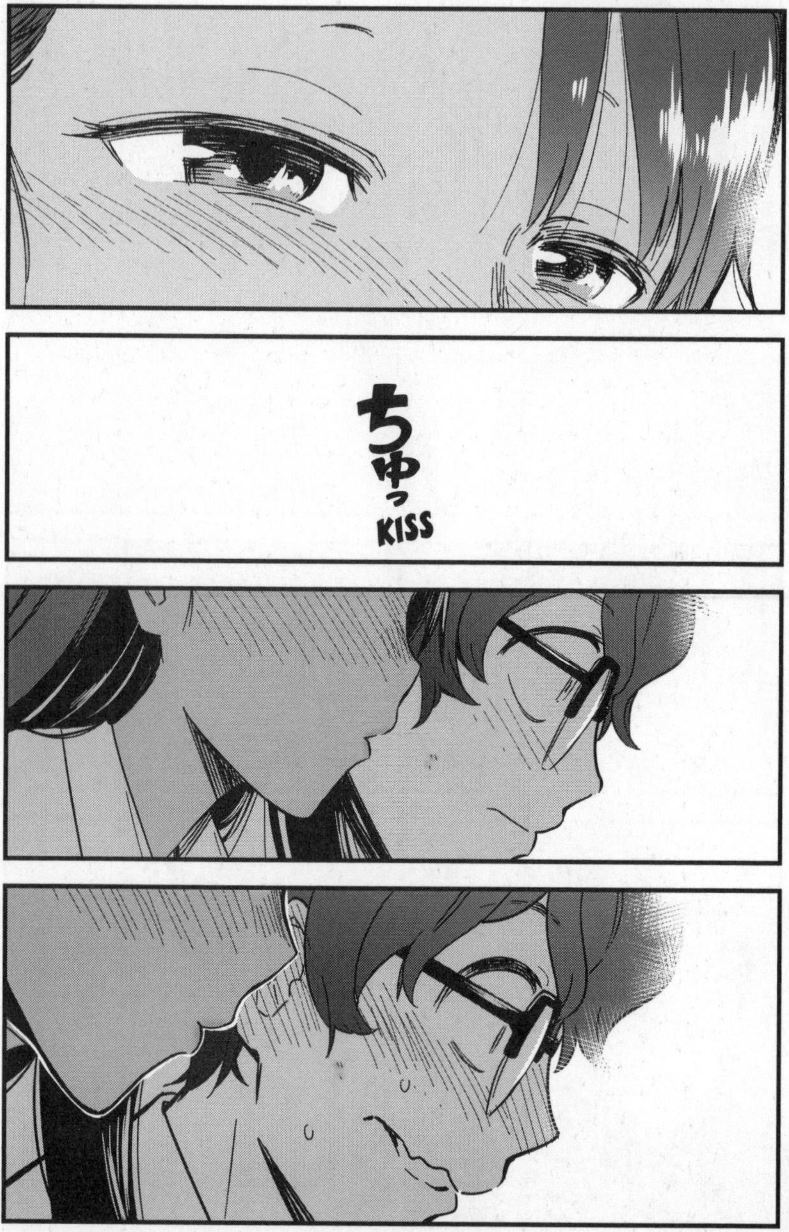
ちゅっ
KISS

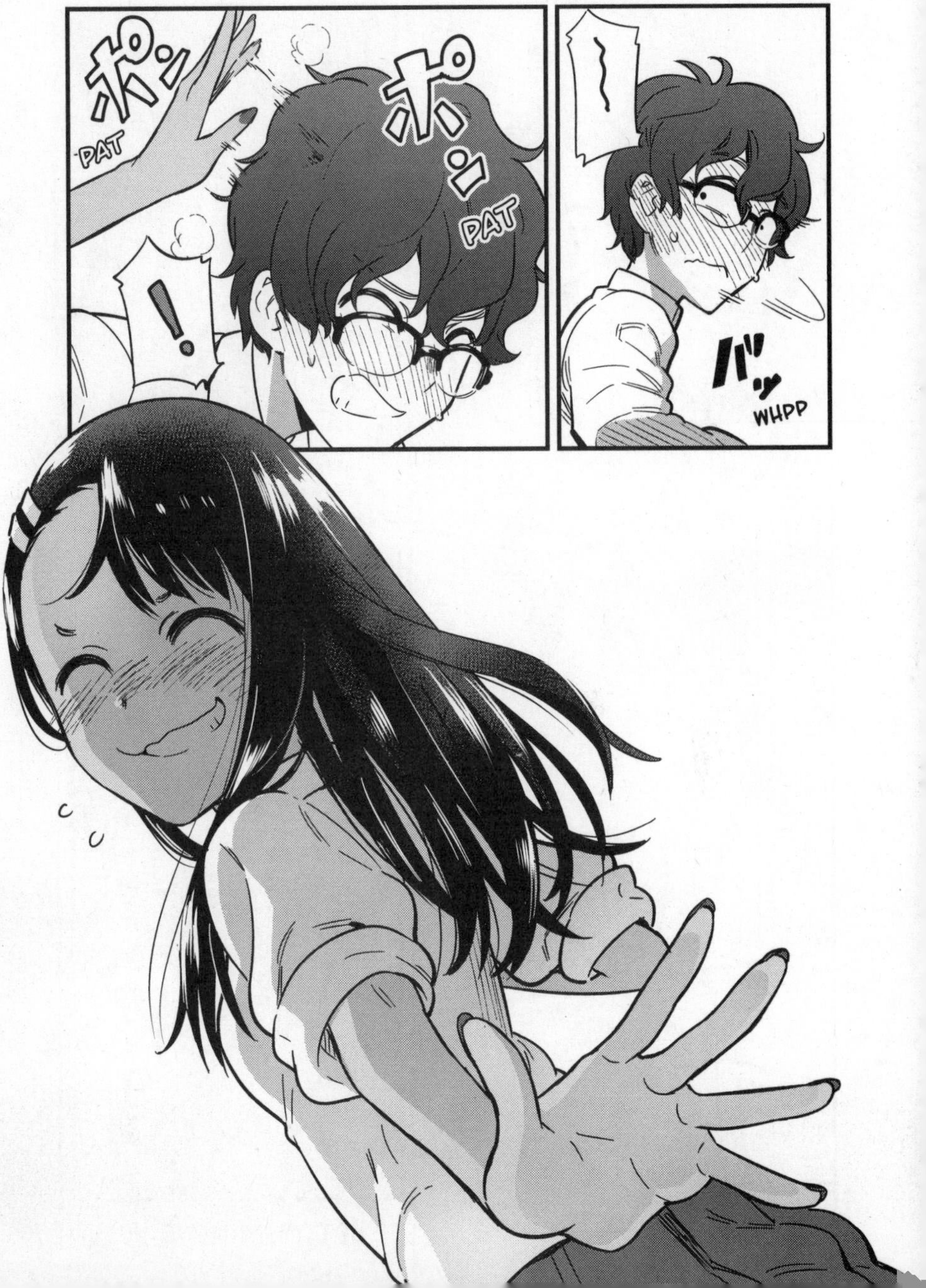
バッ
WHPP
ポン
PAT
ポン
PAT
!

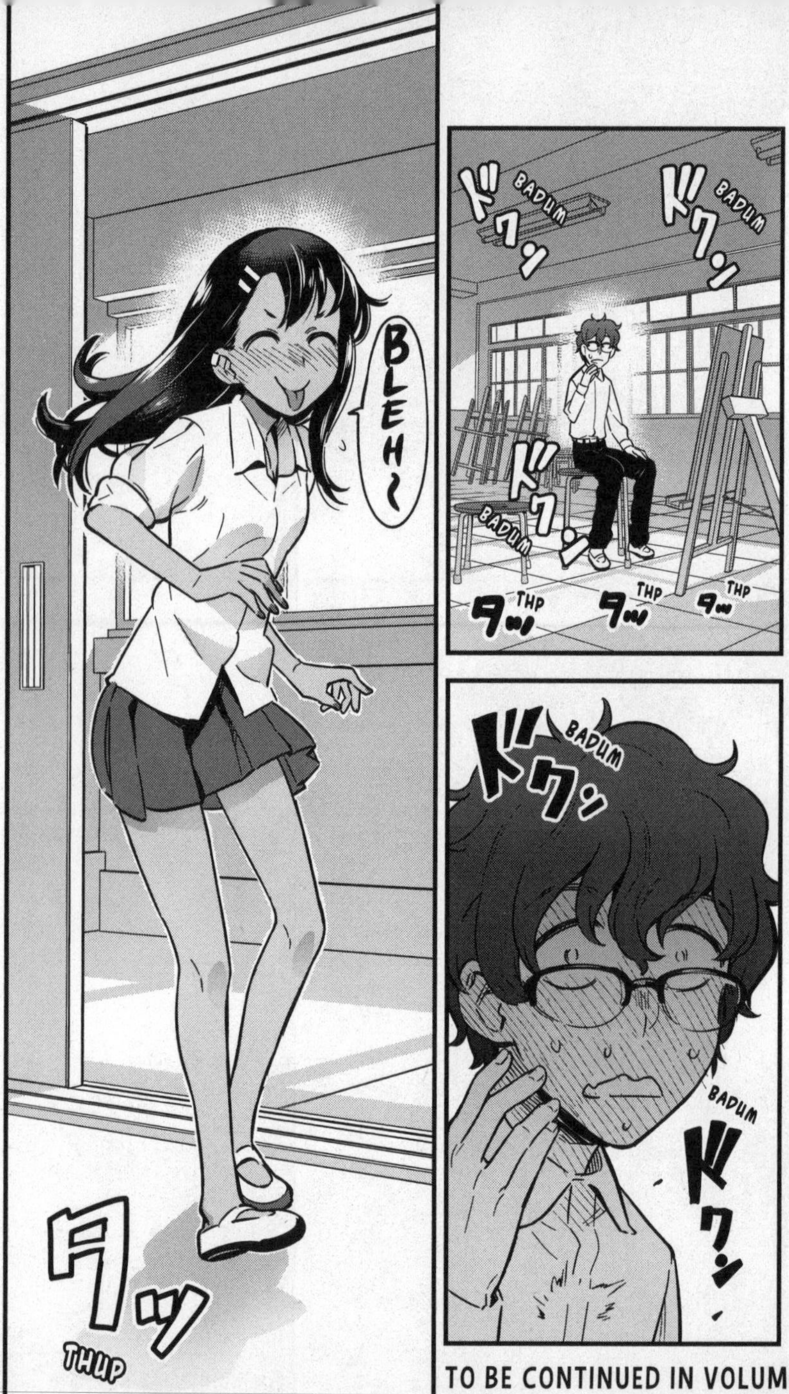

ドクン
BADUM
ドクン
BADUM
ドクン
BADUM
タッ
THP
タッ
THP
タッ
THP
ドクン
BADUM
ドクン
BADUM
BLEH~
タッ
THUMP

TO BE CONTINUED IN VOLUME 2!

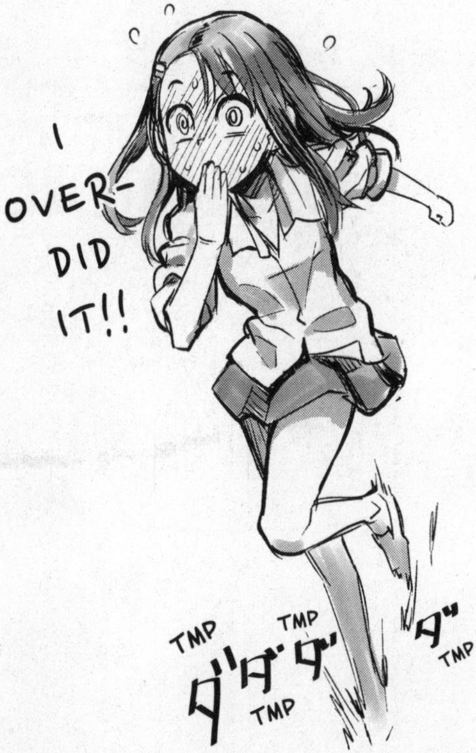
I OVER-DID IT!!
ダ
TMP
ダダダ
TMP TMP TMP

DON'T TOY WITH ME,
MISS NAGATORO

BONUS ①: DID SOMEONE GIVE SENPAI CHOCOLATE...?

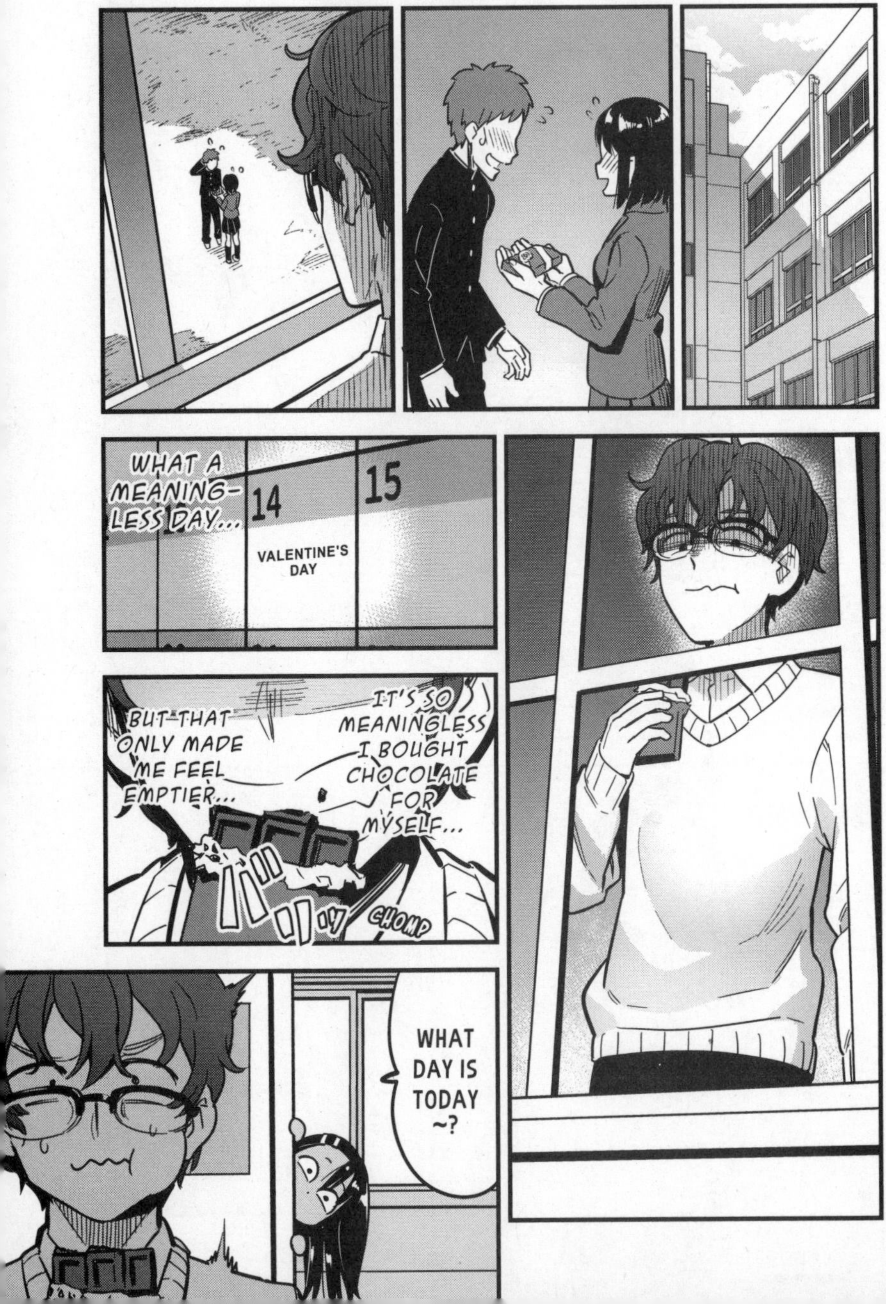
15
14
WHAT A MEANINGLESS DAY...
VALENTINE'S DAY
IT'S SO MEANINGLESS I BOUGHT CHOCOLATE FOR MYSELF...
BUT THAT ONLY MADE ME FEEL EMPTIER...
CHOMP
WHAT DAY IS TODAY ~?

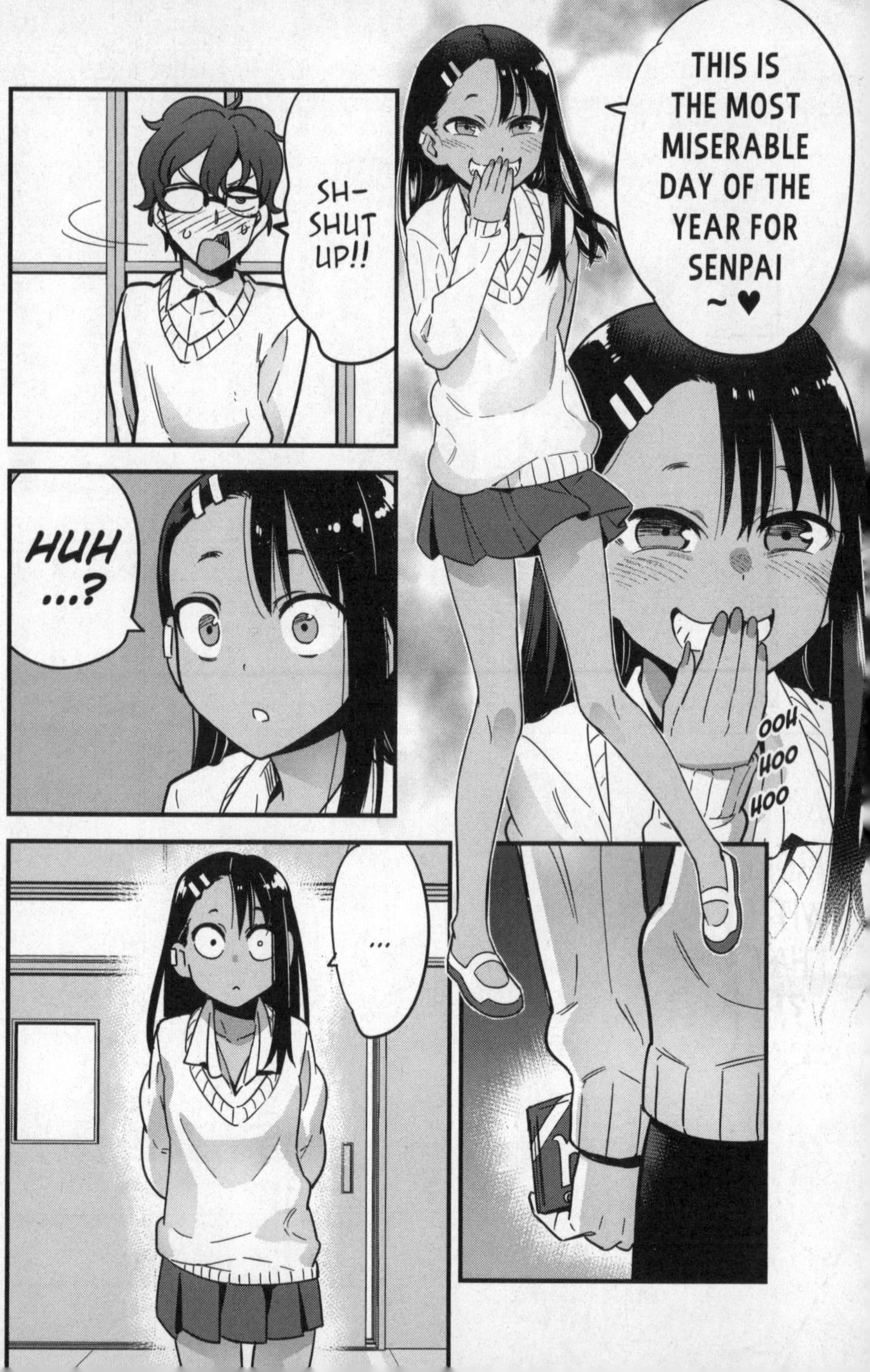
THIS IS THE MOST MISERABLE DAY OF THE YEAR FOR SENPAI ~♥
OOH HOO HOO
SH- SHUT UP!!
HUH ...?
...

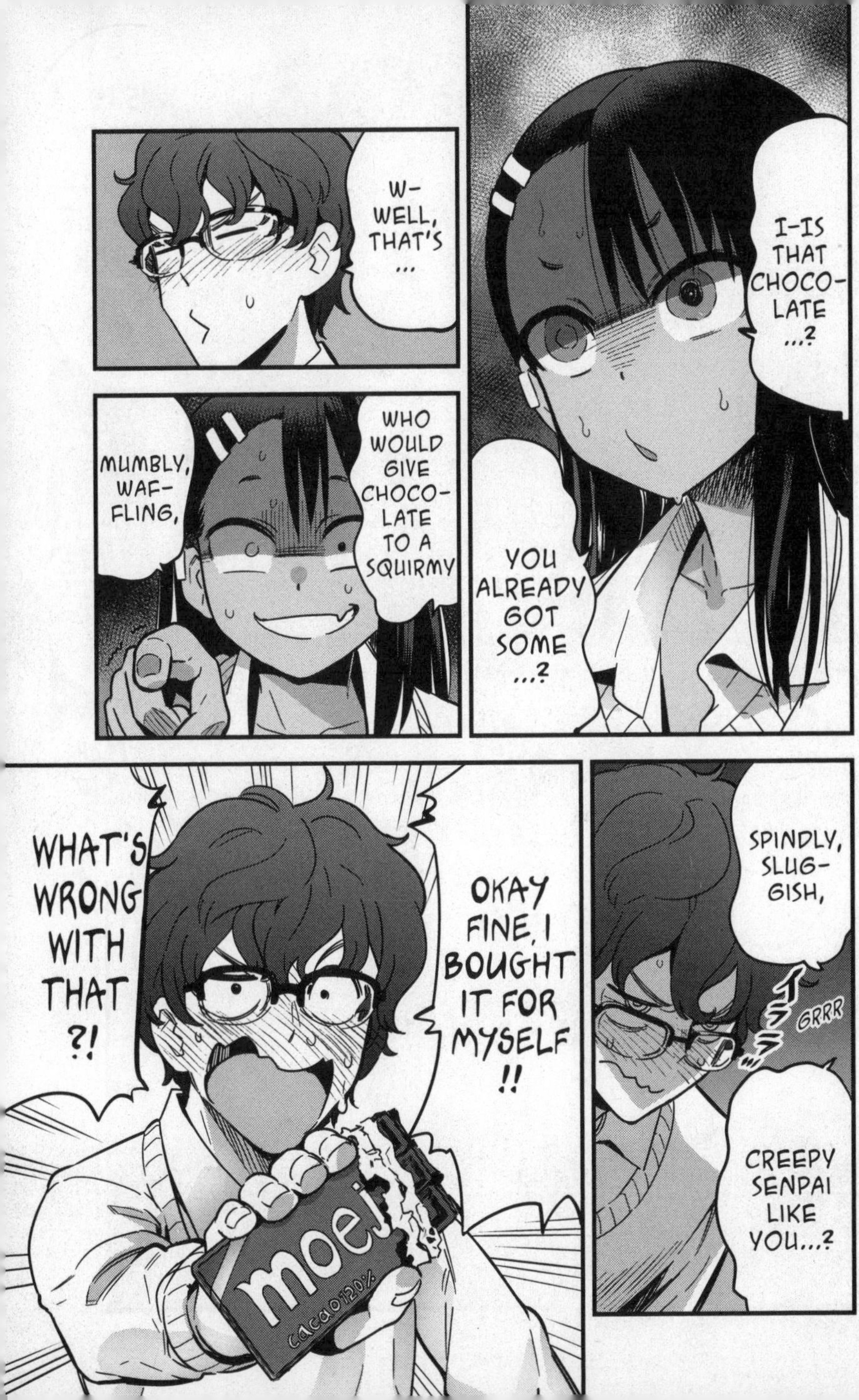
I-IS THAT CHOCOLATE ...?
YOU ALREADY GOT SOME ...?
W-WELL, THAT'S ...
WHO WOULD GIVE CHOCOLATE TO A SQUIRMY
MUMBLY, WAFFLING,
SPINDLY, SLUGGISH,
GRRR
CREEPY SENPAI LIKE YOU...?
OKAY FINE, I BOUGHT IT FOR MYSELF !!
WHAT'S WRONG WITH THAT ?!
moej
cacao120%

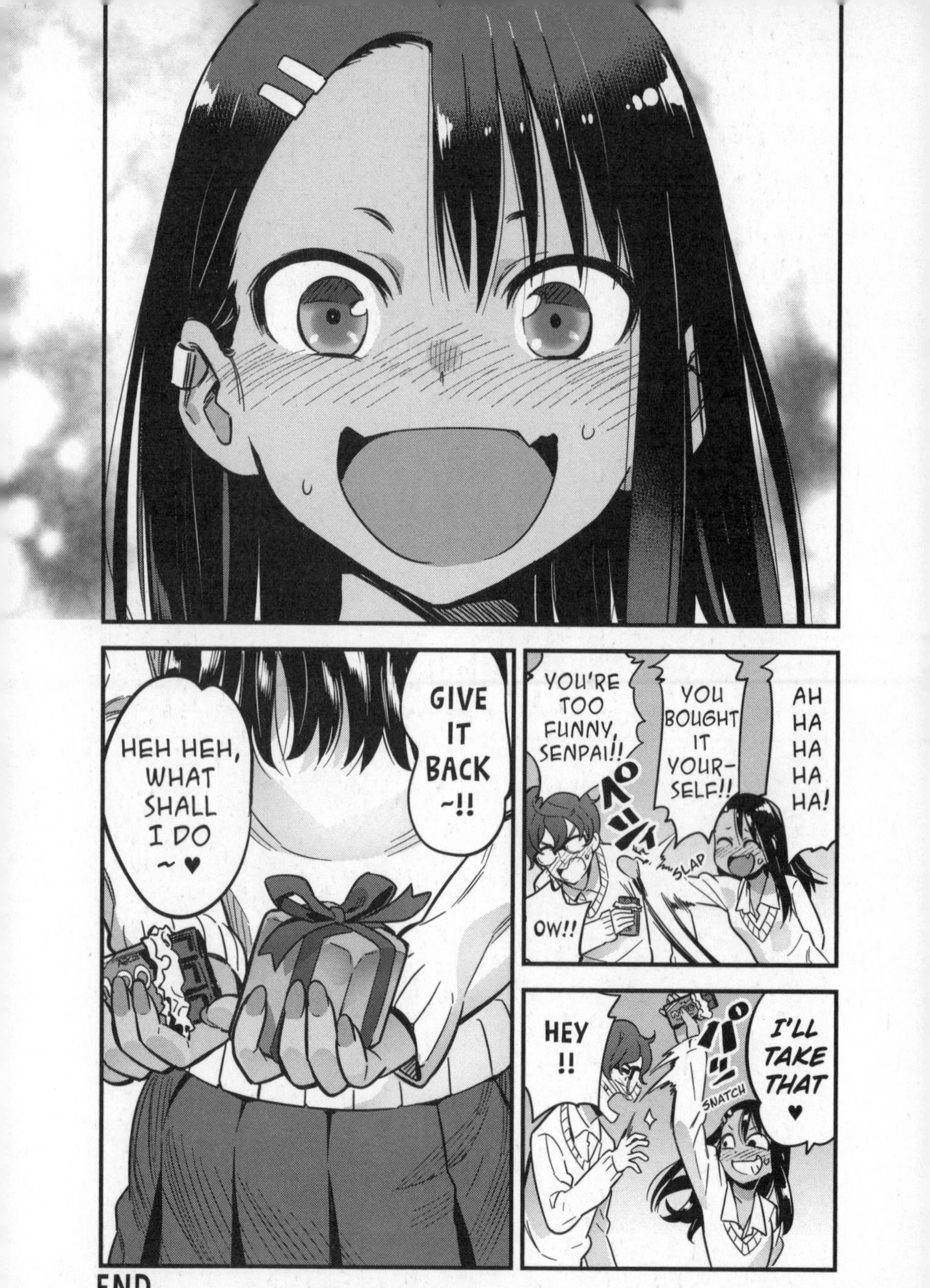
AH HA HA HA HA HA!
YOU BOUGHT IT YOURSELF!!
YOU'RE TOO FUNNY, SENPAI!!
SLAP
OW!!
I'LL TAKE THAT ♥
SNATCH
HEY !!
GIVE IT BACK ~!!
HEH HEH, WHAT SHALL I DO ~ ♥

END

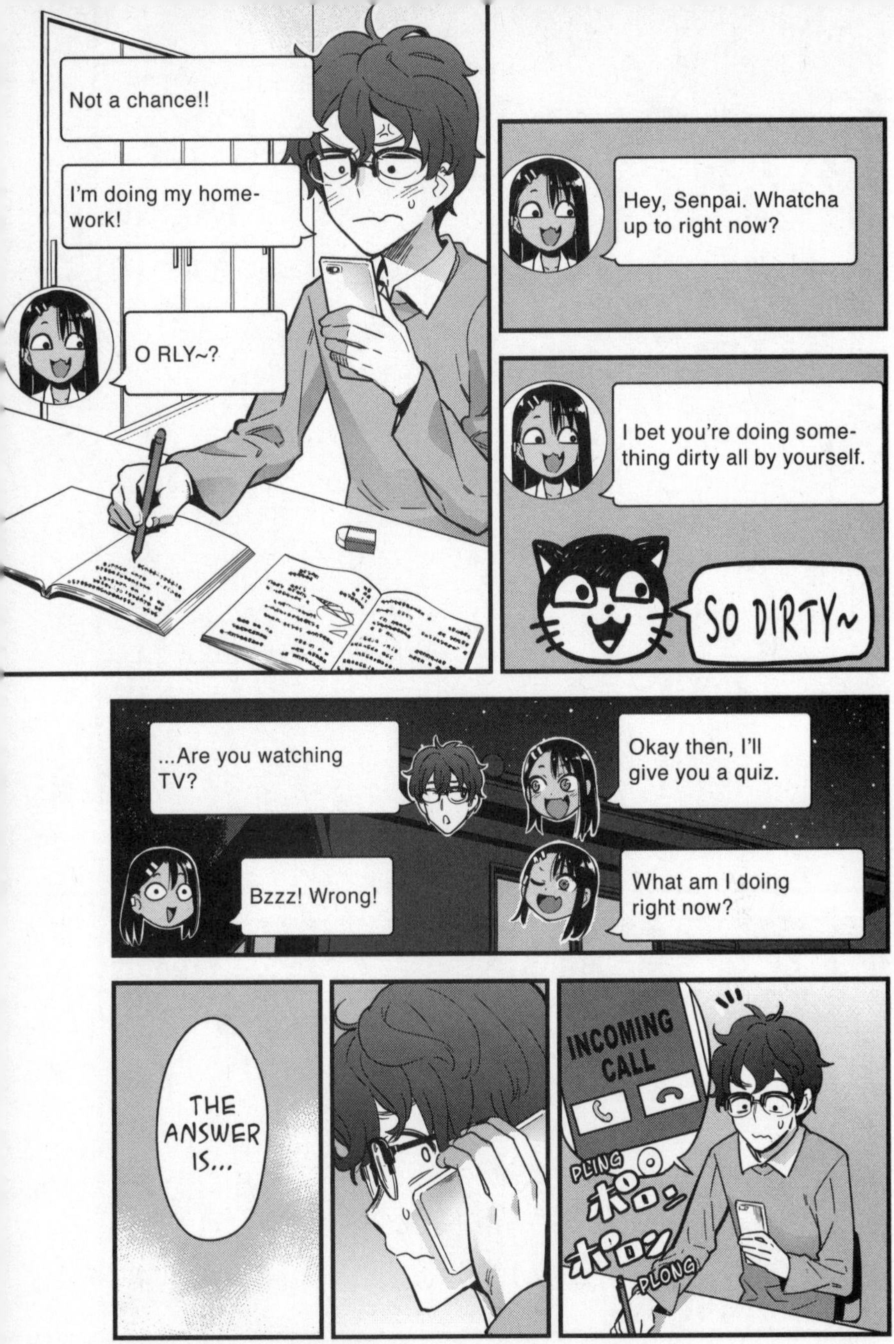
Hey, Senpai. Whatcha up to right now?
I bet you're doing something dirty all by yourself.
SO DIRTY~
Not a chance!!
I'm doing my homework!
O RLY~?
Okay then, I'll give you a quiz.
...Are you watching TV?
What am I doing right now?
Bzzz! Wrong!
INCOMING CALL
PLING
ポロン
ポロン
PLONG
THE ANSWER IS...

BONUS ②: I'M BEING DEFILED BY SENPAI~♥

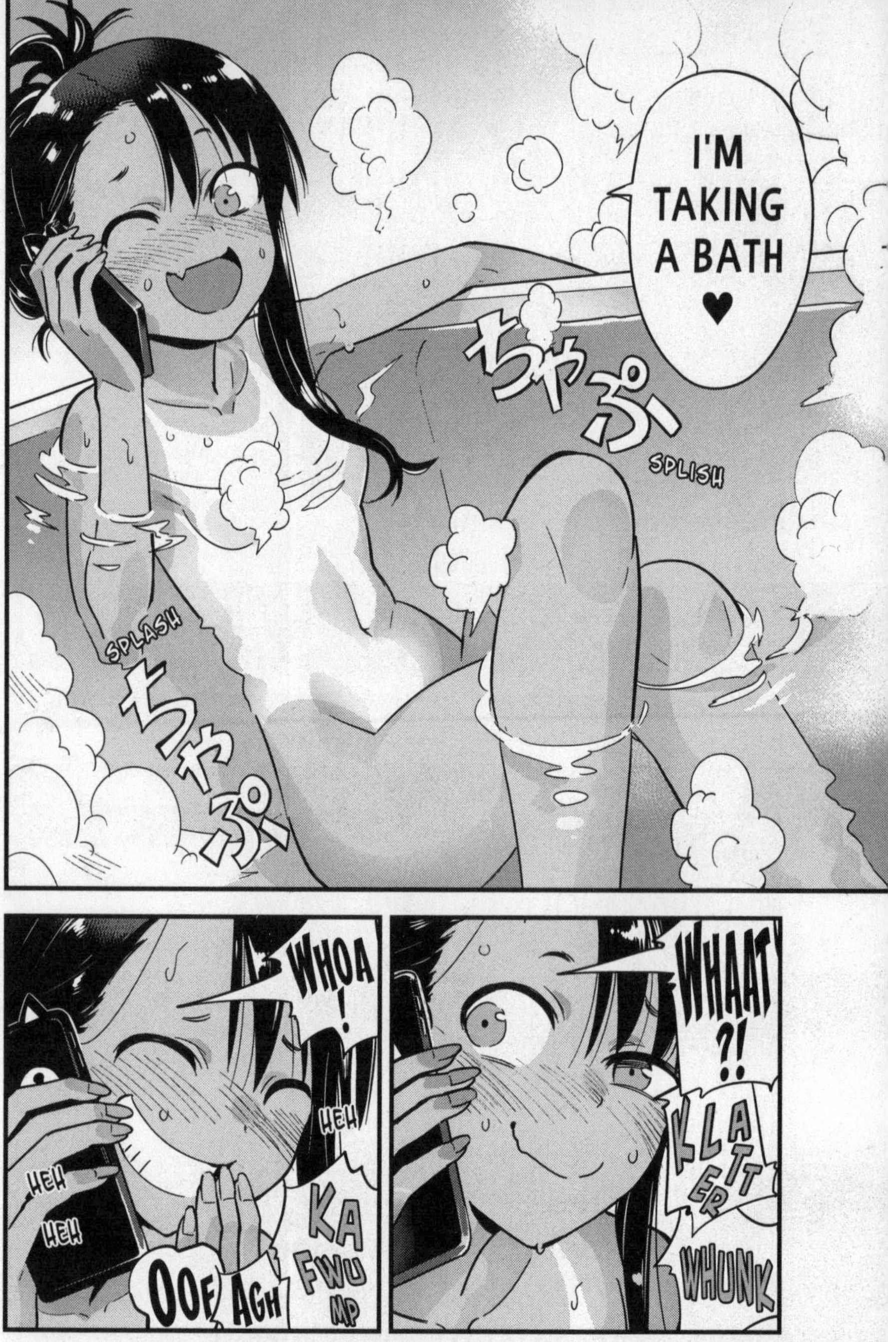
I'M TAKING A BATH ♥
ちゃぷ
SPLISH
SPLASH
ちゃぷ
WHAAT ?!
KLATTER
WHUNK
WHOA!
HEH
HEH HEH
KA FWUMP
OOF
AGH

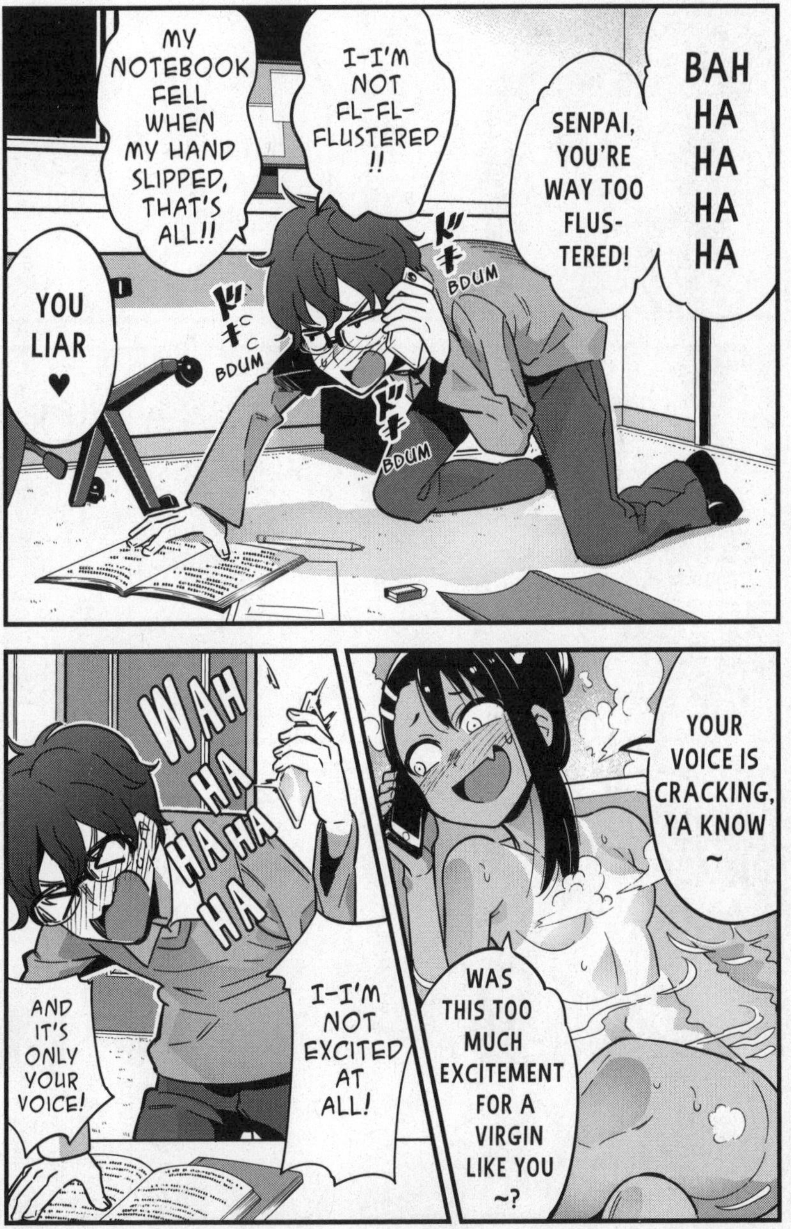
BAH HA HA HA HA
SENPAI, YOU'RE WAY TOO FLUS-TERED!
I-I'M NOT FL-FL-FLUSTERED !!
MY NOTEBOOK FELL WHEN MY HAND SLIPPED, THAT'S ALL!!
BDUM
BDUM
BDUM
YOU LIAR ♥
YOUR VOICE IS CRACKING, YA KNOW ~
WAS THIS TOO MUCH EXCITEMENT FOR A VIRGIN LIKE YOU ~?
WAH HA HA HA HA HA
I-I'M NOT EXCITED AT ALL!
AND IT'S ONLY YOUR VOICE!

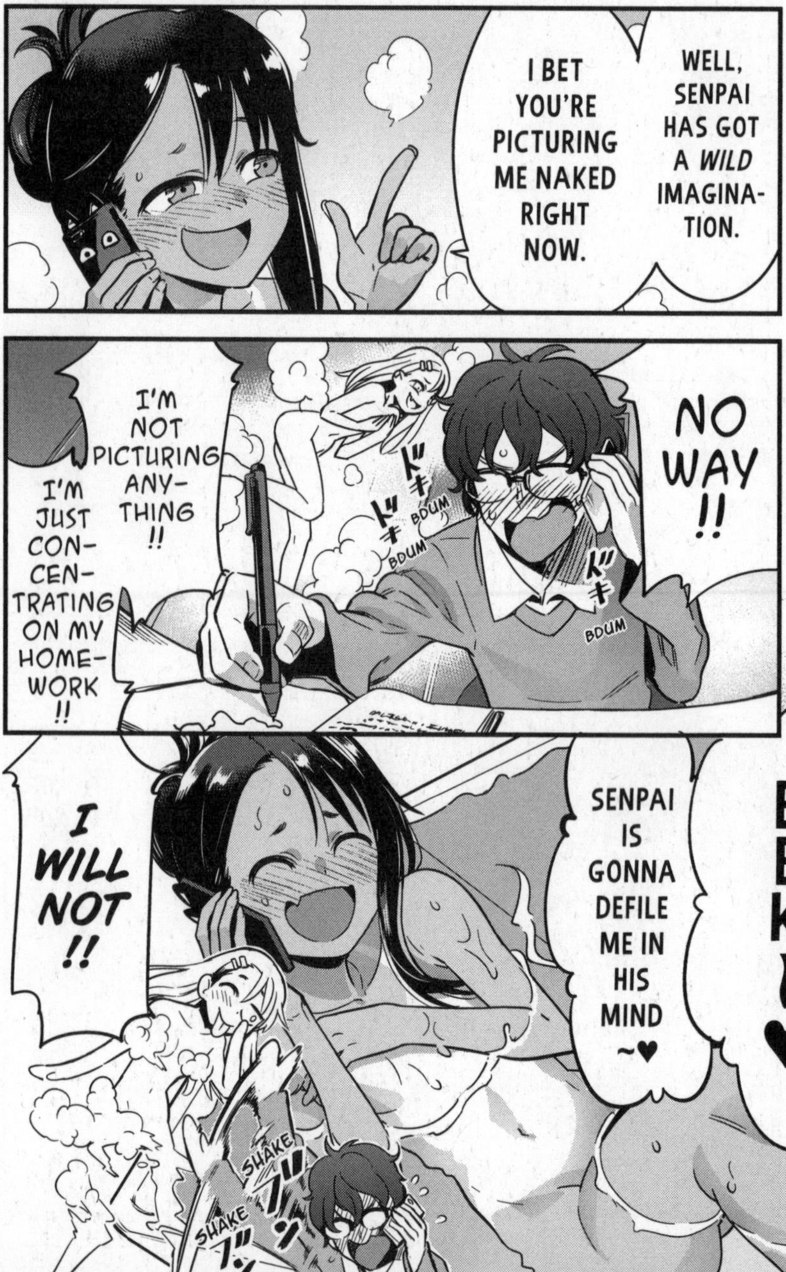
WELL, SENPAI HAS GOT A *WILD* IMAGINATION.
I BET YOU'RE PICTURING ME NAKED RIGHT NOW.
NO WAY!!
BDUM
BDUM
BDUM
I'M NOT PICTURING ANYTHING!!
I'M JUST CONCENTRATING ON MY HOMEWORK!!
EEK~♥
SENPAI IS GONNA DEFILE ME IN HIS MIND~♥
I WILL NOT!!
SHAKE
SHAKE

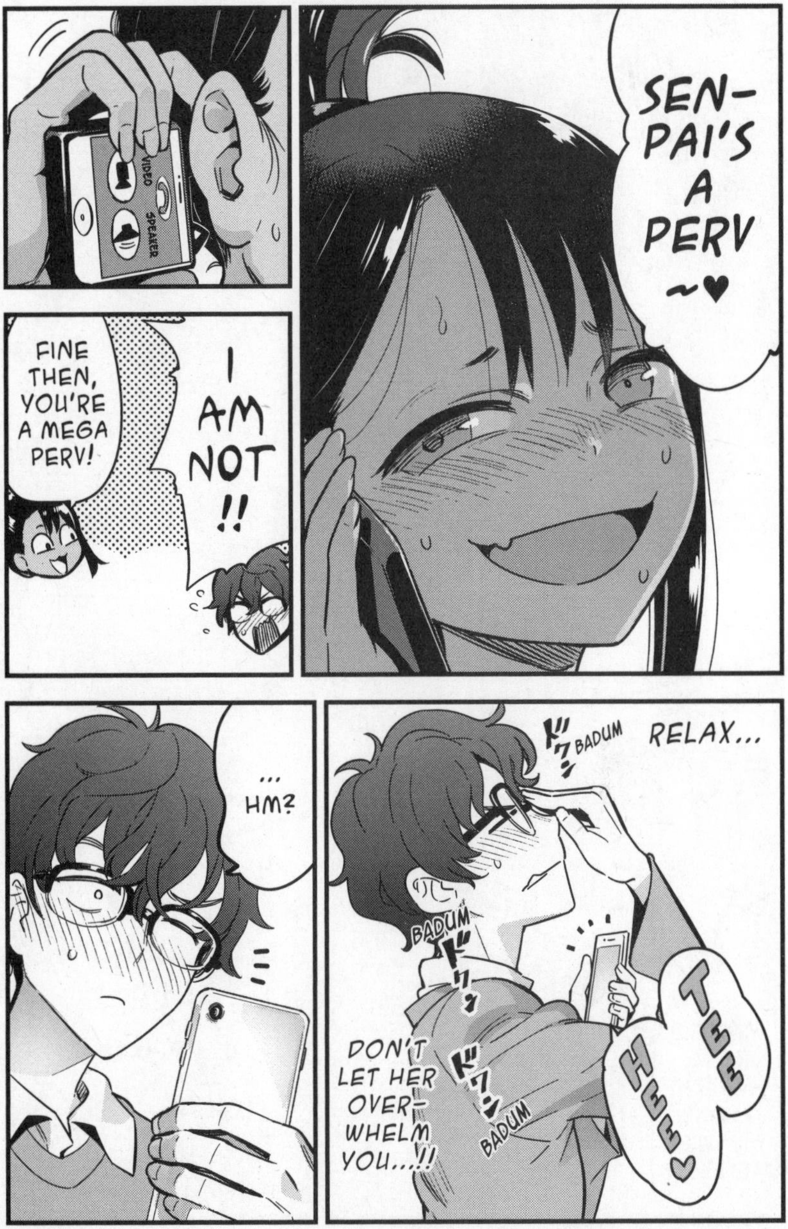
SEN-PAI'S A PERV ~♥
VIDEO
SPEAKER
I AM NOT !!
FINE THEN, YOU'RE A MEGA PERV!
BADUM
RELAX...
BADUM
DON'T LET HER OVER-WHELM YOU...!!
BADUM
TEE HEE ♥
... HM?

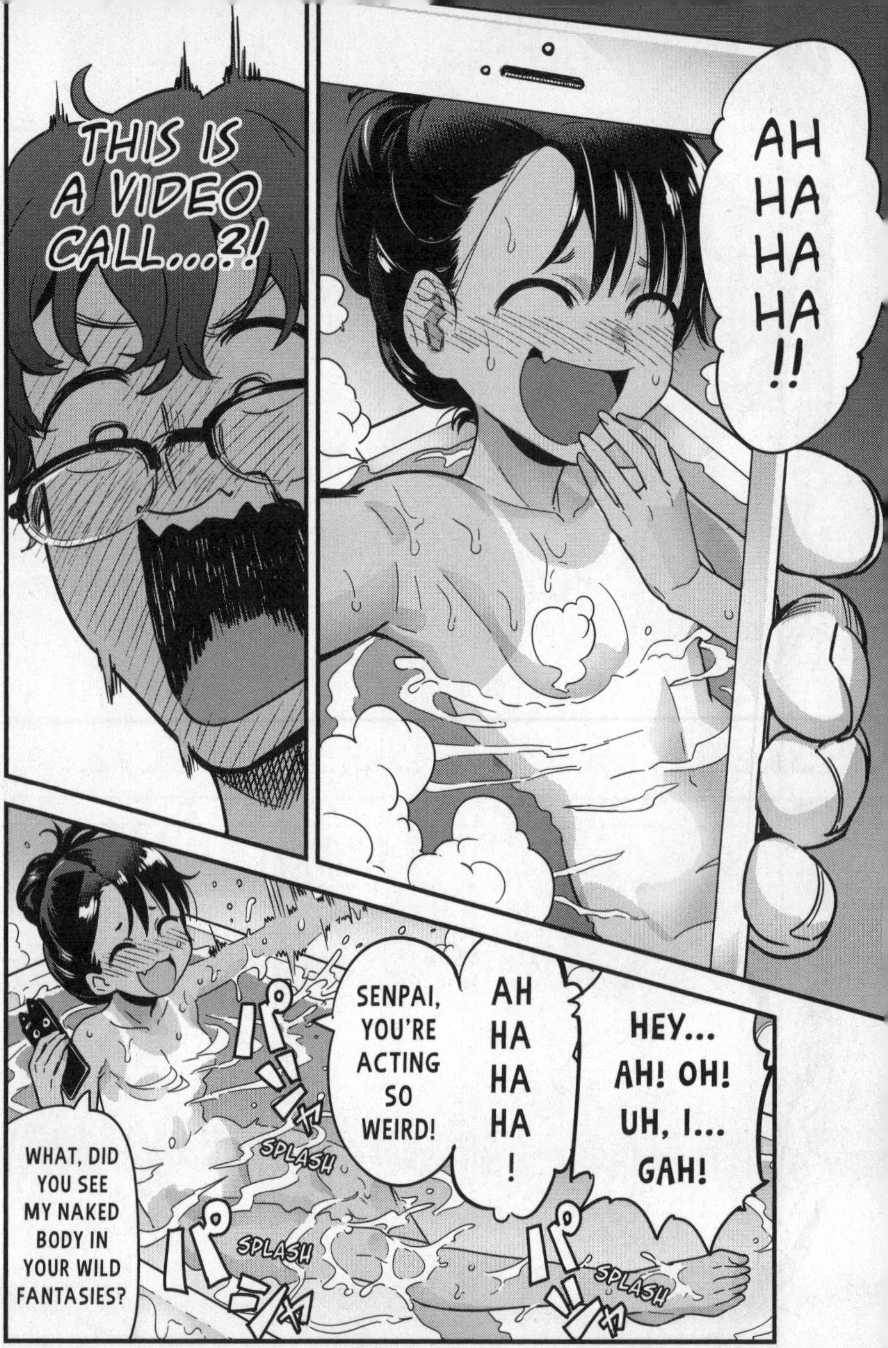

AH HA HA HA!!
THIS IS A VIDEO CALL...?!
HEY... AH! OH! UH, I... GAH!
AH HA HA HA!
SENPAI, YOU'RE ACTING SO WEIRD!
WHAT, DID YOU SEE MY NAKED BODY IN YOUR WILD FANTASIES?
SPLASH
SPLASH
SPLASH

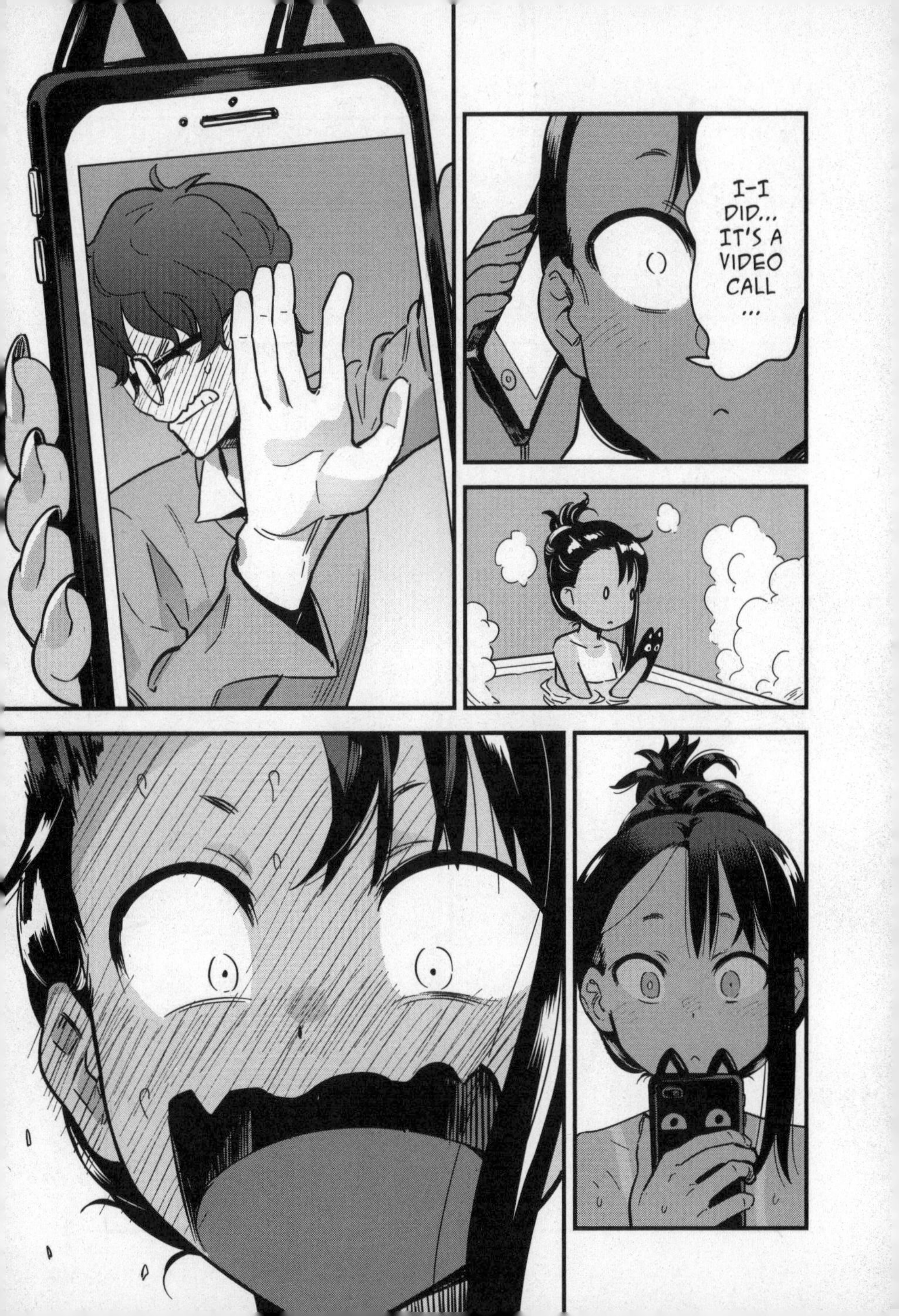
I-I DID... IT'S A VIDEO CALL ...

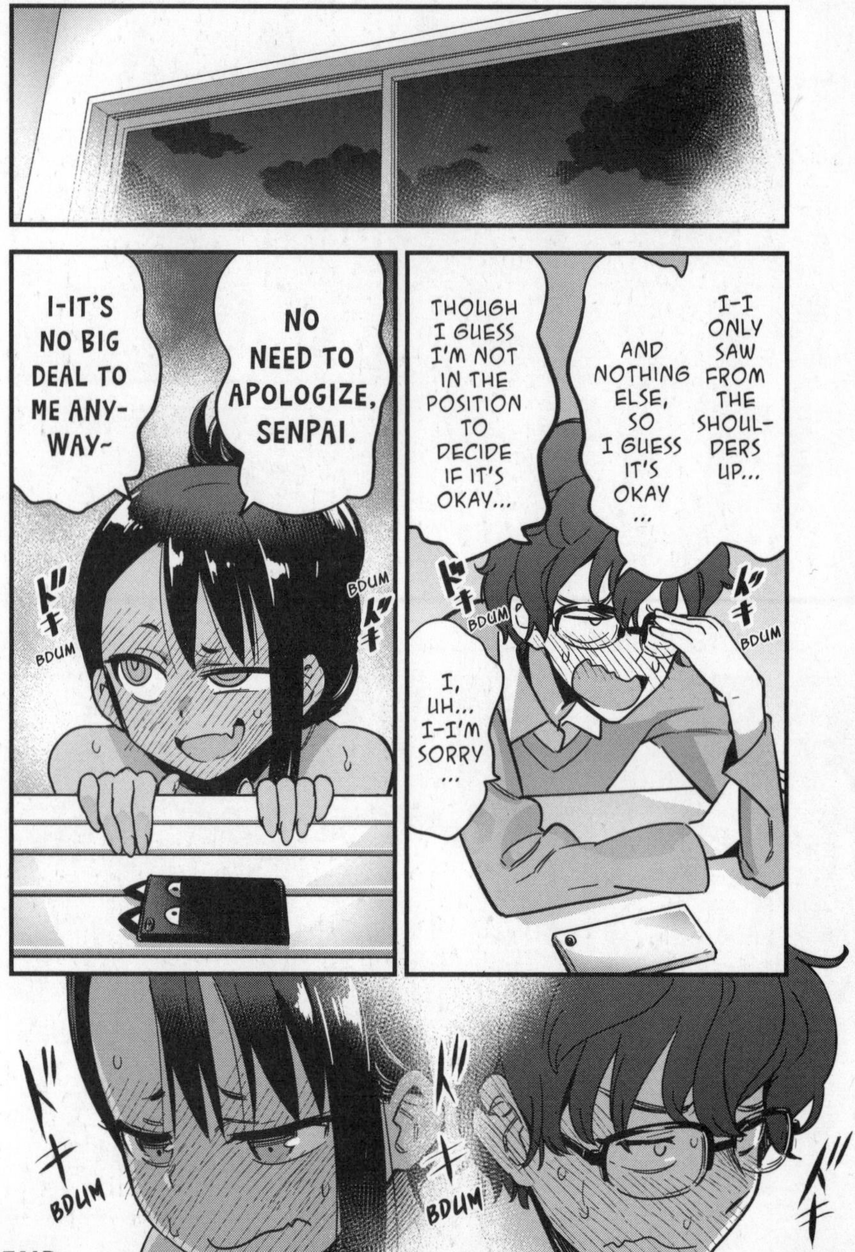
I-I ONLY SAW FROM THE SHOULDERS UP...
AND NOTHING ELSE, SO I GUESS IT'S OKAY...
THOUGH I GUESS I'M NOT IN THE POSITION TO DECIDE IF IT'S OKAY...
BDUM
BDUM
I, UH... I-I'M SORRY...
NO NEED TO APOLOGIZE, SENPAI.
I-IT'S NO BIG DEAL TO ME ANY-WAY~
BDUM
BDUM
BDUM
BDUM
BDUM
END

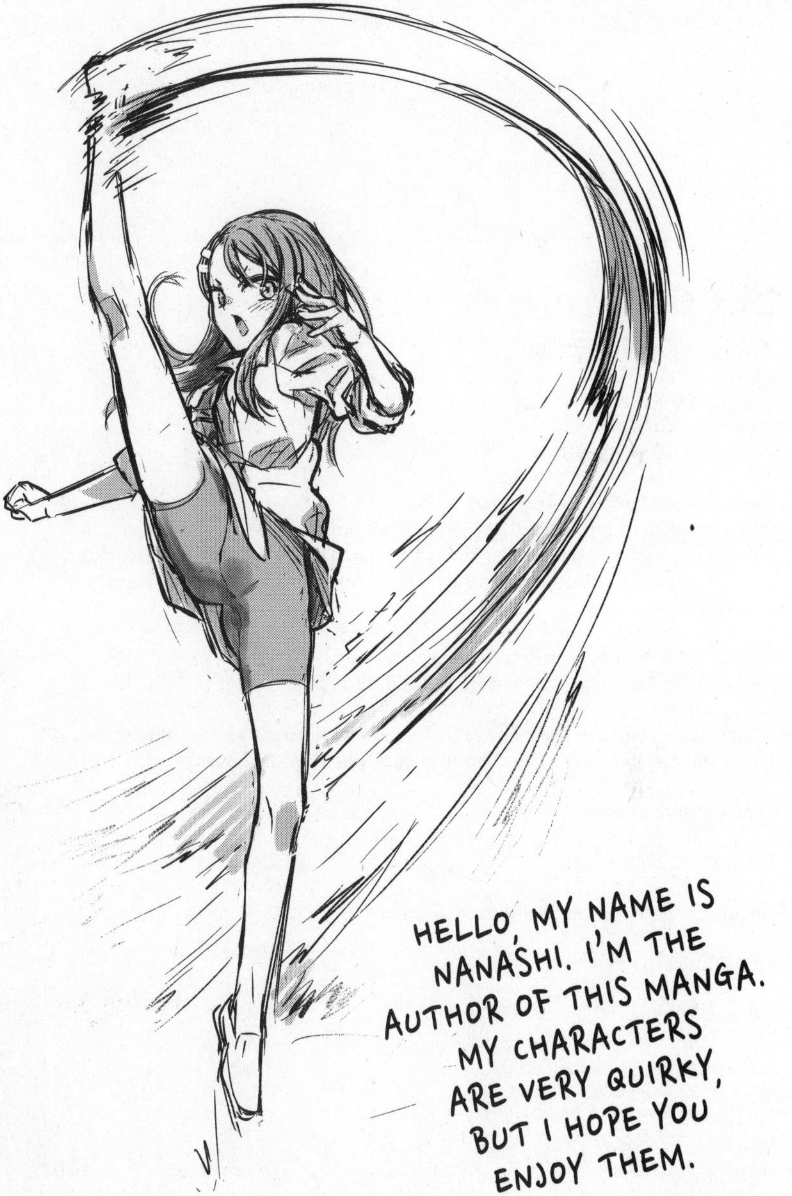
HELLO, MY NAME IS NANASHI. I'M THE AUTHOR OF THIS MANGA. MY CHARACTERS ARE VERY QUIRKY, BUT I HOPE YOU ENJOY THEM.
- NANASHI

Don't Toy With Me, Miss Nagatoro 1

A Vertical Comics Edition

Translation: Kristi Fernandez
Production: Risa Cho
          Eve Grandt

© 2018 Nanashi. All rights reserved.
First published in Japan in 2018 by Kodansha, Ltd., Tokyo
Publication rights for this English edition arranged through Kodansha, Ltd., Tokyo
English language version produced by Vertical Comics, an imprint of Kodansha
USA Publishing, LLC

Translation provided by Vertical Comics, 2019
Published by Kodansha USA Publishing, LLC, New York

Originally published in Japanese as *Ijiranaide, Nagatorosan 1* by Kodansha, Ltd., 2018
Ijiranaide, Nagatorosan first serialized in *Magazine Poketto*, Kodansha, Ltd., 2017-

This is a work of fiction.

ISBN: 978-1-947194-86-1

Manufactured in the United States of America

First Edition

Seventh Printing

Kodansha USA Publishing, LLC
451 Park Avenue South
7th Floor
New York, NY 10016
www.kodansha.us

Vertical books are distributed through Penguin-Random House Publisher Services.